Bernard Berenson and the Twentieth Century

Mary Ann Calo

Bernard Berenson and

the Twentieth Century

Temple University Press · Philadelphia

Temple University Press, Philadelphia 19122
Copyright © 1994 by Temple University. All rights reserved
Published 1994
Printed in the United States of America

The paper used in this publication meets the minimum requirements of
American National Standard for Information Sciences—Permanence of
Paper for Printed Library Materials,
ANSI Z39.48-1984 ∞

Library of Congress Cataloging-in-Publication Data
Calo, Mary Ann, 1949–
Bernard Berenson and the twentieth century / Mary Ann Calo.
p.   cm.
Includes bibliographical references and index.
ISBN 1-56639-116-4 (cloth).—ISBN 1-56639-117-2 (pbk.)
1. Berenson, Bernard, 1865–1959.   2. Art criticism—United States-
History—20th century.   3. Art historians—United States—
Biography.   I. Title.
N7483.B47C36 1994
709'.2—dc20
[B]   93-15584

For Michael, Ryan, and Nina

Contents

Acknowledgments

This book would not have been written without the encouragement, cooperation, and support of numerous individuals and institutions. Among the many who provided me with information and access to collections, I would like to extend special thanks to the staff of the Villa I Tatti, particularly Dottoressa Fiorella Superbi Gioffredi, Curator of Collections and Archives of the Fototeca, whose courtesy, patience, and knowledge of the Berenson Archive were a constant source of wonder during my many hours in Settignano, and to Walter Kaiser, director of the Harvard University Center for Italian Renaissance Studies. Thanks also to Randy Bond, art librarian at Syracuse University, Leigh Bullard Weisblat, researcher at The Phillips Collection, and Ronna Roob, archivist of the Museum of Modern Art, who were especially helpful.

I wish to thank the President and Fellows of Harvard College for granting me the right to publish photographs and letters from the Berenson Archive. I am also grateful to the following institutions for making material from their collections available to me and for granting me permission to quote from primary sources: the Museum of Modern Art, for quotations from Alfred H. Barr, Jr.'s letters and Margaret Scolari's letters from the Alfred H. Barr, Jr., Papers and the Margaret Scolari Barr Papers, Museum of Modern Art Archives; The Phillips Collection, Washington, D.C., for quotations from the correspondence of Bernard Berenson and Duncan Phillips from the Duncan Phillips Papers; the Lilly Library, Indiana University, for quotations from Mary Costelloe Berenson's letters and diaries from the H. W. Smith Papers; Barbara Strachey Halpern for quotations from Mary Costelloe Berenson's letters and diaries; Yale University Library, for quotations from Bernard Berenson's letters to Royal Cortissoz and to Hutchins Hapgood and Mary Berenson's letter to

Hutchins Hapgood from the Yale Collection of American Literature, Beinecke Rare Book and Manuscript Library; and the Archives of American Art, Smithsonian Institution, for quotations from Berenson's letters to William Ivins from the Williams Ivins Papers.

For consenting to be interviewed for this study, I wish to thank John Walker, Sidney Alexander, and Giovanni Colacicchi, who offered many valuable insights. An informal discussion with Leo Steinberg was also illuminating, as was my correspondence with Barbara Strachey Halpern. Special thanks to Clement Greenberg for sharing his impressions of Berenson with me in a lengthy and particularly instructive interview.

I had the good fortune to discuss this project with many colleagues and would especially like to thank the following for useful information and suggestions: Ellen Oppler, Gerlinda Sanford, Peg Weiss, and Antje B. Lemke of Syracuse University and Eric Van Schaack of Colgate University, whose encouragement and good humor were also much appreciated. For their close reading of the manuscript in its form as a dissertation and their astute criticism, I am indebted to Mary Lou Marien, Catherine Lord, and Gary Radke, all of Syracuse University.

To David Tatham of Syracuse University, who served as director of my dissertation on Berenson and offered helpful advice long after its completion, I owe a debt that is immeasurable. His wisdom, generosity, and inexhaustible patience made him an ideal mentor and his exemplary professionalism continues to inspire me.

I wish to acknowledge the contribution of my parents, Peter and Mary Vinciguerra, for their unfailing support during the course of this study. To my husband, Michael, and my children, Ryan and Nina, who help me keep things in perspective, I am eternally grateful. This book is dedicated to them.

Bernard Berenson and the Twentieth Century

Introduction

About the "current," there is a
thought of Nietzsche's which goes
somewhat as follows: if you want to
be distinguished from the crowd it
can be for two reasons; either
because it disgusts you or because
you want to put yourself at its head.
This second motivation has never
been mine; I have always
remembered that the first in a flock
is still always a sheep.

1931

The trouble with the vegetable analogy is the fact that a man has a much larger number of possible moves than a plant.

1901

In the current climate of the humanities in general and art history in particular, Bernard Berenson is a perfect antihero. Consider this statement from the foreword of what Berenson hoped would be his great theoretical treatise on the decline and recovery of the figurative arts.

> In every instance we shall begin with the decorative
> elements, and while doing so we shall ignore the other
> elements whether spiritual or material, social or politi-
> cal. Nor yet shall our attention, except in a cursory way,
> be given to technical questions of why things happened,
> or with attempts at metaphysical or ethical explanation.
> We shall have our hands full studying the succession
> of changes that took place in the art phenomena of the
> twelve centuries above indicated. When they seem prom-
> ising, we may glance at other fields, whether of place
> or time, to inquire if a like sequence of changes occurs
> there as well.[1]

Add to this manifesto of formalist methodology Berenson's unwavering defense of Western civilization and the classical tradition, his antidemocratic worldview, and his devotion to the rarified "fine art" object and his entire career becomes a perfect paradigm of the alleged evils and shortcomings of elitist art history. Furthermore, Berenson's lucrative involvement with the art market and his notorious pandering to the actual and would-be aristocracy of his day make him an object of intense curiosity, as well as loathing. For most of his long life and much of its aftermath, Bernard Berenson has been a man people love to hate.

Although Berenson has always aroused animosity in those for whom the sale of knowledge is an unimaginable crime and the exaltation of Western civilization an untenable position, he has been resurrected of late by others who would remind art historians that looking at art should be central to what they do.[2] Berenson's legacy to art history is that the object speaks to the viewer in a unique way, and although he exaggerated the absolute priority of visual elements in the appreciation of art, a position he would come to regret, he never abandoned this belief. It is fitting that Berenson, who in his youth railed against the practice of reducing art to social, cultural, and political ideals, should be remembered in an age which again seeks its significance primarily in these things.

In reviewing the first volume of Ernest Samuels's indispensable biography of Berenson, Robert Hughes noted that since the end of World War II writing about Berenson had become a subgenre of American journalism.[3] Given the tremendous number of pages devoted to sorting out the Berenson myth, surprisingly little has been written about the influence of his general ideas. This is certainly due in no small measure to the exaggerated interest (regrettably, by both specialists and the general public) in the grandeur of his lifestyle and the financial repercussions of his personal conduct as an expert involved in the trade. Within the field of academic art history, where his impact has been most directly felt, Berenson's theoretical writings have failed to command serious attention. Aside from the usual accolades for his connoisseurship and his contributions to the systematic study of Italian art, Berenson's connection to twentieth-century art and criticism remains poorly understood and, in the main, undervalued.

Recent attempts to associate Berenson with an attitude toward art and history that current wisdom seeks to undermine have concentrated mainly on his activities as an expert and arbiter of taste. A persuasive case, for example, has been made for the fundamental relationship between connoisseurship as Berenson practiced it and the development of formalist art history. Also, studies that seek to ascertain the extent to which the business of attributing paintings has contributed to the commodity status of art in late bourgeois culture have assigned to Berenson a role of central importance.[4] Although Berenson's material wealth and his reputation rested on his undisputed skill as a connoisseur, it is widely known from his autobiographical writings that he remained largely dissatisfied with his professional life. Berenson had hoped to be remembered as a man of letters or as an art theorist, and in his last years he repeatedly deprecated his reputation as a narrow specialist.

The reasons for this relative neglect of Berenson's general ideas are complex, but surely the most compelling is that, by his own admission, Berenson's intellectual development seems to have been arrested early in his career.

> As an organism that took in and gave out, as an instrument, I was complete at five and twenty, and this instrument has worked and preserved its identity for more than fifty subsequent years, in the face of all the forces pulling and pushing, forward and backward. It has changed little if any, although much it dealt with has disappeared, and much that was not there has taken its place.[5]

While he admitted his estrangement from the modern age, Berenson could not resist the impulse to be censorious. Most of his late books, ostensibly concerned with art and theory, are thinly concealed indictments of what he regarded as the abysmal state of modern art and culture.

Berenson's interest in the theme of decline, so much in evidence during the second half of his life, was clearly stimulated by his perception of the twentieth century. He believed that the best approach to understanding a given epoch was through an age that mirrored it. Thus, the strong affinity Berenson sensed between the Italian Renaissance and the late nineteenth century of his youth kindled his desire to come to terms with the achievements of both. In similar fashion, his understanding of the fourth century as an age of barbarism and descent from an ideal culture was reinforced by his apocalyptic view of modern life.

It annoyed Berenson that he could not disengage himself from the present and bask in the celebrity of his old age. Very aware that his social values were anachronistic, he became more or less resigned to his public image as a curious remnant from a forgotten age. But in matters of art he refused to grow old quietly.

> My century, my own, is the 19th. I am and remain a mid—or at best a late Victorian—not Edwardian, let alone Georgian. I try to encounter the events of the day, but my attitude toward them, no matter how sympathetic and benevolent, is a 19th century one. On the other hand, towards the arts I am neither sympathetic nor benevolent but without understanding and therefore contemptuous and hostile. Yet while I grant that con-ceiv-ably [*sic*] my feelings about events and ideals political are outmoded and I should accept those of today (in moderation), I can admit no such participation in the art of today, really of today alone.[6]

Berenson's frequent, vehement outbursts against modern art in his old age were disproportionate to the amount of harm it could have caused him. Surely he took it far too personally.

If Berenson overreacted to the changes that took place in twentieth-century art and criticism, it is in part because he bore a certain measure of responsibility for them. The serenity of his last years was disturbed by many things, not the least of which was an awareness that the cohesive theory of humanistic art he hoped to leave posterity was never realized to his satisfaction, and that what he left instead was an approach to criticism and aesthetics that anticipated, if it did not actually make possible, the modernist art he loathed. Berenson, normally quick to take offense when not given the credit he felt he deserved from other scholars, deeply regretted what the twentieth century would do with what he regarded as his ideas. He realized almost immediately the potential abuse of his early theoretical positions and spent a good deal of his remaining years correcting for this misunderstanding.

To grasp fully the significance of Berenson's ideas and their relationship to the broader currents of modern art and criticism it is necessary to examine his intellectual life in its totality; to consider him within the context of his long life. Few writers on Berenson have challenged his contention that "as a contributor to thought I doubt whether my death soon after fifty would have made the slightest difference."[7] Despite his insistence that he belonged to an age which ended with World War I, it is impossible to ignore that he lived more than half his life in the twentieth century and, as a result, had a chance, indeed was forced, to come to terms with the consequences of these ideas.

Berenson began his career in eager anticipation of a new artistic age and ended it haunted by the fear that he had witnessed, and perhaps helped to create, a tragic mistake. The one dimension of his legacy that remains largely unexplored is the process through which Berenson, who was receptive to the climate of change in which modernism took root, and who, because of his approach to criticism and aesthetics, was uniquely equipped to understand it, came to assume such a reactionary position. A close analysis of the works written at both the beginning and the end of his life, which include frequent comments on recent art, demonstrates that Berenson's hostility toward modernism was inconsistent with his critical methodology and to a certain extent his aesthetic theory. It has its roots, rather, in a profound resistance to the social, cultural, and political changes that threatened his way of life and, perhaps even more fundamentally, in his intellectual ambition.[8]

Although a great deal has been written about Berenson, his relationship to the modern age is rarely addressed. Be that as it may, it is almost impossible to imagine that there are aspects of Berenson's life or thought which remain "undiscovered." Ernest Samuels's exhaustive two-volume biography is as much a thorough history of Berenson's intellectual development as it is a chronicle of his life. The rationale for this study, therefore, is less a matter of disclosure than a shift of emphasis. Berenson's youthful interest in modern art was no secret, but it was subsumed under his prodigious work as a connoisseur of Italian painting. Similarly, the essential modernity of his criticism has long been eclipsed by the enduring image of Berenson as a spokesman for classical humanism.

Because I examine both the development of Berenson's critical writing and the events of his life brought to bear on this development, my methodology necessarily combines text analysis with narration. My consideration of Berenson's biography is highly selective; while it leaves out a great deal, it brings to the foreground some aspects of his life that have remained fairly obscure. For example, in an effort to document the probable impact on his thinking of artist-friends such as Hermann Obrist and Egisto Fabbri, something which is generally neglected in the Berenson literature, I include a detailed account of these personal relationships. The correspondence between Berenson, his wife, Mary Smith Costelloe, and Obrist is largely unpublished and is here examined in depth for the first time.[9] I give less attention, however, to such authors long recognized for their contributions to Berenson's thinking as Walter Pater, William James, and Adolf Hildebrand, and to Berenson's celebrated (and well-documented) relationships with Bertrand Russell, Edith Wharton, and Vernon Lee (pseudonym for Violet Paget).

A comparable asymmetry could be said to exist in my analyses of Berenson's writings. His early essays on Italian art, affectionately referred to by his followers as "The Four Gospels," have been widely studied for their contribution to the historiography of Italian Renaissance painting. I make no attempt to evaluate them in this regard; instead I focus on the modernity of Berenson's critical methodology and the implications of his aesthetic principles for later art and criticism. Thus I consider his early writings for the first time strictly within the context of aesthetic modernism, rather than the usual frameworks of Renaissance art history or connoisseurship.

Although the late books were widely reviewed, they have never been studied systematically and only rarely are they placed in the broad context of Berenson's oeuvre. I do both and in doing so assume, contrary to the vast majority of opinion, that the last works are as significant as the first. Once again, it bears repeating that the cogency and accuracy of Berenson's historical observations are not addressed here, but rather the shift in critical and aesthetic priorities attributable to his increasing political, social, and artistic conservatism.

Given the frequency with which Berenson referred to recent art in his writings, it would be impractical to attempt an exhaustive survey of his critical remarks. What I present must be viewed instead as a representative sample, a summary of his attitudes toward those modern artists and modernist styles about which he had the most to say. Berenson repeated himself a great deal, both in his diaries and in his critical essays; thus I condense his frequent and often random comments on modern art and culture into several fairly consistent lines of argumentation.

Finally, it should be noted at the outset that Berenson's critical language was at times incompatible with contemporary usage and could well have been a source of confusion in the understanding of his aesthetic theories. Especially relevant in this respect was his use of the words "decoration" and "illustration" to distinguish between the form and content of art. In the context of late nineteenth-century aesthetic theory and criticism, the term "decorative" was typically understood as a reproach, applicable to visual expressions somehow lacking in substance or significance. After the work of later formalist critics such as Clive Bell, both "decorative" and "illustrative" (narrative) can be understood as pejoratives in the consideration of modernist art. By "decorative," however, Berenson did not intend the mere reduction to superficial ornamentation or pattern but rather artistic properties in a more general sense. As categories, "decoration" encompassed the formal qualities of art while "illustration" referred to aspects of subject, or more specifically, to the nature of the representation.[10]

1. Appraising Berenson

The great majority of art critics are people who adapt a different jargon from mine to expound ideas which were mine but which I discarded years ago.

1933

I am prepared for history to be unaware of what others owe me, how much they parade in my clothes.

1957

Berenson and Early Modernism

The connection between Berenson's theoretical writing, modernist art, and criticism was noted early in this century. Period reviews of his volumes on the Italian Renaissance published between 1894 and 1907, tend to stress his modernity in terms of the method of scientific connoisseurship; but after World War I, both his critical sensibilities and his theories of art appreciation were being considered within the climate of early modernism. Carrado Pavolini's treatise on early modernist art, *Cubismo, Futurismo, Espressionismo,* published in 1926, suggests a relationship between Berenson's critical and aesthetic priorities and the search for a new reality and sense of the significant that occupied recent artists.[1] So prevalent was this perception of Berenson as a pioneer modernist that in 1939 *Time* magazine could state in a discussion of his theory of tactile values: "Naive tourists have consequently stood before masterpieces in the Florence Academy waiting for their palms to tingle, and some critics have unkindly laid on Berenson responsibility for later 'abstract' jargon."[2]

These sentiments continued to be expressed in the numerous appreciations of Berenson that appeared in the popular and art press after his death in 1959. An obituary in the *New Republic,* for example, noted that the "defense of a great amount of non-representational painting rests solidly on principles established by Berenson, but Berenson was the first to see that such puritanical application of principles ended by denying the very 'life enhancement' for which the principle existed."[3] By 1963 the American writer Sidney Alexander could make the extraordinary claim that "the entire abstract and nonobjective movement in modern art is a grotesque overdevelopment of one limb of Berenson's aesthetics—his stress on 'intrinsic' values, the value of the work of art as contained entirely within itself."[4]

That modernism was a distortion of his ideas was a claim Berenson himself had made, and it was more often than not echoed by writers, such as Alexander, who shared his distaste for nonrepresentational art. It is worth remembering, however, that even the American art historian Meyer Schapiro, who was otherwise unsympathetic to the notion that Berenson had done something to foster the development of modern art, conceded that Berenson's aesthetic "with its categories of 'Form, Movement, and Space,' and his stern insistence on the highest values of art, seems in the line of thought which produced modern painting."[5]

Schapiro also pointed out that Berenson's emphasis on the significance of form in painting paved the way for the later formalist critics Clive Bell and Roger Fry, an observation made frequently by Berenson's close friend, the British art historian Kenneth Clark, and one that warrants greater attention than it has received. Fry in particular occupies a position as progenitor in the history of formalist art criticism that arguably belongs to Berenson, when one considers the similarity of their ideas and Fry's dependence on Berenson during his formative years.

More recent investigations into the history and dominance of abstraction in twentieth-century art theory have similarly acknowledged that Berenson's ideas were of seminal importance to Fry. In Linda Nochlin's influential essay, "The Realist Criminal and the Abstract Law," Berenson is included, along with Fry and Bell, in the roster of antirealist critics who furnish modernism with its historical pedigree.[6] Finally, Paul Barolsky, in what is the most extensive discussion to date of Berenson's relationship to modernist criticism, argues that Berenson's emphasis on formal qualities and impersonality in art, which to a large degree derive from his reading of Pater, have earned him an important intermediary role in a critical tradition, rooted in eighteenth century neo-classicism, that looks forward to the work of T. S. Eliot and Clement Greenberg.[7] Although Barolsky exaggerates Berenson's influence, he correctly identifies him as a pivotal figure in the history of modernist criticism and as a theorist whose critical sensibility was determined by his experience of recent art.

Berenson as a Theorist

Given the consistency with which Berenson's ideas have been related to the climate of early modernism, it is indeed curious how little systematic study they have received. Undeniably, Berenson made a much greater effort to assert himself as a humanist than as a theorist for the avant-garde, but this cannot account for the fact that his recognition in the latter context frequently amounts to no more than a passing nod. For an explanation it is necessary to examine the general terms in which Berenson's strengths and weaknesses, and his historical legacy, are typically discussed.

There is consensus, among his admirers and detractors alike, that although Berenson was an extraordinarily gifted connoisseur who brought to the study of art one of the finest sensibilities ever known, he had no gift for the formulation of complex theoretical arguments. Of this he was well aware.

> The paradox is that I have a very low opinion of my
> abilities when I think of myself in the absolute, as it
> were, without comparing myself to others. . . . My
> thinking is saltatory, inspired, not logical. For which
> reason I am short of breath intellectually, and have little
> to develop and argue on any subject.[8]

An unmistakable air of false modesty hovers over much of Berenson's autobiographical writings, but one can only believe he meant this quite sincerely, for it is corroborated by many who knew him.

Only the most naive of Berenson's many observers, or those prejudiced by an unqualified admiration for his humanism, have insisted on the superiority of his intellect. That he was remarkably learned is beyond dispute, but, as many who have written on him attest, he was not a rigorous or systematic thinker. Individuals close to Berenson, such as John Walker and Kenneth Clark, repeatedly praised his memory and powers of observation but did not hesitate to point out that he had no capacity for abstract thought.[9]

Clement Greenberg admired Berenson as a critic, but he too noted that despite Berenson's desire to leave a philosophy of art for posterity, his aptitude was not for conscious reasoning and he had always been more of a sensibility than an intellect.[10] Unsympathetic reviewers of Berenson's late books were far less generous, accusing him of "hardening of the intellect" or maintaining that "outside his professional corner he had always been a second-rate brain-power, made impressive by large curiosities and the will to act on them."[11]

Berenson's own doubts regarding the rigor of his intellect were made clear by his legendary hostility toward philosophy. Although he counted a number of important philosophers among his friends, he was frequently dismissive of and impatient with their work. As Ernest Samuels correctly pointed out, whenever Berenson philosophized, it was as a pragmatist; Berenson felt William James was the only philosopher who had anything to offer that he could use. His diary entries indicate that he read a good deal of Henri Bergson and Friedrich Nietzsche, and his principle of life-enhancement has been associated with both, but there is very little evidence that his understanding of either was in any way profound. When he spoke of philosophers, it was typically to describe certain affinities he may have felt for their ideas, rarely to elaborate on specific concepts or arguments.

When introduced to Bergson in his youth, Berenson was immensely gratified to learn that the philosopher had read his books and had even expressed admiration for their sound thinking on aesthetics. But he admittedly struggled to understand Bergson's works and recalled with great embarrassment his inability to hold a satisfactory conversation with him.

> He had read me, which made me happy, and remarked
> that much of my work was concerned with discovery
> and establishing identities. But what were identities and
> how did we recognize them? I remember looking at him
> fatuously, and answering that it was by comparing detail

with corresponding detail. Of course; but that was not
what he had in mind, and I have never got over being
ashamed at the puerility of my answer.[12]

He also had an uneasy relationship with the Italian philosopher
Benedetto Croce. Berenson, through his personal secretary Nicki
Mariano, met Croce in 1926. He was unsympathetic toward Croce's
theories of aesthetics, which he viewed as narrow and antiempiri-
cal, but it wounded him to think that Croce cared so little for his
own theories. Although he admired Croce personally and realized
the extent of Croce's influence on the intellectual life of modern Italy,
Berenson resented his apparent lack of interest in what he felt or
thought.

The philosophers with whom Berenson had the most personal
contact, aside from William James, were Bertrand Russell and George
Santayana. He was related to Russell by marriage, and Santayana had
been a classmate at Harvard. For the duration of Russell's marriage
to Mary Berenson's sister Alys, Berenson and Russell were close.
They drifted apart, however, after the marriage disintegrated, and
Berenson later regretted that personal factors had interfered with this
relationship and had denied him Russell's stimulating companion-
ship.[13]

It is well known that Russell took issue with Berenson's theory
of tactile values and life-enhancement when first consulted about it
by Mary Berenson.[14] One of Russell's chief objections was to Berenson's insistence on the universality of the empathetic response to art.
He claimed that it may account for Berenson's pleasure, but not necessarily for that experienced by others who lacked his sensibilities.
Russell clearly included himself as one of the latter and he was very
conscious of his inability to appreciate art.[15] Russell attributed his
lack of aesthetic sensibility to the fact that he had a poor visual imagination. In William James's theory of imagination Russell had found
justification for what he regarded as a fundamental incompatibility
between the capacity to think abstractly and the ability to visualize.

This could account, at least in part, for his failure to be impressed by Berenson, since Russell associated abstract thought with mathematics, which was his chief preoccupation.

The strained relationship between Berenson and George Santayana has also been well documented and was complicated by the fact that Santayana had applied himself to aesthetics with what Berenson thought were largely unsatisfactory results. In a 1912 letter Santayana described life at I Tatti as a "stream of distilled culture flowing over us continually in the form of soulful tourists and weary *dilettanti* who frequent this place." [16] It would seem from this remark that Santayana already saw in Berenson's situation the potential for sinking into a dangerously shallow intellectual life. By then, Berenson was involved with the art dealer Joseph Duveen and, as he himself claimed and as many others confirmed, this association may have had a decisive effect on his intellectual development.

Berenson's autobiographical writings are filled with expressions of regret about his decision to become an expert in the attribution of Italian paintings; he viewed this decision as a major deterrent to developing his general ideas into a significant theoretical treatise. Ostensibly he lamented the loss of his time and energy to the narrow task of attribution, but it is evident that connection with the trade affected his development in a far more integral way. In the opinion of many who knew him, the wordly aims encouraged by Berenson's involvement with the art market soon contaminated his intellectual goals. This view of Berenson has gained currency in the present climate of hostility toward his financial success, resulting in an unfortunate tendency to attribute all of his shortcomings to such involvement. [17]

Berenson as a Writer

Berenson believed he was born to talk and to look, not to write. One of the great paradoxes of his career was that in the face of this he still harbored a life-long ambition to become a writer. This drive to publish, which continued long after it was necessary for him to uphold his professional reputation, has been the subject of much speculation. Berenson seems to have been haunted by the conviction that writing, especially writing for publication, was the only way for him to legitimize his interests—interests that must have seemed, in the context of his Boston upbringing, perilously frivolous. Aesthetic contemplation was not a profession, and Berenson realized early, again from his experiences in literary Boston and Cambridge, that his credibility, livelihood, and, to a certain extent, self-esteem would depend on a reputation created and sustained by publication.

Despite Berenson's desire to become a literary presence, the vast majority of his publications are concerned with technical matters of attribution. His manifest inability to apply the rigor and logic that he brought to connoisseurship to the development of his general ideas might have been less of an impediment to his literary ambition were it not coupled with a debilitating sense of inferiority in regard to his powers of expression. If Berenson has failed to command serious attention as a writer of theory, it is in part because, as he well knew, he simply could not articulate his ideas.

> Where I fall down utterly is not knowing how to arrange and develop what I want to communicate. I have failed to discipline myself, to marshall my arguments in the most effective, the most persuasive and most memorable way. . . . The result is that the few, the very few, ideas I have launched have but seldom reached the cultivated person, and then distorted by my failure to present them adequately.[18]

Berenson's habitual practice of telling his readers and correspondents what he was working on or what he had hoped to produce as a companion to the technical writing he published stemmed, no doubt, from this lack of faith that his writing skills would enable him to see a project through to its completion. Although he was always eager to let people know what he was thinking about, he rarely succeeded in giving more than fragmentary shape to his ideas.

Berenson did not always feel this way about his writing. As an undergraduate he made regular contributions to the *Harvard Monthly,* and he embarked on his "grand tour" of Europe intending to become a literary critic, a plan he surely would not have made without some belief in his gifts as a writer. His confidence seems to have been eroded in no small measure by contact with his wife and her family. Kenneth Clark observed that Berenson's chief misfortune as a writer was to be surrounded by natural stylists; both Mary Berenson and her brother Logan Pearsall Smith wrote well and easily, and Mary Berenson, at least, convinced Berenson that he did not. In 1930, many years and publications later, she expressed to her sister Alys Russell continued astonishment at his rhetorical ineptitude.

> It is an absolute mystery to me how he cannot at least
> say things in a straightforward manner and how he, who
> I know is so extremely sensitive to bad style in what he
> reads, crowds his pages with confused and ungrammati-
> cal sentences. The worst, or perhaps the best of it is that
> in the midst of all this dull writing, every now and then
> he strikes out extraordinarily original and suggestive
> ideas, any one of which would be enough for a historian
> or critic to seize upon and use as the basis for a whole
> treatise. He really does say things that nobody else says
> or thinks, and it seems a pity that they should be buried
> away like this under masses of detail and frightfully
> wearisome connoisseurship, and presented, when they
> are presented, in an insignificant and sometimes almost
> repulsive fashion.[19]

Mary Berenson clearly shared her husband's concern that his general ideas were fair game for appropriation by other writers better equipped to develop them, a possibility that was made clear to them in an infamous episode involving the writer Vernon Lee.[20]

Berenson's desire to write theory was also seriously undermined by a clear preference for aphoristic expression and by his fundamental, if paradoxical, belief that writing about art interfered with the appreciation of it. In 1950 he wrote in his diary:

> I enjoy epigrammatic and aphoristic writing. . . . Elaborate writing is the product of a convention to put through a dialectical process the flashes of intuition that inspire one. To me either an idea is axiomatic at first flash or it never comes home, no matter how much it is coaxed by blandishing arguments. If I was living up to my conviction I would put down all I have to say in a few sentences.[21]

Berenson was equally unfaithful to his belief that "art cannot be correlated with thought. That is why so little can be said about it—except by the people to whom it does not reveal itself."[22] This conflict between the cognitive and the aesthetic appeal of art can be seen throughout Berenson's entire career and is a central theme of many who write on his legacy.

Characterizing Berenson's Achievement

Finally, any appraisal of Berenson's contribution to the study of art must necessarily address two fundamental questions: How can we best characterize his achievements, and how can we assess the role Mary Berenson played in them? Ultimately, these issues are related, for if Berenson is to be remembered strictly as a connoisseur, then unquestionably his wife is deserving of a large measure of his glory.

Samuels's biography of Berenson provides ample proof of Mary Berenson's status as a full collaborator in his professional life. She was no mere assistant but an active participant, sharing in his discoveries, in the making of attributions, and in the writing of his publications. Evidence suggests that the essay for Berenson's first volume on Italian painting, *The Venetian Painters of the Renaissance,* was largely written by Mary Berenson (then Mary Costelloe) and that his chief contribution was in editing and adding the lists. The publication would have borne both their names had her mother not feared the potential scandal of her daughter, who was then still married to the Irish barrister Frank Costelloe, being linked so blatantly with the young American who improperly occupied most of her time.[23]

If Berenson is to be granted a prominent place in the history of art theory and criticism, however, there is no reason to believe that Mary Berenson must also share in this honor. She considered herself a competent connoisseur but consistently deferred to Berenson when it came to the discussion of general ideas, crediting herself only with the ability to understand the concepts he originated. This feeling is most evident in her letters to the German sculptor and designer Hermann Obrist, with whom she had a brief affair and who probably made a substantial contribution of his own to Berenson's theories.[24]

In the summer of 1895, when Berenson was struggling with the essay on the Florentine painters, which contains the first statement of his theoretical principles, Mary Costelloe wrote to Obrist, pleading with him to join them in Florence so that he could act as midwife to Berenson's ideas. Her letter insisted that Berenson needed "manly resistance" to his thought, that what he met in her was a "mush of concession," causing him to advance slowly.[25] It is beyond question that Berenson's future wife, given the nature of their relationship, was being expedient in representing herself as his (and by implication Obrist's) intellectual inferior, an impulse she could not have escaped no matter how strident her feminist upbringing. There is, nevertheless, no evidence to contradict her stated perception that the role she played in the formulation of these ideas was secondary. It is tragically ironic that Mary Berenson, who denied herself the ability to originate thought, was the chief instrument through which Berenson's ideas were rendered intelligible to his readership.[26]

The matter of how best to characterize Berenson's achievements is not as simple as it would seem, although within the field of art history there is widespread agreement that his chief importance was in the realm of connoisseurship.[27] Essays on Berenson and connoisseurship, such as those by Sydney Freedberg and the important study by David Brown, have contributed a great deal to our understanding of the way Berenson's unique gifts worked in tandem with the traditions of Walter Pater and Giovanni Morelli to make of him the precision instrument on which his unrivaled stature as an expert rested. Berenson's strength as a connoisseur depended on the profitable interaction of late nineteenth-century aestheticism with the scientific method of attribution. As Brown put it, Berenson's aesthetic sensibilities served him as a connoisseur precisely because "the process by which he claimed to enter into the spirit of a work became, in practice, a careful scrutiny of it."[28]

Whether applied to appreciation or attribution, there can be no doubt that Berenson's visual memory, his sensitivity to works of art, and his dogged determination to come to terms with his response to them were his singular gifts and his most salient characteristics. But despite the importance of these qualities to the practice of connoisseurship, it has never been possible to define Berenson narrowly as a connoisseur, no matter how great his influence in that arena. Many of the obituaries that flooded the popular and art press in the years after his death stressed his humanism as much as his connoisseurship, and he is described as a critic or art historian as often as an expert. In a 1955 review of several of Berenson's late books, Clement Greenberg prophesied that posterity would value Berenson more for his criticism than his expertise, an astonishing notion coming from a critic whose own formidable critical apparatus was marshaled in defense of the kind of art Berenson spent nearly half his life discrediting.

What enabled a writer like Greenberg to value Berenson's criticism (which is of course inseparable from his connoisseurship) was their mutual emphasis on the importance of taste, artistic quality, and the priority of visual evidence. Greenberg was able to see beyond the normative standard that Berenson allowed his theory of aesthetics to become, toward a critical methodology that, Greenberg believed, with philosophical refinement, could be broadly applied. That Berenson himself refused to see beyond it was his greatest failing as a critic. Greenberg faulted Berenson for his inability to formulate a theory that would serve as more than an "ad hoc means of praising specific works of art," and he had no patience with Berenson's dogmatic insistence on the canons of classical art that formed the basis of his aesthetics.[29]

Greenberg believed that Berenson was at his best, not in his theoretical generalizations, but when he articulated appreciations of individual works, and in this he was not alone. The wry comment by Gertrude Stein that "[Berenson] thinks he is great all the time but it isn't his mind; it is his moments of exquisite creative perception that completely expressed themselves" reflects an estimation that is nearly universal in the literature.[30] A consistent theme among Berenson's appraisers has been that he need not have regretted his decision to become an expert, because his time was most profitably spent in the formal analysis and criticism of individual works of art, not in the articulation of theory.

Berenson's theories of art and aesthetics, outlined in the essays on Italian Renaissance painting and elaborated in his last books, are now regarded mainly as curiosities, vestiges from another age that have no validity when applied outside the narrow range of art for which they were developed. Based on the principles of psychological aesthetics current in the late nineteenth century, these theories assume that human beings respond physically, or with a kind of unconscious self-identification, to certain formal elements in art, and they have proven to be useful and enduring guidelines for the appreciation of Florentine Renaissance painting. Their limitations became evident almost immediately, when Berenson insisted on applying them as a normative standard by which to judge value and quality in the figurative art of all ages.

The premise that we experience tactile values and movement as "ideated sensations" when we look at a painting is very limited as an aesthetic theory. It is more suitably defined as a theory of art appreciation and criticism based on viewer response. Its detractors have demonstrated that it is not a theory or a philosophy of art with universal implications. The discipline may not have lost a great theorist in Berenson, but many art historians were clearly dismayed, especially in Berenson's last years, by the emphasis that both Berenson and his popularizers placed on the shallow ideals of art appreciation.

In a statement written shortly after Berenson's death, the art historian Creighton Gilbert lamented the numerous reminiscences, encouraged by the remarks in Berenson's published diaries, that tended to exalt Berenson's aesthetic sensibilities at the expense of proper recognition for his learning and scholarship. Gilbert feared that the often-repeated observation that Berenson taught us all the importance of "seeing" art carried with it the danger that this accomplishment would be trivialized, resulting in a deflection of interest—and resources—from serious scholarship in favor of a more accessible form of "visual education" for the general public. Berenson's "appreciation course," according to Gilbert, was not very good, but it derived its power and credibility from the background of Berenson's original scholarship.[31]

In the popular imagination, Berenson's theories of art appreciation were linked with more than the priority of seeing and experiencing the work; they were inseparable from the humanism he claimed as the guiding principle of his life. The most enduring image, before that of the Faustian art dealer of recent years, was of Berenson as the last great humanist, hiding out in the ivory tower at Settignano, watching Western civilization sink into ruin. He has been compared with everyone from Petrarch to Boccaccio and liked to think of himself as a modern day Winckelmann or Goethe.

The principle of life-enhancement through art was the most deliberately philosophical part of Berenson's theory of aesthetics and is largely responsible for the general impression that this theory is badly dated and prejudicial, especially as it applies to his understanding of the humanistic function of art. His insistence that art must manifest its grounding in visible reality in order to effectively engage the viewer led him to dismiss all abstract art as "anti-art," a position that does not seem illogical within the context of his empathetic response theory. While other theorists encouraged expansion of the concept of aesthetic empathy (living into a work of art) to include response to formal values in the abstract, divorced from naturalistic representation, Berenson further narrowed the concept to the point where nobody expected him to approve of modern art. At the end of his life he became a standard-bearer for a coherent set of values in the face of chaos, stubbornly upholding the canons of classical art that had enhanced his life. But his refusal to accept modern art was not simply a matter of it having rendered his aesthetic theory useless; he also could not see how this kind of art contributed to what he liked to call the "House of Life."

*   *   *

There is, then, a troublesome inconsistency in the current understanding of Berenson's legacy to modern criticism and the implications of his general ideas. It is argued that his aesthetic principles would not allow him to concede any ground to modernism, and this is certainly reinforced by his outspoken disapproval of nonrepresentational painting. But paradoxically, these same principles helped to create the climate in which modernism could flourish, and to a large extent they informed its critical vocabulary. Berenson's enjoyment of art turned on an acute sensitivity to its intrinsic formal qualities, but his belief in classical humanism would not allow him to ignore its extrinsic or associative qualities. Art must do more than enhance the senses; it serves a higher purpose.

It is precisely the position that the aesthetic experience requires some sort of justification, a stance he went out of his way to decry in his youth, that separates Berenson from the school of criticism he helped found. By insisting on humanism as the philosophical basis of art, Berenson betrayed his critical sensibilities and assumed what Clement Greenberg has aptly characterized as a "posture" regarding modern art that is only marginally related to Berenson's aesthetics.[32]

The common assumptions about Berenson and the twentieth century, that he helped make modernism possible and that he could not be expected to accept it, are both correct. If there is a contradiction in his historical legacy, it has arisen because a critical method was transformed into a moral position posing as a theory of aesthetics.

2. Defining Berenson's Modernity

Yes, it was in my youth that I accepted the exile of staying here in Florence, and now I have become accustomed to it as though it were my true home. It was an exile into which I moved from Paris, where my impulse had been to study the art of the nineteenth century.

1931

Pictures are classified on almost any principle except the aesthetic, the only legitimate one in matters of art; a masterpiece runs every risk of being stuck, like a postage stamp, on a wall covered with paintings that have nothing but historic or archaeological interest to recommend them, instead of being, as they should be, isolated in a special niche like the image of a jealous god.

1898

Introduction

It is virtually impossible to write about Berenson without having to impose some sort of order on his prodigious career.[1] There are a number of ways to apportion his professional activities, but none are without difficulty because his career did not develop in a linear fashion. In retrospect, Berenson regarded his decision to become an expert in the connoisseurship of Italian painting as a turning point in his career. His explanation that attributions consumed all his time and energy, thus undermining his literary ambition and distracting him from the goal of pure appreciation, was clearly self-serving. However, attempts to focus on the financial rewards that accompanied Berenson's decision, in order to expose alleged flaws in his character, are neither objective nor particularly helpful. If Berenson's career had a pattern, it was perhaps better characterized by individuals such as Kenneth Clark and John Walker, who were close to him and privy to his wide-ranging and constantly shifting interests.

Berenson published in book form mainly in the first fifteen and last fifteen years of his career. In the intervening decades any influence he had outside the arena of picture dealing was mainly limited to his rich conversation and is therefore difficult to assess. There can be no doubt that his most influential works were the early books and essays on Italian painting, written between 1894 and 1907. Most of Berenson's writing during the years of his involvement with Duveen (from about 1907 to 1937) was concerned with technical matters of attribution and with revisions of the lists that had accompanied his four original books on the regional schools of Italian painting. The essays that served as introductions to these lists were never revised, assumedly because, as Berenson once remarked to Meyer Schapiro, he thought of them as "classics" with which he should not tamper.

In addition to the four volumes on Italian Renaissance painting, during these years Berenson published the two-volume study *The Drawings of the Florentine Painters* (1903), widely regarded as his most significant contribution to art historical scholarship; a monograph on Lorenzo Lotto (1895, revised 1901); and numerous periodical articles, some of which were collected in the anthology series entitled *The Study and Criticism of Italian Art* (1901, 1902, 1916). Although his book on Sassetta, *A Sienese Painter of the Franciscan Legend,* bears a 1909 publication date, the original articles appeared in *Burlington Magazine* in 1903 and should be considered in this aggregate of early works.

Most of Berenson's general ideas on art, aesthetics, and connoisseurship are introduced in these books. A great deal has been written about the intellectual climate in which they were produced, both from the standpoint of influences on Berenson and from the general state of art study and criticism at the turn of the nineteenth century.[2] Berenson's originality as a writer on art rested largely on the distance he willfully placed between himself and the followers of John Ruskin, whose literary, moralistic approach to art was the dominant critical mode of the late nineteenth century in England and in the United States.

The autonomy of art and the notion of disinterested aesthetic pleasure were the cornerstones of Berenson's early critical position and are clearly rooted in the progressive art for art's sake milieu he embraced as a youth. His aestheticism, which manifested itself not only in epicurean idealism but also in a critical method that relied on an intense awareness of his own sensations and the desire to sustain a heightened state of responsiveness, has its origins in Walter Pater, whom he claimed as his greatest influence and inspiration.[3] He also acknowledged a great intellectual debt to William James, who, as Samuels notes, inadvertently reinforced in his Harvard classroom the psychological reality of experienced sensations that were crucial to Pater's aesthetics. Berenson's dependence on Giovanni Morelli, founder of so-called scientific connoisseurship—the study and attribution of paintings based on careful scrutiny of morphological detail—has been extensively documented, as has his frequent departure from the narrow constraints of this method.[4] Finally, Berenson's assimilation of the cultural and artistic values of the elite Bostonian society that nurtured him in youth and lionized him in maturity requires no further elaboration.[5]

Berenson's interest in German aesthetic theory has been the subject of much speculation, and it is still not well understood.[6] His hostility toward anything German and his unsympathetic attitude toward philosophy could not conceal an obvious affinity between his own approach to aesthetics and the psychological theories of aesthetics that were current in his youth; he read German with ease and no doubt had access to these German texts. Establishing a line of direct influence, however, has proven slippery and inconclusive. Berenson's proposal that certain formal artistic qualities stimulate ideated sensations in the viewer is commonly held to be an obvious derivative of the theory of empathy explored by German aesthetic philosophers such as F. T. Vischer, Theodor Lipps, and Johannes Volkelt. Late in life Berenson would claim to have been ignorant of Volkelt and to have read only portions of Lipps before writing his own theoretical treatise. His diary entries contain references to both Volkelt and Heinrich Wölfflin as German theorists who anticipated him in matters of theory, but nowhere does he acknowledge their direct influence on his thinking.[7]

The Germans who most influenced Berenson's thinking were not philosophers but practicing artists who were also interested in art theory. Among them were Adolf Hildebrand and Hermann Obrist. Hildebrand's small pamphlet *The Problem of Form in the Figurative Arts,* published in 1893, influenced an entire generation of art theorists and critics, including Heinrich Wölfflin. Hildebrand's practical approach to aesthetics was concerned with finding a working method for artists by analyzing the basic elements of perception and then ordering them into a separate formal reality.[8] This practice was far more compatible with Berenson's mind than the metaphysical abstractions of aesthetic philosophers. Hildebrand's emphasis on the priority of perceived values of mass and space in both the creation and the apprehension of works of art no doubt fell on sympathetic ears in Berenson, who was already predisposed to think of art in terms of identifiable psychological or physiological responses from his reading of William James and from his familiarity, however superficial, with current German theory. Even more important was Hildebrand's availability; he lived in Florence and could discuss his theories in the presence of the works of art from which they were derived.

There is no reason to believe that a mind like Berenson's, nurtured on the notion of Paterian ecstasy through engagement with the work of art, engrossed in the disciplined visual analysis demanded of the Morellian connoisseur, hostile to the abstract argumentation of philosophy, would have gained more from reading aesthetic treatises than he did from talking to artists about art. Even his understanding of empathy probably owed a great deal to the interpretation given it by artists such as Obrist, who was a frequent companion of Berenson's during the mid-1890s when the small volumes on Italian art were in progress. The first fifteen years of Berenson's adult life were spent reading, talking, and looking, and what emerged by way of written theory must be understood as a confluence of essential activities that if considered in isolation are rendered unimportant. Berenson understood theory chiefly by applying it to actual works in the presence of a stimulating companion. His articulation of aesthetic concepts, at least initially, was motivated by the desire to come to terms with his own responses, given what he held to be plausible notions of how art worked.

The Venetian Painters of the Renaissance

Because of Berenson's unrivaled fame as an expert on Italian Renaissance painting, it is easy to forget that his first great passion when he arrived in Europe in 1887 was modern French art. Even after his decision to devote himself to connoisseurship, there continue to be frequent references in his letters, and in Mary Costelloe's, to their mutual enthusiasm for advanced Parisian painting. Berenson's letters to Costelloe and to his sister Senda, as well as Costelloe's letters and diaries, provide ample documentation to support the view he advances in both *The Venetian Painters* and *Lorenzo Lotto: An Essay in Constructive Art Criticism* that the most significant art of the past is that which anticipated the best art of the present. His great enthusiasm for Venetian painting and his explication of its charm, though clearly indebted to Pater, stand as persuasive appeals to his readership to become aware of the developments in recent art. A central theme of both books is that the importance of Venetian painting rests in its modernity.

When Mary Costelloe began to travel with Berenson in 1891, she wrote to her family often of visits to exhibitions of recent art, and she frequently compared what she saw of the old masters to her favorite moderns. Both Costelloe and Berenson cast aspersions on the French Salon, preferring the impressionist paintings they saw regularly at Durand-Ruel gallery and at the various international exhibitions they made a point of attending on the Continent. From Munich Costelloe complained to her sister Alys Russell of her ponderous note-taking on the Italian paintings in the Alte Pinakothek, while she and Berenson were both secretly "dying" to get to the exhibition of modern pictures.[9] The standard of excellence for Costelloe at this time was clearly Claude Monet, and when she admired art of the past, such as that of Frans Hals or the late Titian, it was because it possessed a similar kind of beauty.

On seeing the art of Renaissance Venice, Costelloe drafted for her family a linear, evolutionary history of art that placed Titian at the beginning of an unbroken chain of development, which, passing through Italy, Spain, and Holland, culminated in the modern French school.[10] In this extraordinary statement, which denies the existence of "free will" in the world of art, insisting that technique was bound to develop and could not stop itself halfway, Costelloe outlined what would soon become the standard formalist rationale for the history of modernism. She also confessed to a preference for Titian's late work, because she could understand it as "pure painting," since it did not depend for its beauty on the fact that it expressed a particular historical epoch with which she was not yet familiar.[11]

Clearly, Costelloe viewed her ability to appreciate French impressionism as indicative of her advanced taste in art. She wrote her family from Paris in 1892 of the shock caused by paintings of Alfred Sisley, Claude Monet, and Camille Pissarro to friends accustomed to seeing nature "a la Barbizon," but she supposed this was inevitable.[12] Impressionism was still viewed in the early 1890s with some suspicion by the British public, who found it wanting in imagination and inept by academic standards.[13] At this time, no doubt with Berenson's encouragement, Costelloe was also striving toward a disinterested aesthetic, thus attempting to free herself of the kind of sentimental conditioned response typical of the Anglo-American spectator.[14]

She was only willing to go so far, however, and the limitations of this advanced taste are also evident in her letters and diaries. Despite her brother Logan's pleading to the contrary, she could see no beauty in the art of the Swiss painter Arnold Böcklin, whose works she referred to as monstrosities and horrors, vigorous and imaginative but careless in technique and not at all pleasurable.[15] Even more telling were remarks made in a letter to her mother in which she promised to forward the family a brief account of the modern French school that she was writing. She asked her mother to tell Logan of her recent meeting with someone who adored Mary Cassatt's paintings because they were "so flat," comparing them to Edouard Manet's *Olympia:* "Perhaps Logan can see light in the comparison. I could not."[16]

To Berenson, as well as to Costelloe, impressionism was a sensate art that rendered reality palpable by the unification of tonal values on the painterly surface. Berenson too sought precedents for this in Venetian and Baroque painting. A lengthy notation made in 1892 testifies to how thoroughly imbued he was with this aesthetic.

> In painting an effect of reality is only to be attained
> through light and shadow, tones, values, and atmo-
> sphere. These it will be observed are the names of the
> principal problems confronted by the mass of modern
> painters in France. . . . I must draw attention to the fact
> that the greatest painters of the past . . . whose works to
> this day produce upon us the effect of the greatest reality
> are precisely those who anticipated modern artists by en-
> countering their problems. . . . [Titian, Hals, Tintoretto,
> Velázquez, Rembrandt] produce their astonishing effect

of reality not it will be remembered through beauty of
line or even color, but through their treatment of light,
values and atmosphere, or at least through their fascinating brushwork. . . . Now modern painting of France
aims at this effect of reality, uses the right means for
attaining this end, and frequently succeeds—not only
in producing this effect but its apparently inseparable
companion beauty. This goes a great way to proving that
modern French painting is at any rate on the right track,
and being on the right track for the attainment of reality,
and considering how full life is nowadays, we need not
despair of seeing works of art produced in the immediate
future which would make us able to dispense, if it were
necessary, with most of the art of the past.[17]

In the summer of 1892 Berenson and Costelloe spent a good deal of
time in Paris looking at modern pictures, and Berenson advised their
friend James Burke on the purchase of some for his collection.[18] By
October Berenson was back in Italy, where he wrote his sister Senda
after a visit to Padua that he found his love for the fourteenth-century
painters growing in exact proportion to "the increase of my interest
in the very latest painters of my own time."[19] He further explained
to her that he had begun to see art differently. Having once sought
only classical ideals of form and Virgilian sentiments in painting, he
now looked to enjoy the "art" in a picture: "The quality of line in
drawing, force, decision mean everything to me." Because he was indifferent to the sentiments of pictures, he expressed his readiness to
appreciate any painting of quality, be it by Edgar Degas, Hokusai, or
Giotto. This letter suggests that Berenson was looking at modern art
with increased rigor and discrimination and that his apprehension
of it exceeded a simplistic understanding of the painterly versus the
sculptural mode of representation.

The Venetian Painters of the Renaissance, published in 1894, was
written by Costelloe and Berenson in the heat of their enthusiasm
for recent French painting. It reflects their unmistakable admiration

for the new and the modern. This is typically regarded as the least original of Berenson's early books, dependent as it is on Pater and the art for art's sake view of modernity that he exemplified. In their view Venetian art was modern because it satisfies the demand for pleasure and beauty without appealing to other instincts. As such, it perfectly mirrors Venetian society, which was characterized by "a love of comfort, of ease, and of splendour, a refinement of manner, and humaneness of feeling, which made them the first modern people in Europe."[20] Unlike the Florentines, who devoted themselves to science and archaeology, the Venetians esteemed beauty. Consequently, they produced art that could never have been made by the Florentines, who were "too much attached to classical ideals of form and composition, in other words, too academic, to give embodiment to the throbbing feeling for life and pleasure."[21] If only for purposes of argument, Costelloe and Berenson made significant efforts in this book to distance the "academic" traits of classicism from the sensuous appeal of Venetian art, and by extension, modern art.

In analyzing the Venetians, the authors were willing to forgive "venial faults of drawing," as long as space and mass are honored, a predictably generous view coming from two progressives well aware that a chief criticism of impressionism from academic circles was its lack of respect for contour and finish. They pointed out that these artists think of the painting as a "cubic content of atmosphere enveloping all the objects depicted," but they also made a case for the essential realism of the Venetian vision: "The eye does not see everything, but all the eye would naturally see along with the principal objects must be painted, or the picture will not look true to life."[22]

Aesthetically, Venetian painting is discussed in terms of what they had come to admire in recent art. We can view the book in part as an apology for this new art: "Indeed, not the least attraction of the Venetian masters is their note of modernity, by which I mean the feeling they give us that they were on the high road of the art of today."[23] Costelloe and Berenson even suggested at one point that both the Spanish baroque and the French modern painters were superior in terms of pure painting technique to the Venetians whose significance lies elsewhere, namely, the perfect way in which they mirror their age.

In retrospect, what has struck readers as anachronistic regarding *The Venetian Painters* is precisely this lingering tendency to treat art as a manifestation of the spirit of an age, appealing to its relevance in the realm of history and ideas. This is in sharp contrast to the formalist approach to Florentine art that Berenson would take several years later. But it is worth noting here that although the theories of aesthetics outlined in *The Florentine Painters* were clearly more radical and original, this appraisal of Venetian painting already places Berenson firmly in the milieu of what would, in 1894, have rightfully been viewed as progressive taste, informed by a vigorous defense of modern art.

Lorenzo Lotto

> Even the critic will always understand best the artist
> who was most like him in temperament, but it never
> occurs to him to limit his interest to that one artist.
> The person who is not a critic does just this and has his
> favorite poet, favorite painter, and favorite musician,
> that is to say the kind of artist he would be himself if
> he were one. If I were one I should be a great deal like
> Lotto allowing for four centuries of difference, an insur-
> mountable gulf. Yet Lotto speaks to me with a directness
> that scarcely any other artist in any other art ever has.[24]

When Berenson wrote these words to his sister, he had settled on the career of Lorenzo Lotto as a vehicle to demonstrate the fertility of the so-called new art criticism, that is, Morellian connoisseurship. In lieu of writing an article on the subject in the abstract, he decided to illustrate how the method worked by attempting to reconstruct the artistic personality of this painter through the close scrutiny of correctly attributed works. The study of Lotto was to provide both a working model and an exoneration of this method at a time when the relevancy of scientific connoisseurship was highly suspect. By using it to gain insight into the artist's personality and epoch, Berenson could justify the labor of making correct attributions.

The selection of Lotto, then regarded as a minor Italian painter, troubled period reviewers, who felt the effort would have been better spent on a more deserving figure. Years later, Kenneth Clark also questioned Lotto as a choice when, considering the nature of the task at hand, he was a poor candidate. Berenson set out to demonstrate that the career of an artist could be reconstructed solely on the basis of evidence internal to the work, without the use of documents or signatures. The Morellian system of analyzing morphological details to determine authorship assumes a fundamental consistency in terms of execution, but, as Clark submits, Lotto was an uneven and stylistically unpredictable painter. Also, a fair amount of his paintings can be authenticated with signatures and documents. Ever mindful of the unreliability of such evidence, the Morellian connoisseur placed more faith in visual evidence, but as Clark and even Berenson himself later granted, the attempted reconstruction of Lotto's personality and career is based on an erroneous assumption about Venetian painting and on several incorrect attributions.[25]

It is evident that Berenson chose to write about Lotto for highly personal reasons, not because Lotto was a particularly good example of how scientific connoisseurship could further art historical inquiry. In looking back on his own youthful days spent with Berenson in search of the work of Lotto, Clark understood well the artist's appeal in these early years. "I was crushed by the intolerable confidence of Titian, but Lotto's uneasiness was sympathetic. Forty-five years later I have come to appreciate the greatness of Titian, and to feel slightly impatient at Lotto's instability."[26]

Berenson, of course, reached a similar conclusion in his maturity and was somewhat embarrassed by his naive enthusiasm for Lotto, but this does nothing to alter the fact that in the 1890s Lotto seemed to him "as modern as Degas" and that this very modernity was at the root of Berenson's affinity for him.[27]

It is easy to read *Lorenzo Lotto* as a kind of self-portrait of the young Berenson and his age. He suggests this as a possibility in the final chapter when he writes that the psychological composite he offers of Lotto as a man can make no claim to scientific accuracy because art traffics in emotion, and

> do what we will to pump ourselves dry of prejudices and accidental feelings, do what we will to be cautious and judicious, our final impression of works of art remains an equation between them and our own temperament. Every appreciation is, therefore, a confession, and its value depends entirely upon its sincerity.[28]

What Berenson prized in Lotto was that he was an artist of great sensitivity who was at odds with the ideals of his own age, a modernist prophet who can best be understood by those who are receptive to the most advanced ideas of the present.[29] It was Lotto's rendering of psychological characteristics, a quality evident in both his religious paintings and his portraits, to which Berenson was particularly responsive and that defined for him the essence of the artist's modernity. He advanced the image of Lotto as a thinker who penetrated his subjects deeply, exposing them to the viewer as gentle, sensitive creatures, horrified by the crimes of their age.

In contrast to Lotto, Titian was the quintessential cinquecento painter who presented his subjects at their best and most attractive in an impersonal manner. Although Titian's work embodied the dominant tendencies of his age, it did not give us access to people's souls. Titian painted ideal types, Lotto real people. Lotto was like a psychologist, interested in the effects of events and things on human consciousness. Our sympathy is won for his sitters because we can relate to their weakness and vulnerability. His people feel as we do.

This comparison relies heavily on the interpretation of subject, a critical method Berenson nominally opposed. As such, it supplies an interesting contrast to the view of the Renaissance that Berenson sketched in *The Venetian Painters*. In the latter, he made a case for Venetian painting as the most complete expression of the modern spirit of the Renaissance, a spirit he claims for his own age: "We, too, are possessed of boundless curiosity. We, too, have an almost intoxicating sense of human capacity. We, too, believe in a great future for humanity, and nothing has yet happened to check our delight in discovery or faith in life." [30]

The scenario painted in *Lorenzo Lotto,* however, reminds us that the Renaissance was also an age of murder and pillage, and Berenson submitted the sensitive souls of Lotto's portraits as restoration of the "human balance" in the face of the sanguine Titian. Berenson's characterization of Lotto betrays more than a hint of the uncertainty experienced by himself and other members of his generation who faced the end of the century acutely aware of their vulnerability in this age of heady optimism. As a pair, these books can be understood as representing the polarities of the Renaissance which reverberate in the modern age: Venetian art appeals because it forecasts positivism and gratifies the senses; Lotto's relevance lies in his penchant for introspection and personal revelation.

Berenson surmised that the psychological character of Lotto's art militated against his enjoying a successful reputation because his values and insights were contrary to the norm. Because of the advances in recent art, Berenson argued, we are able to admire in Lotto qualities that in the past would scarcely have commanded serious attention. He noted, for example, that Lotto's painterly technique, suggestive of Manet and Degas, was scarcely popular with contemporary viewers. Thus it is not hard to imagine its meeting with scorn in the Renaissance; even the famed Titian was destined to have his late works regarded as unfinished sketches. By expanding the pantheon of the arts, Berenson asserted, we can begin to "understand the greatness of some of our living painters, instead of waiting until death calls attention to their genius, and to find in certain Italian master's beauties workmanship un-appreciated by their contemporaries." [31]

In terms of formal analysis, *Lorenzo Lotto* does not show evidence of much change from the aesthetic priorities Berenson set forth in *The Venetian Painters*. It is, of course, replete with conspicuous Morellianism, but when Berenson referred to the modernity of Lotto's technique, he was still thinking mainly of loose brushwork and tonal integration. Only in a few isolated instances did Berenson attempt to deal with formal qualities in Lotto's work that are not related to his painterliness or to specific morphological traits. In discussing Lotto's difficulty with the integration of figures in an architectural setting, for example, Berenson reprovingly noted Lotto's spatial distortion: "To lean back ten feet with bodies not measuring six and yet remain perpendicular sounds like a tale from Alice in Wonderland, but is a miracle performed even nowadays by painters of the best standing, so that we must not be too severe on Lotto."[32]

It is tempting to see in such a statement an early (if intuitive) awareness of the more profound pictorial distortions that would pervade progressive art of the 1890s, but it is likely that Berenson was simply complaining about the ineptitude of many academically trained salon painters.

More interesting are his remarks on Lotto's sense of decoration, which he compared to that of modern and Japanese artists. Lotto's decorative sense was ruled by fancy rather than by geometry, and "because he was a person who was wont to project his own states of feelings into inanimate things about him, we can never quite tell just where in his decoration ornament or trimming ends and symbolism begins."[33] The projection of human feeling into inanimate things and the symbolic use of ornament had particular relevance in the fin-de-siècle ambience of Symbolism and art nouveau and are related to Berenson's own theory of empathy soon to take shape in *The Florentine Painters*.

The case made for Lotto's modernity involved more than a plea for an enlightened aesthetic. Berenson used Lotto's paintings as evidence of a personality whose extreme introspection and penchant for psychological penetration bear an uncanny resemblance to what was distinctively modern.

> Even if modern art were not educating us, as it is, to
> appreciate the technical merit of work such as his,
> nevertheless, in any age personality moulding a work

of art into a veritable semblance of itself is so rare a
phenomenon that we cannot afford to neglect it. Least
of all should we pass it by when that personality hap-
pens to be, as Lotto's was, a type towards which Europe
has moved, during the last three centuries, with such
rapidity that nowadays there probably are a hundred
people like Lotto for one who resembled him in his own
lifetime. His spirit is more like our own than is, perhaps,
that of any other Italian painter, and it has all the appeal
and fascination of a kindred soul in another age.[34]

The strategy Berenson used in *Lorenzo Lotto* was to seek out the
offbeat in the past for the purpose of understanding the present and,
in so doing, to elevate the standing of the unconventional past because it is like the present. It is the same strategy that would result in
revisionist views of Italian Mannerist painters who, with their figural
distortions and heightened expressionism, seemed to anticipate artists such as Vincent van Gogh. Similarly, the displacement in the early
twentieth century of Domenico Ghirlandaio by Piero della Francesca
as the preeminent quattrocento painter can be explained by an increased admiration for the architectonic qualities of the latter and
their resemblance to like characteristics in the work of Cézanne.

Accounting for the present by affirming its connection with the
past became standard practice among early modernist critics, and this
has been a powerful device for the legitimation of much twentieth-
century art. Berenson's efforts in this regard were not lost on the
reviewers of *Lorenzo Lotto,* who made frequent reference to his
pleading for the artist's modernity. They did not always agree with
Berenson's psychological reading of Lotto's art, or that he was worthy
of the attention and praise Berenson lavished on him, but they clearly
recognized Berenson's intentions.

Something might be said in criticism of the author's references to modern painting, his comparisons being at
times a little hasty. But one welcomes the growing sense

among students of ancient art of the fact that painting
is an art with a continuity of inspiration, and not an art
desecrated by modern practice.[35]

Most reviewers of *Lorenzo Lotto* dwelled on the relative merits
of the "new art criticism" as they were manifest in this study, for
the essence of Berenson's professional modernity rested in his practice of Morellian connoisseurship. There was general agreement that
the close reasoning and acute detailed analysis necessitated by this
method were not likely to be of interest to the general reader. The
reviewer for *Atlantic Monthly* maintained that the increased knowledge of Lotto furnished by Berenson's study did not result in a greater
sympathy for the painter. Only the final chapter, "Resulting Impression," was recommended to the nonspecialist for the insight Berenson yielded into Lotto's character and cultural milieu. Berenson was
taken to task for creating a "wilderness of details," compiling facts as
if he were a German, and boring his readers with "dead learning." The
New York Times charged him with lapsing into poetic license when
it came to his judgment of Lotto's gifts, and the *Spectator* accused
him of overreading the psychological character of Lotto's work.[36]

The image of Berenson forged from the reviews of both *Lorenzo
Lotto* and *The Venetian Painters* is of an able practitioner of scientific connoisseurship, who in matters of appreciation still depended
on the interpretation of subject and on a conventional view of art as
the embodiment of things external to itself. In *Lorenzo Lotto* Berenson made an effort to understand the man through his work, but
his conclusions were psychological not aesthetic. In these two works
Berenson applied formalism chiefly as a method of attribution; he
had not yet extended it to include the appreciation of art beyond the
aesthete's vague notions of art as a source of pleasure.[37]

Accusations that Berenson's activities as a connoisseur did little
to increase the reader's appreciation of art confronted him with a
formidable challenge. He attempted to rise to this challenge in the
remaining books of this period. When he eventually addressed himself to fundamental issues of aesthetics, Berenson chose to minimize

the emphasis on psychological character and zeitgeist that informs his first two books. His approach in the ensuing volumes is to use the close scrutiny of the work itself as a tool to explain the enjoyment of painting. The mixed response to these first publications taught him that unless the new criticism contributed in some discernible way to the appreciation and understanding of art, it would forfeit all possibility of influence and success. In his next books, Berenson places the formalist method of Morellian connoisseurship at the service of a system of appreciation and, in so doing, elevates it to the stature of an aesthetic theory.

Egisto Fabbri and Hermann Obrist

It is not without significance that the preface to *Lorenzo Lotto* acknowledges a debt to Vernon Lee and Hermann Obrist, fellow members of the expatriate community in Florence and Berenson's close friends. Beginning in 1893, Berenson and Costelloe, when residing in Florence, spent a great deal of time with this art-intoxicated group. Costelloe's diaries from the mid-1890s furnish a fascinating record of the role their relationships played during this crucial period in Berenson's intellectual development. Berenson's ideas about aesthetics and art appreciation crystallized in his daily contact with individuals such as Lee and Obrist, as well as with the poetic duo known as "Michael Field," the German sculptor Adolf Hildebrand, and the American-born Italian painter Egisto Fabbri. Lee and Hildebrand produced significant publications to which Berenson could refer; as a result, his affinity with these writers has been studied in some detail. But the extent to which the artists Obrist and Fabbri influenced his thinking, though no doubt great, can only be assumed from the brief and often fragmentary comments that have survived in correspondence and diaries, and this has received far less attention.

Berenson evidently met Egisto Fabbri in the spring of 1893 through their mutual friend Enrico Costa. Shortly after making Fabbri's acquaintance, Berenson wrote to his sister of a young painter who had lived in the United States until the age of seventeen and who had since been a pupil of Pissarro. In this letter he also mentioned "wrangles" with Fabbri on questions of art and aesthetics that sometimes went on all night.[38] Costelloe's diary entries for the spring months of 1893, 1894, and 1895 record numerous meetings between Berenson and Fabbri, with references to their constant art talk. By 1892 Berenson had begun to reserve special praise for Degas and Pissarro among the French impressionists, and Berenson and Fabbri's mutual admiration for these painters probably helped cement their relationship. They continued to see one another regularly for the next decade, both in Florence and in Paris, where Fabbri maintained a studio.

Because Mary Costelloe does not seem to have been especially interested in Fabbri, his contribution to the formation of Berenson's thought is particularly difficult to measure. She observed that Fabbri and Berenson talked about art and aesthetics constantly, but she neither corresponded with Fabbri nor elaborated on these conversations in her diary. Whereas there are lengthy entries recording the exchange of ideas between Berenson, Lee, and Obrist, Fabbri's visits were simply noted, and it can be assumed that Berenson's conversations with him were largely private. Berenson described him as being in perfect sympathy with his own ideas. In the rare instances when Costelloe is specific about Fabbri, it is usually to describe his taste, which was entirely consistent with Berenson's at this time: He measured all painting against Pissarro, Degas, Velázquez, and the Japanese and preferred Sandro Botticelli to Giovanni Bellini.

In contrast, Costelloe wrote at length about Obrist to her family and in her diaries, and she corresponded with him for a number of years. Berenson's relationship with Obrist was extremely complex because of Costelloe's infatuation with him, and we cannot always assume objectivity when Obrist and Berenson discussed one another's ideas. The rivalry for Costelloe's affection, as well as her own emotional entanglements with Obrist permeate the records of their exchanges but do not diminish them as compelling evidence that Obrist was one of Berenson's most astute critics.

Obrist moved to Florence from Paris in 1892 and Costelloe met him in February 1893, when she was urged by William James, then visiting Florence and in Berenson's frequent company, to talk with Obrist at a dinner party. She wrote in her diary that during the course of the evening she laid down pure "doctrine" as he sat flabbergasted and the company listened silently.[39] Thereafter, they spent a good deal of time together and both she and Berenson became enthusiastic about Obrist's work. In April 1894 Costelloe noted in her diary that Obrist's current project, a fountain design, was a perfect illustration of all that Berenson had been preaching about relief for the last months.[40]

Obrist's letters to Costelloe when he returned to Germany during the summer and fall of 1894 contain exchanges about recent art in Germany and Paris, as well as thinly veiled attempts to undermine her respect for Berenson's critical acumen. He estimated that she and Berenson operated from a strictly Parisian, and thus narrow, point of view and prodded them to expand their horizons. In a lengthy letter of this time he tried to convince her that sometimes the freshest responses to art came in the presence of people she (and Berenson) would dismiss as hopeless provincials. Obrist invited Costelloe to ask herself from whom she had heard the most hideous nonsense about art, a cultured intellectual like Lee or a fresh, naive person of simple character, knowing full well that the couple made a practice of deprecating Lee.

Critics who associate the understanding of art with an advanced level of culture, Obrist argued, were misguided. He compared this to the rightness of enjoyment brought to art by an adolescent as opposed to an adult who cannot judge freshly but thinks himself better because he can talk, reason, and explain the excellence of the work: "We don't want critics so much to tell people what they are to like as to tell them little and to say out always simply what they [crossed out 'think'] feel really."[41] Obrist also tried to assure Costelloe that he was au courant in terms of what was happening in Paris and lectured her on her ignorance of the decorative arts outside the narrow sphere to which she was exposed there.

Obrist's populist view of art stemmed no doubt from this commitment to the decorative arts, which became his preoccupation when he returned to Germany. He was at the very heart of the Munich craft movement in which the abstract art of Vasily Kandinsky took root, and Obrist has been granted a seminal role in its development.[42] The admiration for the primitive and naive within this milieu requires no further elaboration, but it is worth noting that Obrist sought to distinguish himself from Berenson in other ways, which can be associated with his progressive and decidedly Germanic point of view.

While Berenson was away on his first return trip to the United States in the fall of 1894, Costelloe wrote to Obrist to notify him of her intention to await Berenson's return before visiting him in Germany. Obrist tried to dissuade her, confessing that he could not bear the thought of her viewing with Berenson a collection of Max Klinger etchings in Dresden that he had introduced to her, and then afterward being forced to discuss them when the three were together again. Obrist felt so strongly about Klinger's expressive power ("he is to me a sanctum sanctorum, a cave of thrills hidden deep down") that he regarded his sharing of the artist as a sacred act, "a spiritual and creative revelation that cannot be talked about and registered."[43]

What Obrist feared most was that while viewing the etchings with Berenson Costelloe would objectify her response to Klinger and suppress the subjective feelings he had once aroused in her. There is more here than a former lover's jealousy over a past moment of intimacy; Obrist intensely disliked Berenson's distant, clinical approach to art and believed it to be in marked contrast to his own more passionate self: "Common sense is very powerful in me, but never will neutralize quite that last lurking wild impulse of fierce subjectivity."[44]

Even if he had less invested personally in Klinger's etchings, Obrist confided to Costelloe that a discussion of expressive artists such as Klinger and Böcklin would force Berenson to realize there were artistic (if not aesthetic) problems that he had not yet begun to explore— and that in such situations Berenson was infuriating. Obrist realized that Berenson was very likely to dismiss a problem that he had insufficiently penetrated, in a clever "froth" of superficial talk. He told Costelloe that he found this intolerable when the issue in question touched him deeply and thus preferred to avoid certain topics with him unless he sensed that Berenson was inclined to investigate cautiously, as if he might have something to learn.

> He who always still confuses his *capacity* for perceiv-
> ing and unraveling a problem, if he sets his mind to it,
> with the fact of *having done so* already, which he often
> has not yet. . . . I never tire of saying that if Berenson
> were (1) forever prevented from talking [and] (2) forced
> to pass eleven friends before jotting down an opinion,
> he would be the chief critic of this end of century and
> at [the] beginning of [the] next. All the vivifying influ-
> ence of his talk would go lost, but his "thinker" and the
> science would profit enormously.[45]

Obrist's sense of Berenson as a young critic was that his arrogance and impatience made him too ready to believe in the universality of his judgment and quick to discard as impertinent that which did not fit into his scheme of things. Correspondence between Costelloe and Obrist during the months when Berenson was at work on the intro-ductory essay for *The Florentine Painters of the Renaissance* reveals the fundamental incompatibility of Obrist and Berenson's critical positions.

In spring 1895 Costelloe reported to Obrist that collectively she and Berenson were undergoing profound changes in their thinking about art. Because for several years Obrist had been one of the people with whom Berenson talked seriously about aesthetics, Obrist was very interested in this transition. He was motivated both by genuine curiosity and by the desire to contribute. Also at stake were ideas of his own that he had already shared with Berenson, and Obrist did not entirely trust him to acknowledge this when the time came to make them public.[46]

During a visit to France in May of that year, Costelloe took elabo-rate notes on the modern paintings in Paris. She sent them to Obrist, disclosing that although a year ago she and Berenson regarded many

French artists as supreme in all qualities that made for great art, the two were now on a different track and grew more difficult to please every day.[47] Obrist replied that long ago he had undergone the upset of standards they were experiencing. Because he had never been especially sympathetic to the modern French art they so admired in Paris, he added that, to a certain extent, a drastic reappraisal had not even been necessary. It pained Obrist to witness an eye trained by Morelli appreciating Pissarro at the same time as Auguste Rodin, Giorgione, Klinger, and Botticelli, not to mention his own work. He had long awaited the time when Costelloe and Berenson would be de-hypnotized by impressionism and ready to move on.[48]

Obrist was also curious about a reference, made by Costelloe in an earlier letter, to Berenson's current thinking about the "genesis" of a work of art. Based on their previous discussions, Obrist was certain he and Berenson would disagree about this. He cautioned her that Berenson should be thinking specifically in terms of the genesis of a work of art in the Italian school, rather than aiming at generalities.[49] Obrist already sensed what would become patently obvious to Berenson's later critics, that Berenson's insistence on the wide application of ideas developed in a narrow context would undermine the potency of his conclusions.

The issue that most divided Obrist and Berenson, however, was Berenson's uncompromising formalism, which became more resolute as the manuscript for the *The Florentine Painters* progressed. When Obrist was approached by Costelloe for ideas about the why and how of art enjoyment, he recommended to her a small pamphlet by a German writer named Lange that, as Obrist warned, addressed the intellectual rather than the psychological side of the problem.[50] Obrist stressed that the simple part of appreciation was the enjoyment of mere form, but no matter how great our enjoyment of what Berenson called the "decorative," there was always "something else." It was clearly the second quality that struck a responsive chord in Obrist, even though, as he chided Costelloe, Anglo-French aestheticians such as herself and Berenson would insist this had nothing to do with painting as art. He urged her to tell Berenson not to "scour" this book in his typical Anglo-French way, coming to hasty conclusions about what it does not say, but instead to try to absorb what it does say. In her own experience of art, which he again insisted was too narrowly restricted to painting, she ought to ask herself, beyond the merely formal aspects she enjoys, where the "something else" comes in, what it is, and why she enjoys it.

Costelloe read the pamphlet, but hastened to tell Obrist precisely what he did not want to hear. She claimed that it was good for the points it made but that it failed to address what Berenson was after, which was the formal element distinguishing good art from bad. Similarly, Costelloe told her mother that Lange's explanation of why we enjoy art was inadequate, largely because it could not account for why people enjoy good art rather than bad, though she was forced to admit that only rarely was this actually the case.[51]

Evident from this exchange is Berenson's intention to develop in *The Florentine Painters* a theory of aesthetics that would function as a normative standard he could apply to all art for the purpose of ascertaining value. That Berenson's theory was narrow and exclusionary was apparent to Obrist, who had more catholic taste and a greater awareness of the complexity of aesthetic pleasure. The distance between Obrist and Berenson was great. Costelloe, by her own admission, was overwhelmed during this period by Berenson's "genius" and by her own excitement at being in on the ground floor of what she perceived as a revolution in aesthetics. She must have been stung by Obrist's insinuation that the appreciation of formal and decorative qualities was simple. Costelloe pointed out to him that, simple as it may be, if she and Berenson were on the right track, it would mean a complete refounding of criticism, an assumption that, in retrospect, has proven to be largely correct.[52]

Berenson and Obrist continued to exchange ideas throughout the summer of 1895, and they then engaged in a kind of postmortem of Berenson's completed manuscript. In October Costelloe made notes in her diary about a recent letter from Obrist that conceded their fundamental incompatibility on the matter of art enjoyment. Referring to a long-standing disagreement between them about the artistic merits of Böcklin and Klinger, a recurrent theme in their correspondence, Obrist claimed that because she and Berenson had made up their minds to attend only to the decorative (formal) elements, they and Obrist could never enjoy the same things.[53] He fully admitted that, above all, what he expected from art was stimulation of visual and emotional fancy, and, if the *Stimmung* was right, he could forgive faults of form.

The upheaval of standards experienced by Costelloe and Berenson was to result in their eventual disappointment with Obrist's sculpture and a consequent strain on their relationship with him. Favorably disposed to the fountain sculpture on which Obrist had been working during his spring 1894 residence in Florence, they regarded Obrist as a compatriot of Böcklin, one with better taste and more feeling for art as art.[54] But year later, when Obrist sent them photographs of a monument to the composer Franz Liszt that he was working on in Munich, Costelloe replied with a disheartening roster of the work's architectonic flaws, which she claimed were obvious to everyone who saw the photographs.

> The first feeling is one of slight malaise, coming from
> the curious fact that the rock gives an illusion of reality,
> of being the actual "Naturewerk," and one begins ir-
> resistibly to speculate "Where is the body inside the
> rock?" . . . We could only think of the body curled up
> like a kind of snake, and it made all our muscles feel a
> little uncomfortable.[55]

Rodin's marble blocks, Costelloe argued, accommodated their figures comfortably, and even when body parts were missing they were so emphatically sculpture that one did not think about it. What she disliked in Obrist's monument was the challenge to see it simultaneously as nature and sculpture. She explained to him that because the rock would seem a part of nature (not a sculptor's block) it would be odd to see a man pushing his head through a real rock. This blurring of the boundary between nature and art made Costelloe uncomfortable. She also thought it an inappropriate gesture, since Franz Liszt, unlike Richard Wagner, was not a great natural force but instead a rather artificial genius.[56]

The one thing on which Berenson and Obrist seemed to have agreed was the inherent expressiveness of decorative pattern. Although Berenson refused to see the vivid possibilities in Obrist's fusion of the human figure with elements in nature, he was receptive to the symbolic use of ornament. Berenson demonstrated this in *Lorenzo Lotto* when he discussed Lotto's sense of decoration as being governed by fancy and the inclination to anthropomorphize. The power of linear pattern to transmit emotion and vitality was a conviction that survived the upsets of this period, and it is not difficult to believe that Obrist made a significant contribution to its formulation. As an aesthetic principle, clearly one of Berenson's most radical, Berenson would explore this idea further in *The Florentine Painters* and in his essays on Sassetta.[57]

Samuels correctly observed that because of Obrist's greater interest in the content than the form of art, he could not have been of much help when called upon by Costelloe in the summer of 1895 to assist in the fine-tuning of Berenson's aesthetic theories. Nevertheless, she was especially eager to have Obrist's thoughts on objections raised by Bertrand Russell to Berenson's concept of aesthetic pleasure as life-enhancement. It is evident from Costelloe's and Obrist's letters that he had previously discussed Lipps's concept of empathy with either her or Berenson, because she now appealed to him to be more specific.[58] Though Obrist's replies do not appreciably increase our understanding of the direct link between Berenson and Lipps, they provide useful insight into Berenson's command of German aesthetic theory, at least as far as Obrist could determine.

In a letter to Costelloe of 6 August 1895, Obrist claims to have been coincidentally reading the work of Arthur Schopenhauer moments before opening her letter. He quotes a particular passage nearly verbatim from the German, describing it as "word for word B.B."[59] This episode led Obrist to reflect on how often it had occurred to him that the Germans had already done all the thinking on aesthetics.

Evidently, Obrist thought himself at a distinct disadvantage, being part German, because, even though he had thought out many of these things on his own, he could not contribute anything original to the literature of aesthetics. Were he a Frenchman, on the other hand, nothing would prevent him from referring to what had already been written by Germans while still maintaining his personal view of the question. The message between the lines of Obrist's letter was that Berenson would do well to avail himself of the literature of German aesthetics to increase the strength of his position.

That Berenson had not already done so was made evident in another letter from approximately the same time.[60] In Costelloe's query about Lipps, she mentions that there were points in his lectures (as Obrist had described them to her) that she would like to have clarified, but she realizes she has no right to his unpublished ideas. Obrist told her she was mistaken, that manuscripts of Lipps's lectures had been available for some time.[61] Obrist went on to say that since Berenson would not read this frightful style or be impressed by the unreadable book, it hardly mattered. In Obrist's mind, the more pressing question was "are we to tell BB that young men of 24, led to it by Lipps' influence, talk with the same words that BB uses as formed by himself! Or are we not to."[62]

After the assaults by Russell on Berenson's ideas, Costelloe agreed with Obrist that Berenson must begin a serious study of aesthetics, so that he might have the benefit of all that had been done in the analysis of pleasure and the psychology of sight before embarking on a major treatise of his own.[63] From this exchange it would seem that what understanding Berenson did have of German aesthetics was at least in part filtered through individuals such as Obrist. If Berenson was not particularly generous in admitting the influence of these writers, it may have been because he did not begin to study systematically many of these authors until after he had written *The Florentine Painters,* and then he did so only to see who agreed with him.[64]

The Florentine Painters of the Renaissance

Berenson began writing *The Florentine Painters of the Renaissance* in May 1895, believing, as did Costelloe, that he was on the verge of a great discovery. As he told his sister, nominally he was writing on the Florentines but his absorbing interest was to know why people enjoyed art, adding that he was more advanced on that point than anyone had ever been before.[65] The winter of conversation and study was spent in the company of Obrist, Fabbri, and Lee, who also believed, and tried to convince Berenson, that he had made a great discovery in aesthetics. This was preceded by several months in the United States, where his enthusiasm for the formal and expressive qualities of Asian art had been reinforced by visits to the Boston Museum of Fine Arts with Fenollosa and the artist-theorist Denman Ross.

Among these and other factors accounting for the realignment of Berenson's taste and priorities, perhaps the one that was to have the most direct bearing on the conclusions Berenson reached in *The Florentine Painters* was his confrontation with the ideas of Adolf Hildebrand, a German sculptor and art theorist who resided in Florence. As I have noted, Hildebrand stressed the process of analyzing perceptual data as the basis for the creation and appreciation of art. Berenson's reliance on this strategy is well known; like Hildebrand, he concluded that the artist's primary task was to create a convincing impression of three-dimensionality and that our enjoyment of art was linked to the viewer's apprehension of mass and space.[66]

Berenson met Hildebrand through their mutual friend Carlo Placci sometime in the spring of 1894. According to Samuels, Berenson read Hildebrand's *The Problem of Form in the Figurative Arts* when it was published in 1893 and drafted a review of it, which he eventually abandoned. On Berenson's initial encounter with Hildebrand, he quipped to Costelloe that the sculptor was anxious to meet a man who had read his book and he probably wanted to convince himself that it had actually been understood.[67] By 1896, after the manuscript of *The Florentine Painters* was complete, Berenson would report that the similarity of their thought, which even found expression in the same phrases, was almost embarrassing.[68]

The theory of aesthetics set forth in *The Florentine Painters* combines the proto-formalist view that visual images can be analyzed and broken down into experiential components such as sensations of touch, movement, and space, with a loose understanding of the empathy principle, the projection of human feeling into an object or situation. The "right track" so often referred to by Costelloe and Berenson presupposed the possibility that one could explain aesthetic pleasure by correctly identifying sensations produced by art and then linking them with specific formal elements.

As Costelloe understood German theory, the pleasure afforded by art resulted from one's experience of being reminded of some primary sensation in an acute or facilitated manner. Berenson's singular contribution to the study of aesthetics, she wrote Obrist, would be to articulate the primary sensations involved and the formal ingredients that invoked them. It was her belief that although the Germans had gone as far as thought and logic could go, Berenson was uniquely qualified to clarify these further points because it was a task requiring aesthetic (rather than intellectual) penetration of the work.[69]

Even at the distance of one hundred years and in light of its obvious limitations, *The Florentine Painters* is persuasive evidence of the essential modernity of Berenson's critical position. His theory is introduced as a prelude to the appraisal of Giotto, for whom he claims a "peculiar aptitude for the essential in painting *as an art*." In Berenson's view the isolation of what is essential to figure painting depends on "psychological" evidence that our sense of the third dimension is governed by visual impressions confirmed by our sense of touch and the muscular sensations of movement: "Every time our eyes recognize reality, we are, as a matter of fact, giving tactile values to retinal impressions."[70] Berenson explained that because painting is a two-dimensional art that attempts to give an abiding impression of three-dimensional reality, the painter's task is to "stimulate our consciousness of tactile values, so that the picture shall have at least as much power as the object represented, to appeal to our tactile imagination." [71]

The concept of tactile values is no more important here than the implicit understanding that the best paintings will be those which solve the problems unique to their art. [72] Berenson sought to offer in this essay an explanation of the kind of pleasure only painting can provide; in order to do this, he identified certain formal characteristics as essential, and then he depreciated those aspects of enjoyment that are not dependent on these characteristics. Because the painters who preceded Giotto did not attend sufficiently to artistic essentials, "their works have value, if at all, as highly elaborate, very intelligible symbols, capable, indeed, of communicating something, but losing all higher value the moment the message is delivered." [73] When Berenson added "it is only when we can take for granted the existence of the object painted that it can begin to give us pleasure that is genuinely artistic, as separated from the interest we feel in symbols," he fully articulated the central tenets of formalist art criticism that remained largely unchanged (if not unchallenged) for nearly a century: Aesthetic pleasure is unique, it is derived from appreciation of formal elements and it is independent of subject or associated meaning.

By contrast, Berenson understood form as the embodiment of material significance and not simply, as is sometimes suggested, as a sense of mass alone. This is confirmed in his attempt to explain the theory of tactile values to his good friend Solomon Reinach in Paris. "My formula is that artistic form skims off the material significance of things, presenting them to us in such a way that we must attend to them as form, and not as in actuality as so many objects appealing at haphazard to one of a million needs." [74]

Fully cognizant of the fact that his readership was accustomed to approaching art from a literary point of view, Berenson hastened to make a distinction between those who demand good illustration from a painting and those capable of receiving direct aesthetic pleasure. When he insists that Giotto and the other Florentines have neglected the "secondary pleasures of associations" in favor of a higher purpose, Berenson could as well be making a case for early modern art.

> Now what is behind this power of raising us to a higher
> plane of reality but a genius for grasping and communi-
> cating real significance? What is it to render the tactile
> values of an object but to communicate its material
> significance? A painter who, after generations of mere
> manufacturers of symbols, illustrations, and allegories,
> had the power to render the material significance of the
> objects he painted, must, as a man, have had a profound
> sense of the significant.[75]

Giotto's sense of the significant extended to his communication of theme as well as objects. His paintings are not without meaning, but this meaning is conveyed without resorting to obvious symbols and narrative allegory, as was true, for example, in the Spanish Chapel of Santa Maria Novella in Florence. In Giotto's work, meaning is embodied in the formal elements. Just as mastery of artistic essentials enables the viewer to realize the material objects with greater intensity, so too we grasp the essential content of the work in an immediate and direct way. Berenson essentially argued that the painting of the Florentines is more powerful because it is better art.

The high premium Berenson placed on significance and essentials led him to undervalue the rigorous naturalism of quattrocento Florentine painting. As I have noted, Berenson's antirealist bias ultimately resulted in his being associated with twentieth-century theories of abstraction. Painters such as Paolo Uccello, who concerned themselves with displays of knowledge, skill, and dexterity, did not produce art of enduring value because they communicated information, not significance. Berenson described the relationship between Uccello and Giotto as analogous to that of a relief map of Giverny to a painting by Monet, adding that taking notes in color and form did not necessarily result in art.

> What the scientist who paints—the naturalist, that is
> to say—attempts to do is not to give us what art alone
> can give us, the life-enhancing qualities of objects, but
> a reproduction of them as they are. If he succeeded, he
> would give us the exact visual impression of objects
> themselves; but art, as we have already agreed, must give
> us not the mere reproduction of things but a quickened
> sense of capacity for realizing them.[76]

Because the twentieth century has so aggressively distanced itself
from the mimetic function of art, it is easy to forget that to condemn
an artist in the 1890s on the basis of his naturalism, as Berenson does,
is both surprising and impressive.[77]

In the passage on naturalism, Berenson first used the expression that would become a permanent fixture in his vocabulary and
that would be forever associated with his philosophy of art: life-
enhancing. The term life-enhancement was a metaphor used by Berenson to characterize the pleasure that he maintained art alone could
provide. As a metaphor, it was a useful device insofar as it enabled
Berenson to articulate the effect painting had on him; his insistence
on its validity as a fundamental principle of aesthetics, however, was
problematic from the start. It was his great misfortune to have built
a theory of aesthetics around a concept that was unintelligible to
many of his closest associates and that could not withstand the careful scrutiny of even an intuitive critic such as Obrist, much less the
rigorous analysis of a philosophical mind such as Berenson encountered in Russell. That a certain kind of art enhanced Berenson's life
in the manner he described is unequivocal; that it necessarily did the
same for others was by no means assured.

The principle of life-enhancement encapsulates Berenson's belief
that the pleasure we take in artistic form differs from the pleasure we
take in objects experienced in their actuality. A good painting is one
that enables us to realize the object represented with greater intensity, and in so doing it "stimulates to an unwonted activity psychical

processes which are in themselves the source of most (if not all) of our pleasures."[78]

It is Berenson's view that because we realize the object more intensely and with greater ease, we are overwhelmed with a sense of our increased capacity and, as a result, the entire personality is enhanced by the experience of art. "Precisely this is what form does in painting: it lends a higher coefficient of reality to the object represented, with the consequent enjoyment of accelerated psychical processes, and the exhilarating sense of increased capacity in the observer."[79] Only a painting strong in the essentials of art, such as tactile values, can furnish this kind of pleasure because we grasp form in art the way we grasp it in nature: by giving tactile values to retinal impressions. When we experience an object in nature, it is more difficult to skim off the tactile values, and thus they reach consciousness in a weakened state. An artist who concentrates them for us in a painting enables us to grasp the object more quickly than we could do otherwise and with greater intensity. Herein lies the secret to aesthetic pleasure: It provides a heightened sense of our capacity, making us feel better equipped for life itself.

It is clear from discussions surrounding this essay at the time of its inception that the biggest problem facing Berenson would be in defining aesthetic pleasure as life-enhancement.[80] In May 1895 Costelloe summarized a conversation with Michael Field about the kind of pleasure obtained from art that moves the viewer on the level of pathos versus art that is great in terms of form. "The Mikes" wondered why being susceptible to the effects of illustration was an inferior form of art appreciation, to which Costelloe responded thus:

> A large element in aesthetic pleasure is being made conscious of a surplus of energy. Cheap effects leave us where we were. Real art makes us work for our pleasure and leaves us with a heightened feeling of intelligence at having been able to recognize its good points. Behind the obvious in Raphael is much that is not obvious, the

> recognition of which requires an immense intellectual
> effort. . . . But you must not be required to work too
> hard and exhaust all your surplus energy.[81]

The obvious distance between Berenson's concept of pleasure, as outlined in *The Florentine Painters,* and this explanation suggests that the notion had not yet crystallized in his mind or that Costelloe did not fully understand it. This statement describes the kind of pleasure that turned on the exhilaration resulting from satisfying effort. The reward of applying oneself to the appreciation of true art is that it makes one feel smarter to have done something difficult. This is inconsistent with Berenson's argument that pleasure derives from ease of apprehension. At this point, their respective notions of pleasure and exhilaration are highly personalized; both Costelloe and Berenson understand life-enhancement as a feel-good aesthetic, but they do not expect to feel the same things. Berenson sought maximum sensation for minimal effort; Costelloe sought the satisfaction of successful quasi-intellectual struggle.[82]

Several days later Costelloe seems to have moved closer to Berenson's position, because she wrote that art adds to life, and "What is life? A sense of functioning and increased life is an increased sense of ease and endlessness in every possible way of functioning. Art enhances this feeling, which is at the bottom of all pleasure."[83] This diary entry was preceded by the record of a revealing exchange in which Berenson, responding to the question of why greater pleasure is taken in art than in nature, explained that "it is a peculiar enhancement of life to know that man did it—not a god. This is an aesthetic emotion insofar as it is a real leap of life upward, giving you a greater sense of power." Although this statement seems curious in the context of Berenson's extreme emphasis on the appreciation of formal values for their own sake, the humanizing power of art will be a recurring theme of Berenson's late works and is essential to the intrinsically moral position his theory of aesthetics would eventually become.

In 1895, however, Berenson was eager to leave this kind of thinking behind in the interest of penetrating the appeal of the purely aesthetic. Two days after Costelloe recorded in her diary that he had begun *The Florentine Painters*, she referred at length to an episode that took place at lunch and seems to have been a turning point in the shaping of the essay.

> Today at lunch Bernard suddenly broke out in praise of the Degas on the mantelpiece—"the greatest of all works of art. Why?" . . . A good deal of hesitation and feeling around, and at last the right reason hit on the head, because it *conveys* life directly. He deserted the theory that art is to "uplift" or "broaden" life—or any hygenico-social or moral view of its mission. That may or may not be—but the essence of essences is to be a sheath, an envelope of just "plain life!" Effects of space and composition belong to architecture, and are rightly called in painting "architectonic." But painting can communicate life—livingness itself. This is the purely aesthetic artistic standard of art. Whether it resembles or not is aside from the mark. Painting can *convey life* more forcibly, more essentially, than the living thing itself.[84]

Costelloe also noted in this entry that Berenson had been reading Nietzsche and that this had helped forward his ideas—because Nietzsche hates what works against life and loves what makes for it, concluding with the remark, "There remains the question whether these 'architectonic effects' are not equally life-enhancing with the suggestions of movements[,] etc.[,] etc., which Bernard calls the heart of hearts of art?"

This extraordinary passage from Costelloe's diary demonstrates that Berenson came to his conclusions about the essentials of art not simply by way of the Florentines but also by gazing at modern painting. Degas was for him the standard of excellence in art, a fact he affirms in the section on Leonardo da Vinci, where he claims that outside of Degas one would look in vain for a more stimulating rendering of tactile values and movement than is seen in Leonardo. Even though Costelloe represented this as a pivotal moment, Berenson had long associated Degas with everything fundamental to art. In 1892 he told Costelloe in a letter that the business of art was to bring us close to life. He referred collectively to the work of Botticelli, Hokusai, and Degas, and "the door at Spoleto" as things that ask for no explanation and are complete in themselves.[85] It would also appear from Costelloe's concluding statement that at this point Berenson was thinking of artistic essentials primarily in terms of tactile values and, especially, movement, the qualities he most appreciated in Degas.[86]

The section in *The Florentine Painters* that addresses movement as an essential artistic quality is the closest Berenson would ever come to admitting that formal properties in the abstract could be life-enhancing for the viewer. It is significant that these remarks were made in a discussion of Botticelli, whose self-sufficiency he had previously compared to that of Degas and Hokusai. Berenson claimed that Botticelli was indifferent to naturalistic representation, causing the viewer to feel either powerful attraction or revulsion for his "types," but instead seemed intent on "communicating the *unembodied* values of touch and movement."[87] He explained that tactile values could be rendered without corporeality if they were translated into values of movement; for example, the roundness of a wrist could be suggested by outline, working in tandem with the movement of a drapery falling over it.

This notion of material significance communicated entirely in terms of movement, carried one step further, could eventuate in "pure values of movement abstracted, unconnected with any representation whatever. This kind of line, then, being the quintessence of movement, has, like the essential elements in all the arts, a power of stimulating our imagination and of directly communicating life."[88] Berenson called this the art of linear decoration, and he claimed for Botticelli no rivals among his European counterparts, although this kind of expression had precedents in Asian art. He used the music metaphor to emphasize that Botticelli, for whom the representative element was a libretto, was at his best when he could make symphonies in which everything was made to yield to the expressive power of line. When Berenson declares that in such paintings the background is simplified or suppressed to prevent the drawing of the eye inward, away from the rhythm of the line, we are again reminded of how effectively his critical language could be applied to modern art.

For Berenson to admit the possibility that line unconnected with representation could directly communicate life was a radical departure from his pseudoscientific tenor in *The Florentine Painters*. Berenson seems unconcerned with exactly what specific capacity such an experience will heighten and gives himself over to the promise of pure aesthetic pleasure, requiring no explanation or justification. The Botticelli section is something of an anomaly in this respect, because the discussion of movement preceding it is wholly consistent with the psycho-biological aesthetics he had employed in the appraisal of Giotto.

Berenson introduced the topic by explaining why a wrestling match, although replete with movement, cannot be enjoyed aesthetically—both because we indulge our dramatic interest in its outcome and because it moves so fast that we exhaust ourselves if we try to empathize with the wrestlers. A painter wishing to convey such an event without causing confusion and fatigue, to make of it an artistic experience, must extract the significance of movement. This is more difficult than skimming off tactile values, because movement involves sequential action. Yet it must be rendered in such a way that the artist, in capturing one particular movement, gives the viewer the ability to realize all potential movements concurrently. When the artist has done this successfully, for example, as in Antonio del Pollaiuolo's engraving, *The Battle of Nudes,* our muscles feel the pressure and strain, and we are able to share in the sensations and pleasures of movement without the exertion.

Here Berenson associates the sense of heightened capacity not only with ease of recognition but also with the conservation of energy. Whereas in the apprehension of tactile values, Berenson discusses life-enhancement in terms of greater psychical capacity, the doubling of mental activity, and being better provided for life, when we are able to experience movement through art, we are also spared the necessity of physical effort. It is as if Berenson thought of this experience as a graceful way to experience life without having to participate in it: "And thus while under the spell of this illusion—this hyperaesthesia not bought with drugs, and not paid for with cheques on our vitality—we feel as if the elixir of life, not our own sluggish blood, were coursing through our veins."[89]

The compensatory nature of Berenson's theories warrants greater attention than it has received. He was slight, physically frail, in chronic ill-health, and (when not aroused to indignation) generally reserved in behavior. One of the things Berenson sought in art was a vigorous sense of the life he was unable to experience in his daily reality, desirous as he was of conserving energy and disassociating himself from the grunts and groans of animal existence. Through art Berenson hoped to do what he would not or could not do. The work of art became for him a magical device capable of producing the physical sensations he craved, without expending the effort they typically required.[90]

Costelloe's 1896 unsigned review of *The Florentine Painters*, which took the form of an essay entitled "The Philosophy of Enjoyment of Art," makes a point of stressing the physicality of life-enhancement. In an earlier article that Costelloe had written in defense of "the new art criticism" she had attempted to explain why it was important to look at correctly attributed pictures.[91] She was basically making a case for the value of scientific connoisseurship in the face of doubts expressed in reviews of *Lorenzo Lotto* and *The Venetian Painters*. One of the reasons Costelloe offered for the prudence of looking at correctly attributed pictures was to avoid wasting one's time and energy or exhausting one's aesthetic capacities in the search for beauty in poor paintings incorrectly attributed to famous names.

Reflecting Berenson's shift from attribution to appreciation, when Costelloe reviewed *The Florentine Painters* she raised questions as to why people enjoy certain kinds of pictures and what pictures they do enjoy. Costelloe furnished the theory of life-enhancement as an explanation, and she, too, discussed aesthetic pleasure in terms of bodily function, stating very explicitly what Berenson's essay implied. "It is the aim of all the arts, Mr. Berenson says, to be 'life-enhancing'; that is to say, to stimulate that healthy functioning of the organism which is the source of most of our normal pleasures."[92] According to Berenson, she continued, representations of form and movement can do this because they arouse greater physical activity than real life can provide, without the disturbing physical sensations.

After reading Berenson's manuscript, Bertrand Russell insisted that this concept of pleasure as increased capacity was by no means universal and that pleasure was more correctly defined as the satisfaction of desire. Russell felt the principle of heightened capacity was too vague, pointing out to Costelloe that pain can also induce a state of intensified awareness and that the capacity had to be for something specific. There can be no doubt that Russell identified the most serious weakness in Berenson's reasoning, for Berenson's own sense of what was meant by heightened capacity did not remain consistent. As it is presented in *The Florentine Painters*, it can be understood as the potential for increased sensual satisfaction with minimal effort or, as Costelloe defined it, as pleasure taken in the healthy functioning of the organism. But it becomes clear by the end of the essay that what Berenson intended by greater capacity for life went beyond these empathetic notions that art affirms the apparatus of the senses.

This is implicit in the concluding section of *The Florentine Painters*, which deals with the art of Michelangelo. Berenson's appreciation of Michelangelo includes a digression on the importance of the nude, a discussion that will remain the core of his critical position with respect to representational art. Berenson calls man a creature who anthropomorphizes: "We realize objects when we perfectly translate them into terms of our own states, our own feelings."[93] The only object not requiring this transformation is the human being. This makes the human form the ideal vehicle for an empathetic response, at once immediate and powerful. According to Berenson, we can live into a nude more easily than anything else in the arts, and it thus possesses the greatest potential to heighten our sense of capacity.

Berenson goes on to say that the importance of the nude is not limited to this. "Not only is it the best vehicle for all that in art which is directly life-confirming and life-enhancing, but it is itself the most significant object in the human world."[94] The power of Michelangelo derives from his feeling for what is materially significant and his ability to convey it in terms of artistic essentials, working in combination with an unequalled "vision of a glorious but possible humanity."[95]

Underlying Berenson's remarks on Michelangelo was his unstated but very clear belief that heightened capacity meant not only the individual's capacity to experience life to the utmost but also the capacity of the human race to reach a higher plane of existence through art. Although he attempted to give it an aura of empiricism by using psychological jargon, in *The Florentine Painters* Berenson is really talking about the power of art to enhance our sense of well-being and to stimulate Western humanity to ever higher plateaus of achievement. Berenson would remain satisfied with art as long as it continued to do both, but when it ceased to enhance his life or, in his view, further the interests of Western civilization and bourgeois culture, he would protest. His future discontent is foreshadowed in a stubborn unwillingness to value the late work of Michelangelo, sensing in it an uncomfortable tension resultant from the disharmonious rapport between the artist's gifts and his mandated subjects. Berenson viewed the *Last Judgment* in the Sistine Chapel as a failure, for which he blamed the inability of an artist whose genius was for arresting the ideal vision of humanity to convey the attributes required in this scene: weakness, submission, and dread.

Berenson's criticism of the *Last Judgment* turned essentially on its failure as illustration, but he admitted that Michelangelo was also capable of formal flaws, especially the late work, in which he was inclined to exaggerate tactile values. This Michelangelo did to make a more powerful appeal to our tactile imagination, in much the same way that Botticelli stimulates our sense of movement. Michelangelo could be similarly indifferent to the requirements of representation. In Berenson's view, such extremes enhanced the appeal of Botticelli, but in Michelangelo he saw it as a defect, because "while there is such a thing as movement, there is no such thing as tactile values without representation."[96]

That Berenson would not admit the possibility of unembodied tactile values, a sense of plasticity in the abstract, explains one important aspect of his antipathy to most twentieth-century art. Echoes of this polarization between the appeal of pure linear decoration and the abstraction of mass would be heard as Berenson faced the next century with a mind at least open to Henri Matisse, while holding Pablo Picasso, and especially cubism, in absolute contempt.

Had Berenson simply suggested in *The Florentine Painters* that art provides a quickened sense of life, his argument would have been far less vulnerable to premature obsolescence. That is fundamentally the aesthete's position, rooted in Pater's insistence on the intellect's need to feel itself alive and his mandate to make the most of each experience for its own sake, positions not at all incompatible with modernism. Berenson dates himself, however, in proposing that the appreciation of art is an accomplishment that increases the viewer's self-confidence and energy and that this heightened capacity for life can only be directed one way. For all his insistent formalism, what Berenson outlines in *The Florentine Painters* is an aesthetic theory which, in the end, turns more on the pleasure taken in the response than in the work of art itself.

After the manuscript was finished, Costelloe and Berenson were still quarreling over the definition of pleasure. She recorded in her diary that the closest they could come was that "pleasure is the feeling accompanying the attainment of the sort of life we desire, or the confirmation of a sense of capacity to attain it."[97] By wedding aesthetic pleasure to increased capacity, to life-enhancement, Berenson in effect sought not only to explain that pleasure but also to justify it. It would appear that justification was ultimately to be found, as Russell had advised them, in the satisfaction of desire.[98]

The Central Italian Painters of the Renaissance

> Recall the summer of 1895. You had *The Florentine
> Painters* behind you. You were a wanderer in Germany.
> You were alone, you had no company but your own
> thoughts. You wanted no other, for these thoughts
> made you happy with what they revealed, with what
> they penetrated, with what they irradiated. Your mind
> worked as never before and, shame, never since. You had
> visions, clear, detailed visions of what you should do for
> years and years to come—a lifetime, in fact.[99]

In old age, Berenson remembered the summer of his thirtieth year
with a romantic nostalgia for his promising youth. His position as
adviser to Isabella Stewart Gardner in the acquisition of Italian paintings for her collection was still relatively informal, and he did not
yet think of himself as an expert in the strictest (mercantile) sense.
Even in the face of criticism offered by various "enemy-friends" and
well-meaning relatives, his belief in the originality and importance
of *The Florentine Painters* did not waver. This moment of supreme
confidence in his abilities became for Berenson emblematic of the
career he might have had. His autobiographical works are filled with
statements of remorse at having been dissuaded from the life plan he
had envisioned at this time. It is often noted that the success of the
four essays on Italian painting illumined two paths for him to follow:
theory and aesthetics (essays) or attribution (lists). That he ultimately
chose attribution, a decision that resulted in, among other things,
his extraordinary accomplishment of *The Drawings of the Florentine
Painters,* was a turn of events that only Berenson himself regretted.

It would be over a decade before Berenson resigned himself to
this choice; in 1895 his mind was still absorbed with the articulation of theory. His next book, *The Central Italian Painters of the
Renaissance,* became a forum for the expansion and clarification of
the ideas set forth in *The Florentine Painters* and an opportunity to

introduce others. He begins here, for example, to use the term "ideated sensations" to refer to the effects of tactile values and movement. Although he approached the project in the wake of this confident summer, Berenson's instincts told him that it would be anticlimactic. As he confided to his sister, he did not expect this book to equal *The Florentine Painters*, much less surpass it.

Berenson's strategy in *The Central Italian Painters* is to identify characteristics that distinguish painters of this school from both the Venetians and the Florentines. This was in keeping with his conception of the four books on Italian art as a series that would establish a strong regional identity for each school in the form of highly specific artistic qualities. His insistence on reducing Italian painting to a matter of artistic essentials and typical characteristics, though it served him well in discussing the Florentines, quickly became a critical albatross. The desire to characterize each geographical group soon came into conflict with the related goal of explaining their singular appeal.

The problem Berenson faced in *The Central Italian Painters* (and again in the final book of this series, *The North Italian Painters*) was that he did not find the works to be strong in the formal qualities he had outlined in his previous book. Yet, as he well knew, these were the most beloved Italian artists of his Anglo-American readership. Thus, Berenson set himself the arduous task of accounting for the almost universal attraction and enduring fascination of a school of painters he did not especially admire. To do this he digressed on a number of fundamental concerns, to which subsequent critics and historians have repeatedly returned. It is not necessary to accept Berenson's ideas to realize that in these four essays he plotted a critical minefield that the twentieth century has not yet defused.[100]

Berenson observed that Central Italian painting appealed to most viewers on the level of representation, or what he called "illustration." He used this essay to further develop the distinction made in *The Florentine Painters* between this and "decoration," by which he meant formal elements, not simple ornamentation. He describes illustration as "everything which in a work of art appeals to us, not for any intrinsic quality, as of colour or form or composition, contained in the work of art itself, but for the value the thing represented has elsewhere, whether in the world outside, or in the mind within." [101] It is appropriate to consider as illustration visual imagery in which "the form has no intrinsic merit"; illustration, in other words, is representation without what Roger Fry and Clive Bell would later call "significant form." [102]

This discussion of illustration and decoration forms part of a digression on the nature of visual images and the mimetic function of art. Berenson argues that because ordinary human beings are mediocre visualizers and struggle to call forth images to match named objects, they are quick to take pleasure in accurate reproduction, even in the crude form of a photograph. But the kind of representation that painting provides, especially in competent hands, supplies more than the information we require to recognize; it stocks our minds with imaginary or idealized images that we admire for themselves.

Berenson was careful to point out, however, that contrary to traditional wisdom, a beautiful mental picture that takes concrete form in a painting is not necessarily art. He was unhappy with the tenacious but outdated concept, preserved primarily by art academies, that "great art would be defined not as the blind imitation of nature, but as the reproduction of the visual images haunting great minds." [103] His requirements were more exacting, and here he found it necessary to distinguish between "aesthetic" and "artistic" pleasure. The latter is restricted to the apprehension of decorative (formal) quality and, although it falls under the domain of aesthetics, it is not dependent on the intrinsic beauty or nobility of representation. Berenson contended that "the work of art, as such, had comparatively little to gain from the attractiveness of the object represented, but that the artist could enhance and glorify almost any object that lent itself to his treatment." [104]

By suggesting that the pleasure taken in idealized representation is aesthetic only in a general way, and is perhaps even intellectual, Berenson distanced himself from the typical genre of praise lavished on artists such as Raphael, making it necessary for him to furnish another more artistically viable reason for their excellence. He drove this wedge even deeper by maintaining that the illustrative appeal is ephemeral but the decorative is timeless. Because illustration hinges on subject, it is inseparable from historical context; it reflects the objects of desire and admiration, the ideals of a given age, and is thus destined to constant oscillation. Decorative elements, on the other hand, are fixed, and their relative merits, bonded as they are to human empathy, do not fluctuate. Berenson upheld that changes in ideals do not effect decoration but that "illustration changes from epoch to epoch with the contents of the mind, the visual part of which it reproduces, and it is as varied as are races and individuals."[105]

In this essay, Berenson characterized Umbria as a region suffering from a paucity of native genius, which imported talent and embraced a diluted version of the Sienese (illustrative) tradition. He claimed that even the greatest of the Central Italians, the hallowed Raphael, who profited from his contact with Florentine art, was at best a mediocre figure painter. What saved Umbrian painting from relegation to the dustheap of mere illustration, what made it properly "artistic," was a pictorial device Berenson called "space composition." This was to be distinguished from ordinary composition, which involved only surface pattern; space composition was expansion of the pictorial design inward. It was the distribution of forms in a coherent spatial container, or in Berenson's words, in the cube not on the surface.

What qualified space composition as an artistic essential was its powerful potential to enhance life.

> Producing as it does immediate effects—how and why
> cannot here be discussed—on the vaso-motor system,
> with every change of space we suffer on the instant a
> change in our circulation and our breathing—a change
> which we become aware of as a feeling of heightened or
> lowered vitality.[106]

Berenson compared the effect of space composition to a similar sensation generated by music and architecture, but he argued that an architectural setting was not necessary for its realization.[107] In fact, he contended that space composition in painting was potentially more musical than architecture because it was illusory, unfettered by the weights and restraints of actual materials, allowing greater freedom for many more instruments to play and "woo us away from our tight, painfully limited selves, and to dissolve us into the space presented, until at last we seem to become its indwelling, permeating spirit." [108]

On one level, space composition was related to the concept of tactile values, insofar as it contributed to the convincing depiction of relief that Berenson prized so highly.[109] But ideated sensations of space composition did more than define mass; they could induce in the viewer a feeling of well-being so powerful that it went beyond life-enhancement. Berenson explained that space composition could remain an artistic sensation or "it may transport one into the raptures of mysticism." He asserted that under the spell of this effect, we not only breathe more easily but can transcend the self, thus experiencing a "feeling of being identified with the universe, perhaps even of being the soul of the universe." Because this sense of identification with the universe was the very essence of religious emotion, "an emotion, by the way, as independent of belief and conduct as love itself," space composition was the most effective means of communicating religiosity in painting.[110]

By giving space composition a spiritual as well as artistic dimension, Berenson could effectively legitimize Umbrian painting both to himself and to his less aesthetically sensitive viewers, who continued to require that "something else" of which Obrist spoke to respond to art. In *The Florentine Painters* Berenson attended to religious content summarily, with broad references to spiritual significance. But Umbrian painting, especially the work of Raphael, was a sacred cow for whom he required an elaborate defense.

Berenson was well aware, and no doubt derisive, of the sort of sentimentality that this kind of religious painting typically inspired. He made a point of explaining that space composition communicated (not represented) religious emotion with such efficacy that even an atheist and villain like the artist Pietro Perugino could produce profoundly religious paintings, referring to this (former) paradox as the "haunting quandary of commonplace minds." In this passage on Perugino, Berenson once again insists on formalism as a method of appreciation that eliminates the need for literal interpretation in terms of subject or even of artist's biography, though he clearly was not ignorant of these alternative strategies.

> If here it were our business to discuss the relation of the work of art to the artist, it could be pointed out that a villain and an atheist might paint sweet, holy people because he preferred them in life, finding them easier victims, lovely, tender, pure women, because they were a rarer or more fragile prey. Finding these people more convenient, he might even be crafty enough to do what he could to add to their number by painting pictures that would wake those who looked on them to a consciousness of preference for a life holy and refined. All this is a quite conceivable, but here at least an unnecessary, hypothesis. Perugino, as I have now said, produces his religious effect by means of his space composition.[111]

Berenson claimed that the feelings associated with the effective use of space composition—freedom, well-being, expansiveness, religious transcendence—were also possible in the direct experience of nature. It is worth remembering in this context the Emersonian Boston of Berenson's youth. But whereas American Transcendentalism found its most perfect visual expression in landscape painting, Berenson hastened to point out that space composition is not synonymous with landscape art. The effect does not depend on topography any more than it does on architecture, and in fact the acquired skills of the landscape painter do little to facilitate ideated sensations of space composition. Berenson thought of it not as a skill or even a science but as an intuitive sensibility, or, perhaps more important, as a pictorial tradition that was not easily learned. The painters of Umbria, for whom this was indigenous, achieved it with the greatest consistency and success.

Even though Berenson acknowledged space composition as independent of the landscape tradition, he insisted that it was essential to its perfection. In what is perhaps the best-known passage from *The Central Italian Painters,* he makes a case for the preeminence of this ideated sensation in a genre that had already undergone astonishing transformation in his own age.

> In spite of the exquisite modelling of Cézanne, who
> gives the sky its tactile values as perfectly as Michel-
> angelo has given them to the human figure, in spite
> of all Monet's communication of the very pulse-beat
> of the sun's warmth over fields and trees, we are still
> waiting for a real art of landscape. And this will come
> only when some artist, modelling skies like Cézanne's,
> able to communicate light and heat as Monet does, will
> have a feeling for space rivalling Perugino's or even
> Raphael's.[112]

This digression concludes with the remark that Nicolas Poussin, J.M.W. Turner, and Claude Lorrain remain the best landscape painters in the European tradition because of their instinctive feeling for space composition and despite their inferiority in other respects to more recent painters.

The notoriety of this passage lies, not in the fact that Berenson here established space composition as an essential of landscape art, but that he introduced the name of Paul Cézanne into the discussion. Scarcely a writer occupied with Berenson's career has failed to take note of it. The significance of his mentioning Cézanne to an English and American audience in 1897 has been the locus of more than one appraisal of Berenson's relative modernity and, recently, his critical acumen. Sympathetic eulogizers, such as Kenneth Clark and Benedict Nicolson, insisted that, when viewed historically, Berenson's recognition of both Cézanne and Monet as the decisive figures of modern landscape painting is extraordinary, especially the reference to the then little-known painter Cézanne.[113] In contrast, Meyer Schapiro and John Rewald, both highly acclaimed for their work on Cézanne and on the history of early modern art, have dismissed Berenson's remarks as of relatively little consequence and, in the case of Rewald, of potential harm in the impression these remarks left on his readers of Cézanne's shortcomings.[114]

Schapiro took it upon himself to "set the record straight" about what he perceived as the preposterous notion that Berenson "discovered" Cézanne, a claim that Benedict Nicolson denied was ever made on his behalf. It clearly vexed Schapiro that a critic as hostile and close-minded to contemporary art as he knew Berenson to be should enjoy any recognition whatsoever as having furthered its interests.[115] But, as Nicolson correctly pointed out, Schapiro's case is spoiled by exaggeration, especially when he insists that by 1897 Cézanne was "well known" through the Gustave Caillebotte bequest to the Luxembourg Museum and the historic 1895 exhibition at the gallery of Ambroise Vollard. Cézanne may indeed have been, as Schapiro suggests, the idol of a generation of younger painters. That particular group, however, did not compose much of Berenson's readership, and, what's more, it was considerably smaller. To the Anglo-American, nonspecialist public to whom these essays (if not the lists) were addressed, Cézanne was obscure. Nicolson is surely justified in his contention that "one would be hard put to it to find any other appreciative response to the painter in English or American art literature before the 20th century."[116]

If Berenson merits distinction as one of the first art writers (in English) to acknowledge Cézanne's importance in print, and the evidence suggests that he does, the question would still remain as to the nature and possible influence of his remarks—whether, as Nicolson stated, they were at all appreciative. This question was also raised by Schapiro, who argued that Berenson demonstrated no awareness of Cézanne's originality and invoked his name as a "bit of up-to-date dressing," as he did James Tissot's later in the same essay. Robert Hughes echoed Schapiro's sentiments when he referred to the Cézanne excerpt as a "warbling palimpsest of incompatible names" and concluded that "No one who imagined that Raphael's idea of space could be reconciled with Cézanne's heroic doubt and deep sense of relativity can be said to have looked much at Cézanne."[117] Similarly, Remy Saisselin faulted Berenson for his failure to apprehend Cézanne's anxiety about painting in the modern world or what he meant to other artists.[118]

That Berenson's understanding of Cézanne and his originality was not profound is beyond dispute and although there is truth to all of these assertions, it should be remembered that Berenson was not alone in this respect. Few painters in the history of art have been more poorly understood than Cézanne. Several generations of artists and critics have fashioned careers out of misrepresenting Cézanne, even with the benefit of decades of hindsight.[119] Berenson can hardly be faulted for failing to grasp in 1897, after a brief exposure to a handful of Cézannes, what is still neither obvious nor accepted truth among scholars who have availed themselves of his entire oeuvre for almost a century. Furthermore, Berenson did more than simply mention Cézanne in *The Central Italian Painters;* both through his critical method and his early familiarity with the painter, he had a direct impact on shaping the first generation of English and American writers who produced Cézanne criticism that is now widely recognized for its insight and consequence, namely, Leo Stein, Walter Pach, and Roger Fry.

The most extensive study of Berenson and Cézanne has been undertaken by John Rewald as part of his important book *Cézanne and America.* Although it furnishes invaluable documentation of the chronology and extent of Berenson's acquaintance with the painter's works, this account suffers from the frequent (but regrettable) tendency to undervalue Berenson's achievements, out of personal animosity.[120] Granting that Berenson was the first American to notice Cézanne in print and that "it was no mean feat at that time to mention Cézanne in the same breath as Michelangelo," Rewald doubts that these remarks did much to further the artist's reputation with his readers because the admiration Berenson expressed was qualified and tentative.[121]

A convincing argument is made by Rewald that the very lack of spatial continuity in Cézanne's landscapes may have prompted

Berenson to bring him into the discussion of space composition, the result being that "Berenson's intriguing paragraph established that Cézanne's feeling for space was wanting, the exquisite modelling and tactile values of his skies notwithstanding, a statement that must have left most students of Central Italian painting completely indifferent." [122] Elsewhere in this study Rewald implies that Berenson did not really think much of Cézanne and was slow to grasp his importance and even his plasticity.

Though there is truth in much of what Rewald surmises, the scenario he constructs is neither complete nor entirely fair to Berenson. In an effort to identify the paintings on which Berenson initially formed his opinion, Rewald cites as possibilities those in the Caillebotte bequest to the Luxembourg Museum or the works shown in Vollard's gallery. Rewald favors the Luxembourg bequest, which included two Cézanne landscapes and was on display by February 1896.[123] Rewald also questioned Berenson's motives for seeking out Cézanne's work in Paris. He wondered if Berenson had been inspired to go to the Luxembourg Museum by the Cézanne-talk in progressive art circles or if he was simply making his routine check of public collections.[124]

Insofar as it is possible to reconstruct (from diaries and letters) the relationship between Berenson and Fabbri during this time, it seems reasonable to assume that it was Fabbri who stimulated Berenson to take an interest in Cézanne on his trip to Paris in the summer of 1896. A Costelloe diary entry of 26 April 1896 notes a visit from the painter at I Tatti during which Fabbri argued with Berenson about Raphael, refusing to admit *La Belle Jardinaire* as a significant work of art.[125] Fabbri may have known about Cézanne earlier because of his contact with Pissarro, but, at any rate, by April he had already purchased his first Cézanne and may well have discussed him with Berenson at this time. Having expressed skepticism about Berenson's insistence on space composition as a separate and essential artistic quality, Fabbri probably encouraged Berenson to examine Cézanne in an effort to reorient him to his original critical priorities of mass and material significance.[126]

A few months later, Berenson wrote Costelloe from Paris of a visit to the Luxembourg Museum where he saw, among other things, the "Sezannes" (*sic*). The same letter also mentions a visit to see the Cézannes at Vollard's gallery, but he told her that nothing entirely won him over.[127] Although Rewald assumed that Berenson first saw Fabbri's Cézannes in 1904 (when he reported to his wife that the paintings were "disappointing"), Berenson actually saw Fabbri's collection much earlier.[128] In the summer of 1897 Costelloe described the Cézannes in Fabbri's studio as a "splendid collection" that had impressed them very much: "They are not 'attractive,' but they were almost *great* art, almost as great in the impersonality as Pier dei Franceschi" (*sic*).[129] Contrary to what Rewald suggests, several years would pass before Berenson would reassess Fabbri's Cézannes as "disappointing," and then not because he failed to recognize their quality but for far more complex reasons.

Berenson may well have been blind to Cézanne's originality, as he had been to that of Degas, whom he admired even more, but he saw and was responsive to the same quality in both painters, that is, a strong sense of what he called material significance. It is not without import that in *The Central Italian Painters* Berenson spoke of Cézanne's "modelling" of the sky, an unusual choice of words to describe the representation of something that has no tangible mass. He noted that Cézanne gave to skies a plasticity and tactility normally reserved in painting for the depiction of three-dimensional objects. This was a characteristic that Berenson seized upon immediately, and, despite his reservations about the painter, it was by no means a flippant or meaningless observation.[130]

Rewald's unwillingness to credit Berenson (respecting his role in awakening viewers to Cézanne) with any more than facts that cannot be ignored, is especially conspicuous in his discussion of the critics who became Cézanne advocates in the early twentieth century. Although Rewald repeats the well-known anecdote concerning Leo Stein's introduction to the work of Cézanne through Berenson's recommendation, he fails to admit the probability that Stein's critical insights were also heavily reliant on Berenson. Furthermore, he barely mentions the relationship between Berenson and Walter Pach and its impact on the subsequent development of Pach's criticism.[131]

Rewald is even more obdurate on the matter of Roger Fry's interest in Cézanne. Though he raises the possibility that Berenson might also have introduced Fry to the painter's works, Rewald concludes that it was not likely and that they probably never even discussed him in conversation. This he deduces by considering the circumstances that would have militated against it, observing that Fry's relationship with Berenson had begun to cool by 1903 (before Fry demonstrated any interest in Cézanne) and that Fry never mentioned Berenson as contributing in any way to his discovery of Cézanne. Rewald then makes the astonishing claim that Fry found his way to seeing Cézanne's gifts unaided. "His sole guide had been the supreme logic of his own sensitivity."[132]

Evidently, Rewald chose to believe that Fry's apprenticeship with Berenson did not prepare him to understand Cézanne's significance, despite the fact that Fry's emphasis on the priority of mass and space in the experience of aesthetic emotion, as articulated in his groundbreaking "Essay on Aesthetics," relies heavily on Berenson's ideas. Also, there is no reason to assume that the painter's name did not come up in conversation; at least once Fry examined a collection of Cézannes in Paris in the company of Mary Berenson.[133] Finally, as Rewald himself admits, Fry deliberately obscured previous occasions on which he might have been led to appreciate Cézanne. It is well known that one of the major sources of conflict between Fry and Berenson was Berenson's suspicion that Fry did not give him proper credit when Fry made use of his ideas and information.[134]

Nevertheless, by the time Roger Fry decided to commit himself to the work of Cézanne and to modern art, Berenson had already begun to close his mind to the possibilities that his own criticism, not to mention the originality of Cézanne, had opened up to the twentieth century. In *The Central Italian Painters,* as in the previous two volumes on the Venetians and the Florentines, Berenson's surprising modernity coexists with an equally startling, but no less dominant, conviction that the frontier of art will and should remain narrowly defined. He claimed for Umbrian painters, especially Raphael, the unqualified admiration of the cultivated (not artistic) public. Although Berenson was not wholly convinced of the intrinsic merit of their work, his allegiance to this audience is undeniable.

In a brief digression into territory that would later occupy such writers as E. H. Gombrich, Berenson explained the appeal of Raphael in terms of post-Renaissance habits of visualization.[135] By this Berenson did not intend simply habits of visual attention; he meant, in a broader sense, the realization of certain ideals and visual types. Employing a familiar argument, he suggested that because the world created by the Renaissance perfectly mirrored the aspirations and desires of the cultivated viewer of the present, it continued to have a powerful grip on the modern imagination.

> Created by Donatello and Masaccio, and sanctioned by the Humanists, the new canon of the figure, the new cast of features, expressing, because the figure arts, properly used, could not express anything else, power, manliness, and stateliness, presented to the ruling classes of that time the type of human being most likely to win the day in the combat of human forces. It needed no more than this to assure the triumph of the new over the old way of seeing and depicting. And as the ideals of effectiveness have not changed since the fifteenth century, the types presented by Renaissance art, despite the ephemeral veerings of mere fashion and sentiment, still embody our choice, and will continue to do so, at least as long as European civilization keeps the essentially Hellenic character it has had ever since the Renaissance.[136]

No one then or since has had the power to break this way of visualizing and, as a result, it has become internalized to the extent that "we have, as a race, come to be more like that type than we ever were before."

Berenson more or less invented the category of space composition to bestow artistic legitimacy on a group of painters he regarded as otherwise mediocre. Although he did not think much of Raphael as a figure painter, he failed to challenge his exalted status to the extent he had, for example, that of Ghirlandaio in *The Florentine Painters,* or will later when he attempts to cast down the much-revered Leonardo da Vinci in his well-known essay of 1916. Berenson claimed for Raphael the distinction as the greatest master of composition ever to live. He did little to undermine the presumption that Raphael is the deserving idol of civilized Western man. Whereas Berenson had earlier made the point that we lose interest in illustrative art once we cease to care about the age it represents, in his discussion of Raphael he insists that the artist's reputation endures precisely because this age, or our desire to identify with it, has not passed.

It is worth noting that in *The Central Italian Painters* the modern world with which Berenson increasingly identified had hardened into a narrow, elitist concept of civilized gentility that he would never abandon. When he wrote on Venetian painting and about Lorenzo Lotto, the essence of his modernity clearly connected him with currents of progressive thought, at least in the domain of art and aesthetics. Whereas Lotto appealed to Berenson because of his penetrating subjectivity, in this book Berenson preaches the importance of impersonality in art, a theme he would return to fifty years later, as he looked back on the storm and stress of the early twentieth century. Impersonality, he claims, appeals to the modern viewer not only because the absence of expressed emotion leaves one more open to the purely artistic but also because we are uplifted by seeing people who do not react to things that would be overpowering in actuality. Heroes are possible only when there is impersonality, and by living into such work we become heroic.

This discussion recalls the final passages on Michelangelo in *The Florentine Painters* and the artist's rendering of a "glorious but possible humanity." By the time Berenson had finished writing *The Central Italian Painters,* his critical method, his formalism, had taken clear and definite shape as a distinctively modern position. His categories of artistic essentials (tactile values, movement, and space composition); the principle of attendant responses in the form of ideated sensations; and his insistent devaluation of subject matter in the process of appreciation will serve as points of reference, not only for his own future criticism but also for that of his contemporaries, most notably Roger Fry.

But what Berenson gained in clarity he lost in flexibility. Although in the years to follow he would become an avid student of Medieval art, he stubbornly refused to admit any form of recent painting that deviated either from the artistic essentials or humanist ideals he had set forth in these early essays. The standards of excellence established in classical antiquity and renewed by the Italian Renaissance became for him inviolate because he had convinced himself that "art teaches us not only what to see but what to be." [137]

3. Berenson at the Crossroads

There is no history without polemic, without an axe to grind, without originating in antagonism to something which exists and which it wants to combat or substitute. So much of my work is polemic, and so much of that has now lost its meaning and importance because it was directed against attitudes and against fashions which by now are defunct (and in great part defunct thanks to my work itself), and now so many people have exaggerated my polemical role that I really should repolemicize against them to set them right again.

1932

Connoisseurship Versus Criticism

> Mr. Berenson is the only connoisseur who has general
> ideas, and the only critic who has the equipment of an
> expert. Our own bias leads us to prefer the critic in him
> to the connoisseur, but doubtless the one is necessary to
> the other. When, as signs seem to show he will, he has
> learned to subordinate the connoisseur to the critic, if
> he can add to both a little more of the artist in letters he
> should become a distinct force in criticism.[1]

This statement, made by Kenyon Cox in his review of *The Drawings
of the Florentine Painters*, mirrored Berenson's own sense that his
priorities and interests were in a perpetual state of conflict. In retrospect it has become evident that Berenson owed his unique métier as
a connoisseur to this confluence of aptitudes. But at the end of the
century, in Berenson's mind, and to an extent in those of his readers,
the businesses of attribution and appreciation were separate and distinct concerns. A fundamental relationship between the two was not
assumed, and it was for this reason that Mary Costelloe took it upon
herself to explain the need for what was then called the "new art
criticism."[2] In her essay in *Atlantic Monthly* she described Morellian
connoisseurship as a form of art criticism that made it possible to
reconstruct artistic personalities on the basis of correctly attributed
pictures. Her goal was to defend the method against detractors who
looked upon it as a specialized research tool that too often yielded
uninteresting information about unimportant paintings.

Costelloe argued in this essay that the establishment of an artistic
personality was an important step toward arriving at an understanding of a painting's relationship to its respective epoch. Great artists
interpreted their age; and the record left to us in the form of a work
of art is unique in that it can be studied with detachment. Unlike
other forms of expression, poetry and music for example, which she
claimed were more susceptible to the imposition of an individual

emotional state or preconception, painting did not change as it was experienced.

> This gives peculiar value to painting as a document in
> the autobiography of the race, and it is this which makes
> the new criticism, in its attempt to edit this important
> document correctly, of such immense service to general
> culture. We have no other source of information about
> the past which is so great an aid to the reconstruction
> of mental life. . . . The effort of the new criticism, then,
> is to lead us to those works of art which are really sig-
> nificant, and to tell us whether they mirror or interpret
> each epoch, whether they express its actualities or por-
> tray its ideals, and thus to prepare us to get from them
> all the enjoyment and all the inspiration possible to our
> temperaments.[3]

Though Morelli had argued against the use of traditional documents in the study of art, Costelloe here implied that because of scientific connoisseurship, art itself can become the most reliable document.

Costelloe's essay seeks to validate connoisseurship on the basis of its contribution to general culture, but it does not address the relationship between attribution and appreciation outside of the broad case made for art as an instrument of learning. When she later reviewed *The Florentine Painters,* in which Berenson had distinguished the enjoyment of art as a unique and vital experience, she approached the problem very differently. In 1895 she had asked the question—what pictures should we look at?—and counseled her readers to seek out pictures with correct attributions because they would be assured more accurate insight into a given historical period. A year later she posed essentially the same question, but her advice was then to look at good pictures, or, using Berenson's terminology, pictures that were life-enhancing. In the interim, as we have already seen, the experience of art and the standards by which it was to be judged, had been redefined for both Costelloe and Berenson. Its value was no longer confined to that of a "document in the autobiography of the race" but instead claims were now made for art as "one of the great tonic forces of civilization."[4]

Aesthetics and the science of attribution are not rendered more compatible in either of these essays. If anything they are driven further apart. Subsequent reviews of Berenson's books are no less divisive, insisting, as did Cox, that Berenson was a kind of split personality who, when confronted with a work of art, could not make up his mind whether to adjust its attribution or assess its aesthetic merits. Nor did Berenson's own expressed ambivalence about the Morellian method and the value of connoisseurship as a worthy undertaking help the situation. With the publication of the first two volumes of the series entitled *The Study and Criticism of Italian Art*, Berenson started what would become a favorite hobby in his old age—the flagellation of his learning and expertise.[5]

Berenson announced his growing dissatisfaction with Morellian connoisseurship in the preface to the first volume of *The Study and Criticism of Italian Art* (1901). Characterizing the early articles collected in this anthology as juvenilia, he confessed to a present conviction that connoisseurship was a worthless endeavor. He basically agreed with critics who had suggested that attribution did little to enhance appreciation. At the same time, however, he upheld the necessity of connoisseurship to art history and asserted that the practice of attribution required training and intelligence of the highest order. In this preface, and again in a previously unpublished essay called "Rudiments of Connoisseurship," included in the next volume of *The Study and Criticism of Italian Art*, Berenson insisted that although an unattributed painting should be subject to the kind of morphological study outlined by Morelli, the final judgment of the connoisseur turned on a sense of its quality.[6] He had become aware of the limitations of this method, especially when a great talent was in evidence, believing that it worked in inverse proportion to the artist's originality.

Reviewers such as Cox warmed to this concession to a sense of quality, which was taken as a welcome humanization of an otherwise bloodless and mechanical approach to art.[7] Cox, who was a painter as well as a critic, was especially comforted by Berenson's acquiescence to critical intuition, a quality Cox claimed had always stood behind the judgments of artists and one the new art criticism threatened to undermine. Even in the face of Berenson's expansive Morellianism, however, Cox continued to question the value of Berenson's findings. The pressing issues remained that all too often this science of attribution was lavished on minor figures, that it was unnecessarily complicated, and that it assumed an unpleasant tone of finality and self-importance about matters of little import to most readers.[8]

Although some writers seemed to take Berenson at his word when he defined connoisseurship as a method of attribution that had little to do with appreciation, Roger Fry, who was closer intellectually to Berenson, knew better. His review of the first volume of *The Study and Criticism of Italian Art* stands in sharp contrast to others by making a case for an essential relationship between the two. Written at a time when Fry was training himself in Morellian connoisseurship, with Berenson as his mentor, Fry attempted to demonstrate that the process of attribution based on purely visual (internal) evidence had direct bearing on the quality and nature of the aesthetic experience. Because attributions were composites of numerous aesthetic judgments brought to bear on a single work, they could stimulate and liberate similar purely aesthetic perceptions. In what is almost a parody of Berenson's theory of ideated sensations and life-enhancement, Fry expounded on the aesthetic relevance of the correct attribution.

> Our aesthetic experience arranges itself in a more orderly manner, and with the increased ease of correlating the aesthetic judgments comes an actual intensifying of our sensations. The relation of this particular picture to others and more familiar ones by the same hand gives us at once the power of bringing ourselves rapidly into sympathy with the mood of the picture, for it is a mood with which we already associated ourselves in other works.[9]

Cox and others were caustic about Berenson's famous creation "Amico di Sandro," the fictitious identity he assigned to a common artistic personality recognized in a group of unattributed paintings. Fry, however, basically accepted Berenson's premise that the name was helpful, though of admittedly less consequence than the recognition of a consistently expressed artistic temperament in an aggregate of works. More than any other writer, Fry was sympathetic to the internal logic of Berenson's critical method, the manner in which, as David Brown explained, Berenson's sustained contact with the work enabled him to classify and appreciate it simultaneously.

For most of Berenson's readership then and since, the critic and the connoisseur came together with greatest efficacy in his monumental study, *The Drawings of the Florentine Painters*, published in 1903.[10] The sheer magnitude of the task was sufficient to guarantee its recognition as a landmark. Cox applauded Berenson for the continued emphasis on a sense of quality and for the use of more accessible language instead of his customary jargon. The separation of attribution and appreciation that seemed to plague the earlier books was here less in evidence. Cox observed that in addition to the compilation of the catalogue, Berenson had examined the drawings with an eye to appraising their aesthetic quality, their insight into artistic personality, and their significance in the development of related masterworks. In so doing Berenson successfully brought together his formidable skills as a critic, psychologist, and historian, a synthesis that has come to define the modern connoisseur, in spite of his own far more limited perception of the practice.[11]

In these volumes, Berenson pioneered a method of study that was to become widespread among future art historians, and the work is considered his most important contribution to the historiography of Italian Renaissance art.[12] Careful scrutiny of the drawings was thought to yield vital insight into the process of creativity, especially with respect to known completed works for which they might have served as preparation. According to Morellian practice, true authorship of a painting is sought in those pictorial details that typically command the least attention. It is in the execution of seemingly insignificant parts of the image, the ears for example, that the artist works by unconscious effort, thus revealing himself through signature habits of execution.

Although this inquiry was undertaken in the spirit of classification and scientific objectivity, Edgar Wind believed that the connoisseur's veneration of drawings was symptomatic of a fundamentally romantic disposition toward art. Wind associated the search for such autograph passages with an aesthetic of freshness and spontaneity, claiming that the Morellian connoisseur above all sought authenticity. This sensibility, he reasoned, which also cherished the moment of inspiration, logically led to a fascination with drawings and was in effect an extension of the romantic "cult of the fragment as the true signature of the artist." [13]

Wind further argued that this fixation on the instantaneous record of pure artistic sensibility led connoisseurs to prize spontaneous expressions over labored finished products, and in this context it is noteworthy that more than one reviewer of *The Drawings of the Florentine Painters* commented on this tendency in Berenson. Cox, a dyed-in-the-wool classicist, complained that Berenson's excessive admiration for sketching and the swift touch made him underrate more finished drawings. And an anonymous reviewer for *Athenaeum* dismissed his unfairness to Fra Bartolomeo as typical of a critic like Berenson who was contemptuous of academic art and indifferent to the pursuit of perfection.[14]

It was through the process of attribution, especially with respect to drawings, that Berenson came closest to making contact with the creative force of the artist. But because of his exigent formalism and distaste for the personal element of art he was unwilling to consider the broad implications of what he experienced. His study of drawings taught him how artists developed ideas, how they gave shape and substance to the images of their fancy, how these were preserved by subsequent generations through artistic habits and convention, and why artists of uncommon ability (or extreme incompetence) were able to break away from established practice. Even though he may also have harbored the romantic notion that his contact with drawings brought him closer to the moment of vision, it did not result in a more generous view of artistic genius or the creative process.

Berenson's involvement with individual works of art, when not strictly professional, was confined to an intense awareness of how they spoke to him. Provided they did not offend his sense of decorum, he worried little about meaning or intention beyond what was immediately apparent. For the most part, he was unresponsive, when not actively hostile, to the nuances of personalized expression. This practice of disinterested contemplation, crucial to his early critical writing, would be seriously undermined by a growing antipathy toward what he regarded as the ruinous path of modern art.

A Sienese Painter of the Franciscan Legend

One notable exception to Berenson's cultivated critical detachment and customary preference for the monumental and silent was his weakness for late Medieval art. Despite the obvious fact that it could never supply the requisite ideated sensations, he was irresistibly drawn to both the decorative and illustrative qualities of Medieval painting, especially in its more mystical strains. Berenson's interest in the Italian "primitives" coincided with, and was no doubt stimulated by, their ascendancy in the market, but his interest cannot be explained as simple opportunism. He was stirred by an acute awareness and appreciation of their distance from the mainstream of classical tradition and their affinity with non-Western, especially Asian, forms of expression. In his early articles on Medieval art and the Sienese we are able to glimpse the critic Berenson might have been had he not allowed his narrow criteria of humanism and artistic essentials to prejudice his judgment.

The most interesting of these studies, *A Sienese Painter of the Franciscan Legend*, consisted of a two-part essay from 1903, originally featured in *Burlington Magazine*. In the preface to the single volume published in 1909, Berenson expressed regrets that time had not allowed him to add other essays that he had hoped to complete on related topics, such as Oriental religious painting and what he called "imaginative design." He defined this latter concept in the context of a discussion of why the Sienese painter Sassetta was better equipped to capture the spirituality of Saint Francis than was the Tuscan Giotto, who so often illustrated the events in the saint's life.

> What I have in mind is the kind of design which, instead of expounding facts, no matter how exalted, makes a direct appeal to the imagination, communicating emotions, feelings, and atmospheres, and exhaling dreams, as fragrant odours are exhaled from sweet-smelling flowers. . . . The resulting picture will give you scarcely less than will the mere representation of the man whose quality is not in his physical appearance, but in his soul's attitude and in his longings.[15]

Berenson argued in this essay that Giotto, who admittedly created great works of art, failed to communicate successfully the essence of Saint Francis's seraphic spirit. Giotto's frescoes at Assisi and in the Bardi Chapel of Santa Croce are convincing narratives that illuminate the fundamental tenets of the teaching of Saint Francis but do not seize the spirit of the man behind them. This required an artist of greater poetic imagination, a symbolist, capable, as Giotto was not, of dematerializing his vision in the interest of conveying pure spirituality.

What precluded Giotto from achieving such an effect was his very embodiment of the canons of Western figurative art, prized so highly by Berenson. In this essay, Berenson expressed doubt that European painters, whose natural tendencies were toward the expression of heroism, grandeur, and physical impressiveness, could ever capture the genuinely spiritual. They were perpetually impeded by the interference of the cognitive and thus were reluctant to indulge their sense of mysticism and ecstacy. Oriental artists were much more successful in this regard because of a greater willingness to give themselves over to the spiritual at the expense of the material.[16]

According to Berenson, Occidental art suffers from an inherent inability to express the spirit because "its essential quality is its constant endeavor to realize the material significance of objects," and to do so it is forced to rely heavily on modeling.[17] This emphasis on mass militated against the convincing representation of intangibles. The realm of the spirit, Berenson claimed, is best evoked by conveying values of movement with incorporeal forms suspended in infinite space. Even an Occidental painter such as Raphael, who was a master of space composition, the one pictorial device Berenson had associated with religious emotion, was inhibited by his facility for illusionistic realism.

Berenson concluded that the European artists who came closest to the mystical inclination and pictorial language of the East would be best suited to convey pure spirituality. Because Sienese art was quasi-Eastern in its pure line, flat color, suppression of three-dimensionality, and emphasis on movement, and because Sienese culture gave priority to the religious over the humanistic or scientific, Siena was the place to look for a painter who could give artistic form to the soul of Saint Francis.

> Thus Sassetta succeeds where Giotto failed; and he succeeded not only because his imagination was better able to penetrate the open secret of Franciscan doctrine, not only because he was more lyrical and rapturous, but also because his instruments of expression did not blunt, as Giotto's certainly would have, but enhanced his vision.[18]

Berenson owned some of Sassetta's panels, and they were unarguably the finest works in his personal collection. His discussion of the panels alternates comfortably between formal analysis and interpretation of religious imagery. These essays on Sassetta are convincing evidence of Berenson's considerable skill in both the exploration of associative meaning and the apprehension of the suggestive formal qualities that empower a symbolic design, unfettered by the requirements to life-enhance through ideated sensations.

The concept of imaginative design, the direct transmission of emotion through unembodied artistic values, was foreshadowed by Berenson's discussion of linear decoration and Botticelli in *The Florentine Painters*. Here his concept is enriched by the suggestion that such a design derives its power from its very abstraction, thus recognizing both the expressive potential and formal attributes of an art addressing itself not to material reality but to the intangible and symbolic. It is worth noting that this essay was written at a time when Oriental art was soon to be supplanted by the so-called primitive or tribal as the non-Western vogue and that while Berenson was receptive to the former, he could not abide the latter. His formulation of the concept of imaginative design and his unwillingness to see its promise as a means of coming to terms with objects produced by these other remote (and in his mind scarcely human) civilizations are indicative of the similarly nonaesthetic bias with which he would regard twentieth-century art.

It was acceptable to Berenson for an Eastern artist to convey the spirituality of Buddha or for a Western artist to express a spirit emblematic of the white man's Judeo-Christian God. But it outraged him that Western artists sought to overturn their indigenous artistic traditions and replace them with a foreign "primitive" idiom in the interest of expressing the "self" or a peculiarly modern notion of anxiety. The "self" that Berenson honored, and the only one that he deemed worthy of attention, was the Hellenic self realized in classical art and Western culture.

Unlike the progressive artists of this generation, Berenson made a sharp, if intuitive, distinction between the "naive" and the "primitive." An artist such as Sassetta personified the spiritual values of Western Christianity, if not the canons of classical art, but he operated outside the mainstream of tradition. Typically, Berenson discussed Medieval art in terms of its underdeveloped sense of form, which he believed resulted in an inordinate emphasis on illustration. He had no quarrel with those who availed themselves of imaginative design to convey meaning, as long as they preceded the Renaissance or were operating outside its center of gravity. But he could not imag-

ine why a modern Western artist would willfully abandon a way of
visualizing and a formal language sanctioned as an artistic canon
advancing the interests of Hellenism.

These essays on Sassetta were a promising but brief interlude. As
Samuels suggests, they more than likely resulted from Berenson's in-
toxication with the panels in his possession and, in a sense, revived
the ecstasy he experienced on his 1894 trip to the United States, when
he reveled in the Asian art he saw with Denman Ross and Ernest
Fenollosa.[19] In 1907 Berenson decided to reread the Sassetta essays
with the hope of developing the concept of imaginative design into a
book. His wife noted that he found he no longer understood what he
meant by the term and that he was troubled by the inelasticity of his
thought.[20] Berenson eventually abandoned the project, perhaps because he realized that it would require him to journey far afield from
his territory and to challenge the certainty of the aesthetic principles
he had already defined.[21]

The North Italian Painters of the Renaissance

In the decade separating *The Central Italian Painters* from the fourth
and final volume of the series on the regional schools of Italian art, a
good deal had changed in Berenson's life. His relationship with Mary
Costelloe, which of necessity had been cloaked in deceit, was finally
legitimized by their marriage in 1900, following the death of her first
husband. Through the publication of a steady stream of books and
articles, he had risen to a position of prominence as an expert in Italian art, enabling him to attain the comfortable life and social standing
he desired.

Berenson's economic dependence on the continued practice of
connoisseurship accompanied a mounting dissatisfaction with its
limitations, the result being an almost perpetual state of anxiety and
frustration about the demands made on his time and energy. The material success and public recognition he enjoyed were compensation
for what he already recognized as encroaching intellectual stagna-

tion, an almost crippling sense that as a theorist he had little else to say. This spirit of malaise and uncertainty hovers over *The North Italian Painters of the Renaissance*, a book he was loath to complete and that is notable primarily for what it reveals about the shortcomings of his aesthetic principles in the face of a revolutionary climate he never accepted or fully understood.

As Samuels has described, Berenson faced the task of writing this fourth volume with extreme distaste; it was an obligation he deeply resented, made more odious both by his ambivalence toward connoisseurship and by his relative contempt for the subject itself. The model of artistic essentials outlined in *The Florentine Painters* had already been problematic in assessing the painters of central Italy, and it was to prove more so here. As early as 1902 he was worrying about how he would stick to his high standards when discussing a school of painters he viewed as parochial and mediocre.

Central Italian painting had been validated by the concept of space composition, but Berenson could come up with no such artistic essential to rescue the painters of the north. To remain consistent with the other essays in terms of identifying a distinguishing characteristic for each regional school, he proposed the quality of "prettiness" for these painters. But, unlike the other principles he had introduced, prettiness was by no means life-enhancing or essential. Berenson discussed this trait as resultant from mediocre painters imitating great art, a practice he viewed as symptomatic of the figurative arts in decline.

The book opens with a reaffirmation of his belief that great art is that which stimulated ideated sensations of tactile values, movement, and space composition, with the resulting effect of a sense of increased capacity in the viewer. Although Berenson's theory remained fundamentally unchanged, he presented it here in an obviously refined state, free of the fragmentary, incomplete thoughts that had rendered the volume on the Florentines in parts obscure and confusing. The only notable modification was in the substitution of the word "happiness" for pleasure. He reiterated the priority of the human figure as the principle concern of the visual arts and the necessity of subordinating all else to humanistic standards. The standards (or ideals) of which he spoke are not moral or utilitarian, "they are standards of happiness, not the happiness of the figure portrayed, but of us who look on and perceive." [22]

According to Berenson, humanistic content is not in itself a sufficient condition for the creation of a true work of art; the figure must also be constructed in such a way that we are forced "to dwell upon it, until it arouses in ourselves ideated sensations that shall make us experience the diffused sense of happiness which results upon our becoming aware of an unexpectedly intensified, facilitated activity." [23] Since nature does not furnish accentuated values of movement, mass, or coherent space, it is the business of art to create conventions through which they may be transmitted. The singular achievement of the Florentines was the successful completion of this task. Here Berenson defined art, more or less, as the construction of conventions for conveying what will make the viewer happy.

Berenson then proposes a set of rudimentary distinctions between the various phases of figurative art in the classical tradition, stipulating that the categories he describes are not bound to a particular historical context. This is a stage by stage theory of artistic development considered in the abstract, although he does associate each phase with a specific historical period for discursive purposes. The three stages Berenson identified are the archaistic, the archaic, and the classic, each one defined by its position in relation to the struggle toward an artistic model that perfectly conveys ideated sensations, in other words, toward significant form.

Berenson's belief, fundamental to this theory, was that the pursuit of artistic essentials unimpeded by requirements to illustrate, will tend toward the classic. He considered the period of discovery, what he called the archaic, as the most vital and stimulating phase. What interested Berenson was the struggle toward pure form, a phenomenon he observed in what he viewed as the high points of Western art: that of ancient Greece, Renaissance Florence, and late nineteenth-century France. The formal model exists in its most refined, perfected state in the classic phase of development; what Berenson called the archaistic phase represents a degradation of the model through mindless imitation. He was careful to point out that although art must first be archaic before it is classic, archaic is not synonymous with the concept of the "primitive." Some periods of artistic activity and striving are never archaic, specifically those outside the mainstream of both the East and West.[24]

In this essay, again as a prelude to the critical appreciation of Milanese painting, Berenson also reprised the discussion of changes in habits of visualization, first undertaken in *The Central Italian Painters*. He now described this process as a transition from the linear to the plastic to the pictorial mode of visualization, citing Venetian painting as a kind of intermediary mode he called the plastic-pictorial.[25] Berenson characterized this method as a "new vision resulting from the almost complete emancipation of colour from the control of plastic form and line."[26] In terms of the rendering of mass and the action of brushwork on the surface, Berenson noted the similarity of this mode to that of certain modern painters, whom he refers to categorically as "famous," not intending the remark as praise.

Berenson treated this reference to the aesthetics of impressionism as a historical observation. It is followed by the admonition that although this was still the reigning mode of visualization in painting, it had been of no help to the mediocre, because it had encouraged them to seek originality when they were capable only of anarchy. Berenson went on to say that if the Italian artists who had developed this method are less renowned than the pioneers of tactile values and movement, it was simply because the greater importance of quality was axiomatic and: "Newness is a very minor consideration in the world of art."[27]

In the context of this lofty theoretical discourse on classical form and visual modes, Berenson's employment of the standard of "prettiness" to assess Milanese art seems inane and almost arbitrary. Because he found the work of these painters lacking in the artistic essentials of tactile values and movement, but without a compensatory strength, Berenson's criticism of the painters of Milan was reduced to what David Brown has aptly described as "footnotes to more general attitude of praise and blame."[28] Berenson identified prettiness as the source of both their popularity and their inferiority. Prettiness resulted when mediocre painters copied classical models (in this case the work of Leonardo) without the concomitant artistic essentials; prettiness is "all that remains of beauty when the permanent causes of the sensation are removed." [29]

Pretty art appeals to the viewer as smooth and refined, in contrast to difficult archaic art, which manifests its struggle in crude but powerful form. But this type of pseudoaesthetic seduction is analogous to that of exaggerated emotional expression, which Berenson summons as the twin of prettiness, in that it appeals on the level of actuality.

> The aesthetic moment—that too brief but most exquisite ecstasy when we and the work of art are one—is prevented from arriving; for the object of vision, instead of absorbing our entire attention as if it were a complete universe, and permitting us to enjoy the feeling of oneness with it, drives us back on curiosity and afield for information, setting up within us a host of mental activities hostile to the pure enjoyment of art.[30]

Neither prettiness nor emotional expression are sources of genuine artistic pleasure, any more than is illustration, which similarly tends toward the cognitive as it moves one to action rather than to aesthetic contemplation.

The limitations of Berenson's aesthetic principles, as evidenced in this essay, were obvious to Roger Fry, who by then had begun to take a serious interest in modern art. In his review of *The North Italian Painters* for *Burlington Magazine*, Fry regretted Berenson's conspicuous compression of thought, no doubt attributable, he asserted, to his need for brevity. Fry politely suggested that in a more expansive format Berenson might have been less inflexible in his critical estimation of the Milanese school. He clearly objected to Berenson's insistence on his formula of tactile values and ideated sensations as a universal standard by which all art can and should be judged.

When it was applied inappropriately, as for example to the work of Antonio Pisanello, this formula resulted in a distorted view of the artist's achievement.

> That he [Pisanello] does not at all fit in with the move-
> ment of Italian and particularly Florentine art is evi-
> dently true, but Mr. Berenson seems to miss the great
> importance of this tentative divagation. That Pisanello
> gave up altogether perspective, so nearly established by
> his trecento predecessors, would alone suggest that he
> had in view an altogether alternative mode of expres-
> sion, one from which European art has studiously turned
> aside, but not, therefore, a negligible one. His credit
> seems indeed to suffer precisely because his art refuses to
> be explained by Mr. Berenson's principles. The employ-
> ment of a more tentative and inductive method might at
> this point have led to an extension of the possible causes
> of aesthetic delight.[31]

Fry believed that Berenson's unwillingness to see beyond his stated requirements also led him to grossly misrepresent the character of Mantegna and to undervalue Correggio. This, he felt, was particularly regrettable in light of the fact that Berenson's appraisal of Correggio's gifts was so acute. Fry points out, for example, that Berenson had been correct to note that Correggio indulged in chiaroscuro for its own sake, but then could not praise him because Berenson had never accepted pure chiaroscuro, unrelated to modeling, as an artistic element. Fry here observed a defect that would reveal itself to many of Berenson's subsequent critics: an astonishing sensitivity toward salient pictorial qualities obstructed by a rigid theoretical bias that sorely restricted the pantheon of great art.

This review was written one year before Fry published his seminal "Essay on Aesthetics" and is compelling evidence of his readiness to supersede Berenson in matters of criticism. Though he repeatedly excuses Berenson on the grounds of enforced concision, claiming that he would surely concede more were he at liberty to be discursive, Fry offers a formidable indictment of Berenson's self-imposed aesthetic intolerance. This article is more than a routine review; it has the tenor of an intellectual challenge. Fry seems to be sizing up Berenson with the rigor one might expect from an apprentice-turned-rival.

Coming as it did on the heels of Berenson's commitment to attribute paintings for Duveen, and Fry's commitment to defend modern art, the review can be taken also as a declaration of war, one that Berenson was destined to lose. In the coming decades, Berenson would watch Roger Fry become what he had hoped to be: a brilliant theorist credited with the redirection of modern criticism. That Fry achieved this distinction in no small measure through the systematic application to modern art of aesthetic principles and a critical method pioneered by Berenson, must have been bitter medicine indeed.

"The Decline of Art"

The concluding pages of *The North Italian Painters,* which represented the end of this series on the regional painters of the Renaissance, contain a brief essay entitled "The Decline of Art." Berenson had incorporated a prelude to this discussion into the text of *The Drawings of the Florentine Painters,* wherein the relationship of mannerism to the art of Michelangelo was discussed in terms of decline. He meant "The Decline of Form" to explicate the extent to which his theories could be used, not only to reveal the essence and appeal of the figurative arts, but also to account for their unmaking in a period of decline.

Central to his argument was the premise that painting would not decline if it held its ground; that is, if it continued to strive toward what he called the classic. Berenson blamed the periodic collapse of artistic form in Western art on the European's incurable need for perpetual change. He did not believe in the common assumption that periods of decline were characterized by a dearth of genius, holding this to be a fallacy attributable to the understanding of genius exclusively in terms of the positive. As long as racial purity was not violated, he upheld, genius would survive. However, it was necessary for one to recognize the destructive, as well as constructive, potential of genius. In this essay Berenson called for a redefinition of artistic genius as the "capacity for productive reaction against one's training," an account that, by implication, suggests that raw genius could further the interests of art or destroy it.[32]

As an illustration of the decline cycle, Berenson referred to the development of Italian painting after the Renaissance. He stressed again the superiority of the archaic phase with its constant struggle toward life-enhancing formal values, notwithstanding its occasional lapses into crudeness and exaggeration. Once essential form and movement had been realized, art entered the classic stage and attention began to be diverted from the means to the adulation of the end result. This set the stage for decline because "the effect is then readily mistaken for the cause, and the types, shapes, attitudes, and arrangements, which have resulted from the conquest of form and movement, come to be regarded as the only possible moulds of beauty, and are canonized."[33]

The generation of artists following a classic phase (such as that of the mannerists) perceives a new goal. These artists, responsive to a populace seduced by the sensual emotion and "prettiness" that can be skimmed off the classic (phase), are also driven by the "instinctive craving for self-assertion." In general, the masses do not take to either the reticent severity of the classic phase or to the awkward continence of the archaic phase. They do, however, encourage younger artists who extract the superficial qualities of beauty and grace to present them in attenuated form. The emergent art is thereby fashioned into a "fully representative pictograph," in which silhouettes and shapes are placed in the service of unalloyed attractiveness rather than ideated sensations, thus signaling imminent decline. "Without realizing whither his [the artist's] applauded progress—which is no more than blind energy—was taking him, he will have got rid of form and movement; he will have thrown art out of the door, and, unlike nature, art will not come back through the window."[34]

Berenson thought of this cycle as inevitable, owing to the "rolling platform of art-reaction" that "facilitates advance in its own direction, while practically prohibiting progress in any other course."[35] In his scenario, art marches on to the next generation, which, in reaction to its predecessor, seeks a return to the classic. These artists, increasingly distant from the battlefield of the archaic phase and the vocabulary of the classic phase, grope with uncertainty, arriving finally at an academic eclecticism personified by the Carracci and the Bolognesi. Their belief that art will be saved by the lifeless combination of classical attributes is equally harmful, rooted as it is in categorical admiration of conventional models without the stimulation of fresh research. Decline can be arrested only with the advent of a new archaic phase and its attendant rediscovery of essential artistic values.

> No amount of rearrangement will infuse life. Vitality will appear only when artists recognize that the types, shapes, attitudes, and arrangements produced in the course of evolution are no more to be used again than spent cartridges, and that the only hope of resurrection lies in the disappearance of that facility which is in essence an enslaving habit of visualizing conventionally and of executing by rote. Then artists shall again attain tactile values and movement by observing the corporeal significance of objects and not their ready made aspects.[36]

Berenson concludes with the pronouncement that such rediscovery has not yet taken place in Italy and explains why, in the last three centuries, it has failed to produce a single great artist.

The theme of decline explored in this brief essay would occupy Berenson for the remaining years of his life. What here served him as further justification of the aesthetic principles he had outlined in these four volumes eventually took shape as an elaborate metaphor embodying his fear for the future of Western civilization. This fear, frequently expressed in letters and conversation, especially after the

First World War, is a recurrent tangent in the late books, where it is distilled into an intense hostility to contemporary art. In its early state, however, the decline theory can be interpreted metaphorically only with caution, for Berenson admitted late nineteenth-century French painting as an archaic phase equivalent to Renaissance Florence.

There is little evidence in this essay of Berenson's future antagonism to modern art, although there are definite premonitions. For example, the distinction between originality and quality, and the insistence on the potentially destructive power of genius, were points that he would make later to castigate Picasso. Nor did the essay seem reactionary to his peers. Hermann Obrist, by then a good friend of Kandinsky and a prominent member of the artistically progressive milieu of Munich, called it a "masterpiece of coming to the point" and expressed his desire to post it on studio doors across Europe."[37] Even Roger Fry, whose review of Berenson's *The North Italian Painters* was harsh, congratulated him on the brilliance of the decline essay, adding that his "rapid survey of the relation of artistic endeavor at each point in its evolution to the emotional demands of the crowd is altogether admirable, and suggests the solution of many of the irritating paradoxes of the story of modern art."[38]

Nothing in this essay would disallow, at least from a theoretical point of view, the future development of modernism. But Berenson clearly sensed danger, and it can be understood as an affirmation of his faith in the artistic traditions of Western classicism at a time when these traditions were under siege. Berenson continued to see Fabbri a good deal in these years and, more important, the art collectors Leo, Michael, and Sally Stein. Shortly after the publication of *The North Italian Painters,* he met Henri Matisse and other modern artists who confronted him with a constant challenge to his system of belief. During the ensuing decade, as Berenson came to terms with the life he had chosen for himself, his aesthetic theories merged with his worldview. They worked together to mold him in the image of the classical humanist that he would become desperate to preserve.

As Berenson further enmeshed himself in the refinement of connoisseurship and in the type of life it brought him, the essence of his modernity would require redefinition. It survived primarily in the form of a critical method that continued to insist on the detached, if no longer disinterested, apprehension of formal values and in a decidedly modern temperament dedicated to the exploration and perfection of the self through art. But his criterion of value and his aesthetic philosophy, both of which he insisted revolved around an unwavering commitment to classical humanism, became increasingly reactionary. He continued his critical practice of keeping the present before the public as he expounded on the past. But when he invoked the modern, with a few notable exceptions, it no longer served him as a means of favorable comparison or validation. Instead it was offered as evidence of decline and, more important, as a warning about the future.

Critical Writing During the Duveen Years

One of the great paradoxes of Berenson's growing antipathy to modernism was its coincidence with the steady rise in his fascination with what he called "peripheral" art and with Medieval painting. During the years of his involvement with the art dealer Joseph Duveen (from about 1907 to 1937) a sizable amount of Berenson's technical writing is concerned with painting that is distinguished by its distance from the classical canons he had sought to uphold.[39] In his early essays on Sassetta, Berenson had admitted the limitations of his normative standards and had argued for the viability of imaginative design as an alternative mode of expression, particularly when the artist's aim was the communication of spiritual values. He faced a similar problem in his writing about both provincial and Medieval painting. At times he was forced to concede the illogicality of taking satisfaction in these clearly underdeveloped artistic forms.

> The physiognomy of the figures is amiably imbecile. The bodies are ill proportioned and undersized. The action and gestures remind one of marionettes fashioned by a

plowman in rare moments of leisure. . . . If the beget-
ter of these paperdolls is not distinguished by depth of
feeling or intellect, neither does he retrieve himself by
any merits as a painter. His technique is embarrassed,
his modelling blurred, his coloring hot. And yet I enjoy these decalcomanias! They appeal to something
invincingly puerile in my nature.[40]

The artistic immaturity of these images was a not an impediment
to his appreciation of them, despite the fact that, as he suggested, one
might be ridiculed for confessing to a liking for the artistic equivalent
of dolls and children's toys.

"Decalcomania," the transfer or tracing of decorative patterns
from paper, was a word Berenson frequently used as a pejorative in
reference to modern art and it is clear from such passages that he
was prepared to accept in earlier art the very formal characteristics
that in recent art enraged him. He discussed the aesthetic he found
operating in Medieval painting in very formalist terms, something he
would never do for modern art, even though the terms would have
been similar. Not only was he willing to admit his attraction to this
work but, in some instances, he was also disinclined to deny the in-
tentionality or even competence of the artist. In a 1921 essay on a
pair of recently discovered twentieth-century panels from Constantinople, for example, he insisted that although one may question the
canon of the human figure, here exemplified, one could not question
the artist's skill. Acceptance of the work on its own terms required
an admission that the artist knew exactly what he wanted to do and
did so to perfection: "Contour, modelling, color make the pictures
what they are, as much as the tesserae make a mosaic, and you cannot think of them as better or worse than the design. They are the
design."[41]

The more intolerant Berenson became of recent art that intention-
ally overthrew the canons of classicism, the more generous would be
his position toward artists of the past to whom these canons were lost
or denied. He never granted modern artists the latitude frequently ex-

tended to earlier painters for the simple reason that he felt they should have known better. The distortions of modern artists could not be blamed on distance from an artistic epicenter (peripheral art) or on the unavoidable circumstances of their chronology (medieval art). Although Berenson would admit to a purposive aesthetic designed to communicate spirituality in Sienese painting, he would afford no such recognition to a modern artist bent on conveying a world of the spirit that was anathema to him.

Many articles written by Berenson during this period are replete with elaborate apologies for his inadequacy in areas of study essential to the appreciation of Medieval art, especially with respect to the interpretation of meaning. Berenson's concession in these essays to the importance of iconography was more than a little hypocritical. It stands in sharp contrast to his disparaging remarks, which continued to appear in letters and conversations, about the corruption of art study by scholars such as Erwin Panofsky, whose growing influence he greatly resented.

Despite these occassional nods to iconography, Berenson continued to resist the impulse toward speculative interpretation. In *Venetian Painting in America: The Fifteenth Century* (1916), for example, he contends that "it cannot be too firmly maintained that a work of art can pretend, as a work of art, to no meaning, broadly human or narrowly artistic, beyond what is spontaneously suggested to the cultivated mind." Berenson felt that sorting out nuances of meaning, symbolism, or "neo-mystical nonsense" was the business of theologians and gossips, not of the humanists, aestheticians and dilletanti to whom he typically addressed himself.[42]

In an essay on Leonardo da Vinci, also published in 1916, Berenson makes a strong case for the importance of "what is spontaneously suggested to the cultivated mind."[43] This essay is the first of many subsequent pleas to restore to art the human values his critical method originally seemed to deny. Berenson's purpose was to debunk the myth of Leonardo's genius; uncharacteristically, he chose to accomplish this by exposing Leonardo's ineptness, not in terms of decoration or form, but instead on the level of illustration.

Berenson realized that his readers might find this strategy unusual in a critic who was distinguished by his insistence on the absolute priority of formal values over illustrative values in painting. He was at great pains to correct what he viewed as an unfortunate misconception resulting from his early polemical writing. The essay opens with a disclaimer. It declares that his intention had never been to imply that illustration was without consequence, and he reminds the reader that in *The Florentine Painters* he placed as much emphasis on spiritual significance as he did on tactile values.

> But the last term was new, mysterious, and promising, and thus ended by attracting all the attention, the more so that I had taken the human interest and ethical appeal in works of art for granted, as calling for no definition or discussion, and had felt free to devote my zeal to the part of the theory whose strangeness demanded exposition and defense. Moreover, I insisted in that volume and in others which followed, that a painting made up almost entirely of illustrative elements could never count as a great work of art, while, on the contrary, a great work of art might be as devoid of intentional illustration, as unconscious nature itself. This also could not but encourage the view that in my opinion the subject did not matter, and that its meaning was of no concern to us.[44]

Although he continued to lament the intrusion of too much meaning into a work of art, Berenson is forced to admit that

> a soul-less dauber may get so absorbed in the mere technique of painting as to remain unconscious of its meaning. But for the rest of us there is no way of ignoring the human appeal of a picture. We may throw it out of our minds, but it comes back through our hearts; and defiantly as we may pretend that it does not matter, its claims are first to demand satisfaction.[45]

Leonardo's *Last Supper* failed to meet Berenson's expectation as illustration in that it contradicted the spirit of the subject represented. His unseemly treatment of the theme, with so much gesticulating and expression, smacked to Berenson of the Italian marketplace rather than the noble and subdued humanity of Christ.

After a decade of struggling with the increasingly arcane language of avant-garde painting, in this essay Berenson announced that the appreciation of art should not require the kind of intense intellectual effort demanded by Leonardo's works. We may assume that he also had in mind their modern equivalents. For example, his chief objection to Leonardo's *Mona Lisa* turned on its legendary ambiguity, a quality that resulted in a plethora of imposed "over-meanings," leaving the public exhausted and confused.

> Looking at her leads to questioning, to perplexity, and even to doubt of one's intelligence, which does not interfere with our being fascinated with her, but does effectively prevent the mystic union between the work of art and ourselves, which is the very essence of the aesthetic moment.[46]

The burden of having to figure out the meaning of a painting, Berenson insisted, worked against true appreciation because the aesthetic experience aimed at immediate ecstacy, not intellectual conquest.

Having established Leonardo's shortcomings as an illustrator, from which the strength of his decorative qualities could not rescue him, Berenson then questioned the reasons for his enduring fame. He attributed this to the fact that Leonardo's technical achievements, specifically the perfection of chiaroscuro and contrapposto, furnished models that made the teaching and practice of art easier. Berenson did not place a high premium on either of these qualities. He believed that the widespread reliance on chiaroscuro, especially by mediocre talents, merely served to mask incompetent drawing and thus actually contributed to the decline of painting.

Berenson's conclusion in this essay is that an artist wholly absorbed in the technical problems of painting, as he held Leonardo (and many modern painters) to be, was destined to neglect the pressing demands of both decoration and illustration and thus could never be satisfying to humanists. Leonardo's most serious transgression, in other words, was to give himself over to science and theory at the expense of art. His tendency toward extreme intellectualism made him lose sight of the aesthetic, the result being that Leonardo's pictures so absorb the viewer on the level of technique that pure appreciation is obstructed. Berenson insisted that art should be neither confusing nor overtly theoretical, claiming that "logic has been the ruin of most of the more ambitious and more intellectual art movements of the last eight centuries, from Gothic architecture to Cubist painting."[47]

This essay functions as a provocative metaphor for Berenson's disapproval of modern art and can be interpreted as a vigorous denial of its claims to legitimacy. Nearly all the ingredients of Berenson's future polemic against modern art are introduced here: unjustified claims to genius, unwelcome obscurity, neglect of humanist values, excessive emphasis on technique, bias toward science and logic, and even the connection between art and barbarism. And, perhaps most important, Berenson judges Leonardo's painting unacceptable, and by extension so too modernist art, not on the basis of what it is but on the basis of what it does not do. Underlying the essay on Leonardo was an obvious attempt at damage control on the part of a critic who was beginning to sense that he might have facilitated the development of an art in which human interest and ethical appeal could no longer be taken for granted.

Unless otherwise noted, all photographs on the following pages are courtesy Villa I Tatti, Harvard University Center for Italian Renaissance Studies.

Berenson in Salzburg, 1936

Drawing of Berenson by Kerr Lawson, 1897

Hermann Obrist, 1895

Matisse landscape (*Trees Near Melun*) purchased by
Berenson from the studio of the artist, c. 1909

Portrait of Berenson by William Rothenstein, 1907

Caricature of Berenson by Walter Tittle, "The Simon
Legree of Italian Art"; inscription by the artist: "The
Berenson, as I thought he would look, before my
delightful disillusionment in London in 1932 !!!"

Christmas card from Margaret ("Daisy") Scolari Barr,
1936; photograph of an unidentified man, Arthur
McComb, Leonor Fini, Margaret Barr, and Alfred Barr
(courtesy Museum of Modern Art Archives: Margaret
Scolari Barr Papers)

Berenson with Barbara and Ursula Strachey, children of
Mary Berenson's daughter Ray Costelloe Strachey, 1919

Berenson with Benedetto Croce, 1945

Berenson, c. 1900

Berenson at I Tatti, 1950, next to a relief by Alberto Sani
(photograph by David Lees)

Berenson, in the garden at I Tatti, 1954

4. Berenson's Last Years

I no longer appeal to a public
supposed to take an interest in what
hitherto has been regarded as art.
Now that people with no mustard
seed of native feeling for art
constitute the overwhelming
majority of the public, they can be
bamboozled into taking for art
cubism, surrealism, abstract art,
and put it on the same level with the
artists of the Renaissance, or even
ancient Hellas. For them, what can I
mean? I who defend certain relative

absolutes or canons in art, and
exclude most of what is done today
as mere artifact and not art at all;
what can I mean to the
public today!

1947

The best historians are those who
even in their dreams do not imagine
that the best of all possible ages is
the age in which they are living.

1933

> It is my ever growing conviction that we, of normal
> growth, give out all the good there is in us before 40
> at least. After that age we are little more than organ
> grinders, grinding out a certain number of turns, fondly
> mistaking the variations of sound produced by the de-
> termination of the machinery, for new notes, unheard of
> variants, precious nuances where of we must not deprive
> our eager public. In fact this public has read us off long
> ago and pays no attention unless we add a performing
> monkey to our hand organ.[1]

When Berenson wrote these words to William Ivins in 1944, he had
just passed his seventieth birthday. Forty seems to have been his age
of reckoning, for elsewhere he claimed that he had accomplished little
since then except to build a library and direct a stream of pictures
to America.[2] Shortly after his fortieth birthday he went to work for
Duveen, and these sentiments clearly reflect his customary practice
of blaming connoisseurship and "expertising" for the inability to fulfill his youthful potential. After three decades Berenson finally broke
relations with Duveen and then experienced a resurgence of his long-
dormant intellectual ambitions. Political turmoil on the Continent,
his wife's declining health, and the outbreak of World War II left
him increasingly isolated from the hordes of visitors and clients who
had occupied most of his time. So Berenson turned his attention once
again to the articulation of general ideas on art and aesthetics, something he had virtually abandoned in favor of the technical writing
produced during the Duveen years.

But as his statement to Ivins demonstrates, he did not face this
with the confidence and certainty that had driven him in the 1890s.
Although Berenson had become somewhat of a celebrity in the eyes
of the general public, he was well aware of the erosion of his influence in the inner sanctum of academic art history and professional
art criticism. The drift toward iconographic studies and, more im-

portant, the critical acceptance of modernist art, left him hostile and defensive. His autobiographical books, drawn largely from the diary he began to keep in 1941, are filled with the sentiment he expressed to Ivins: that he feared he had nothing left to say that anyone would care to hear. Paradoxically, there are also repeated allusions to his manifest inability to remain silent, even on those matters in which his competence was questionable. The drive to publish prevailed, and in the final decades of his life modern art became Berenson's "performing monkey," a way to assure himself an audience in an age that otherwise might have ignored him.

Evidence of the magnitude of Berenson's actual exposure to modern art in his final decades is difficult to come by. His diaries and letters make occasional mention of exhibitions he attended, but these rarely include references to specific artists or paintings, as they did, for example, in the decades before World War I, when he was still willing to look earnestly at recent art. One encounter with contemporary art that seems to have made an impression on him was his visit to the 1948 Venice Biennale, where, among other things, he saw Peggy Guggenheim's collection of abstract and surrealist paintings. In her amusing account of this meeting, Guggenheim noted that Berenson liked best the works of Max Ernst and Jackson Pollock, though he objected to the sexual content in Ernst's work.[3] This was later corroborated in a conversation between Clement Greenberg and Berenson, wherein the latter mentioned that the paintings by Pollock were the best works Guggenheim owned, a statement Greenberg did not think was meant necessarily as a compliment.[4]

Berenson visited the Biennale in the company of Alfred Barr, the founding director of the Museum of Modern Art, and his wife, Margaret Scolari Barr, and it is reasonable to assume that they were a major source of information for him on modern art.[5] He began corresponding with Margaret Barr in the mid-1930s, and in the ensuing decades she regularly sent him copies of exhibition and collection catalogs published by the Museum of Modern Art. On at least one occasion, Berenson was called upon to intercede on the museum's behalf with an Italian collector who owned some modern paintings that were needed for an exhibition.[6] When Alfred Barr was preparing his monograph on Matisse, he questioned Berenson about the landscape he once owned and his meetings with the artist.[7] Margaret Barr reported to Berenson on her meetings with various modern artists, especially Picasso, and also introduced him to artists and writers with an interest in modern art. Among them was the art historian Leo Steinberg, who evidently made quite an impression, for Berenson would later query the American painter George Biddle as to what he knew about him, a gesture he made only when a new acquaintance seemed worth investigating.[8]

Margaret Barr suspected that Berenson rather enjoyed their friendly banter over modernism, and at times she sent things with the intention of provoking him. Included with an essay on contemporary art by James Thrall Soby, for example, was a note to Berenson that states: "I know you will loathe the contents but this loathing or this act of loathing I think gives you a certain amount of pleasure."[9] But when it came to her husband, she was protective, and Alfred Barr did not meet Berenson until she had known the older man for over a decade, despite the Barrs' frequent trips to Europe together. When Berenson once reminded her to send some Museum of Modern Art publications that she had been promising, she declined, admitting that

> I have not sent you catalogs because I like your fulminations, only when the lightning does not fall on my immediate family. If this family too must be stricken then, say I heroically, let the arrows fall on my sinful head. I shall circumvent the difficulty by sending you catalogs of American exhibitions. I cannot believe that they will annoy you very much. The catalog sent to Nicki [Mariano] will be sufficient all by itself to give you the measure of the horrors that in its daily routine the museum documents.[10]

For his part, Berenson was intent on giving Margaret Barr the impression that he "kept up" and frequently mentioned the exhibitions of modern art he saw during his travels. As late as 1950, he wrote to her of a trip to Paris, where he claimed to have spent hours looking at recent art and was less shocked than he expected to be, though no less bored.[11] When Alfred Barr went to Taormina in 1954 to proofread a new book on the museum's permanent collection in honor of its twenty-fifth anniversary, Berenson even suggested to Margaret Barr that he stay in the *villino* at I Tatti and do his work in his library which, he claimed, was pretty well stocked with books on modern "non-art."[12] In the year before his death, he confided to Margaret Barr once again that he tried to keep up with what was going on in the art world but added that even she must feel outmoded by what was being done today.[13]

Berenson was no doubt referring to abstract expressionism, which he had the opportunity to see during his periodic visits to the Venice Biennale. Notwithstanding his remark about Peggy Guggenheim's Pollocks, it was abstract art that incurred his greatest wrath. Despite Berenson's distaste for unpleasant subject matter, he seems to have had less quarrel with surrealism. Margaret Barr sent him the catalog of the historic exhibition "Fantastic Art, Dada, and Surrealism," and in 1938 she tried to arrange a meeting between Berenson and Salvador Dali.[14] Possibly stimulated by his study of this publication, Berenson remarked to the Italian writer Umberto Morra that Dali was a good draftsman, given to incongruous themes, and in all probability had, like Picasso, acted with total cynicism.[15] Later Berenson noted in a diary entry his discovery of the surrealist intent to recall dreams. He admitted that because even in dreams, no matter how absurd, we do retain a certain sense of the probable, surrealist art did not offend him as much as nonrepresentational art.[16]

According to Berenson, surrealism was chiefly a form of allegorical art and, as such, it was significant as illustration but did not represent a new artistic vision. For Berenson the crucial distinction between abstraction and surrealism remained the continued presence of recognizable subject matter. Although surrealist painting was absurd and disturbing to him, it remained art, of sorts, if it had vitality of detail (form). Nonrepresentational art, on the other had, was in Berenson's scheme a "contradiction in terms."[17]

Berenson's contempt for modern art in these years was legendary.

All of his late books, though ostensibly concerned with art history and aesthetic theory, carry the same message: Modernism was symptomatic of Western civilization in decline. He tried to deal with this on an intellectual level by searching for historical precedents. During the last half of his life his interest in past art, as exemplified by the holdings of his library and the records of his travels, grew to embrace virtually the entire history of the visual arts. In the decades between the world wars, the decline of form became a major theme of his discontent, dominating his conversation, correspondence, and, eventually, his publications. As he told Umberto Morra in 1937,

> My center of interest is now directed at a pathological
> age so my eye is open to all its manifestations and I could
> study for hours some scribble which would seem utterly
> futile to the eye of any expert who was not impelled by
> the same motive that I am. My pleasure, however, knows
> no limits of time and place . . . without boasting I can
> say that I am a free citizen in the kingdom of art. . . . The
> thing is that the civilization which we consider historical
> is a single whole, and is maturing at its various spatial
> points according to the same process of development.[18]

Excluded from the "whole" of this civilization were, of course, modern art and the tribal objects on which he felt a good deal of it was based.

For Berenson, the last great age in this kingdom of art was the nineteenth century. But his cyclical view of history provided little comfort as he watched the twentieth century rage around him. He believed in the absolute superiority of Western classical civilization and considered himself lucky enough to have been born in one of its shining moments. Like many members of his generation, World War I was the great watershed of his personal experience. Despite his perception of forty as the pivotal age in the life of the intellect, the turning point of Berenson's life was closer to his fiftieth year, or, specifically, the outbreak of the war.

It was during and immediately after the war that his discouragement about the future of art, manifest in his hostility toward cubism, merged with a pronounced fear for the survival of civilization as he knew it. Berenson emerged from the years of the war with a profound sense of alienatiôn from modern culture that would haunt him the remaining four decades of his life. He wrote to the American art historian Frank Jewett Mather in 1919 that the events since the armistice gave him a horror of present culture from which he would never recover and made him yearn for the Middle Ages, which he felt, though no less barbaric, were at least not hypocritical.[19] At about this time Berenson began to urge his protégés, such as Royal Cortissoz, to write their memoirs lest this chapter in the history of the West, which was clearly coming to an end, be lost to future generations who might benefit from their wisdom.

In the decades that followed, it became evident that Berenson's alarm over the future of humanity was in no small measure informed by fear for his own survival, professionally, economically, and socially. His published remarks were concerned primarily with the crisis of humanism and its implications. Privately, however, Berenson deeply resented the undermining of his influence and his standards in a society that showed increasingly less respect for the elitist concept of culture to which he had devoted his life. He told William Ivins in 1931 of his displeasure at being sacrificed to an "abjectly lower standard of civilization," particularly since the exemplars of this "lower state" were never likely to make contributions superior to his own. Much of the barbarization of Europe by the Nazis, he added, was due to the alienation of "unseriner," Berenson's pet expression for people of his own kind.[20]

Berenson expressed similar feelings to his old friend Hutchins Hapgood, of whom he was very fond, despite Hapgood's progressive social ideas.[21] Both Hapgood and Mary Berenson had been liberal reformers in their youth, but they could never successfully interest Bernard Berenson in their causes.

Mary Berenson kept in touch with progressive thought through her daughters Ray Strachey and Karin Stephen, both of whom had married into the Bloomsbury circle and had literary careers of some distinction. In 1931 Mary Berenson wrote Hapgood of a debating club at Oxford, where one of her daughters participated in a discussion of whether the present represented the end of civilization or the end only of the old civilization. She marveled at the younger woman's lack of interest in the outcome of the question and took it as a readiness to grapple with whatever came her way.

> This is not the case with BB and myself. We are living rather anxiously from day to day, not at all sure that the coming society will have any niche for us. . . . We are not in sympathetic touch with the post-war mentality of the young. As it shows itself in regard to art, it consists in indifference to, or scorn for, all classic, all established art, and in experiments inspired by the achievements of barbaric and uncivilized races; and literature and morals seem to be going the same way. BB frets his gizzard mightily about it.[22]

Hapgood's populist notions, which he vigorously espoused as a young man, were also eroded by the crises of the early twentieth century and in their late correspondence Bernard Berenson and Hutchins Hapgood complained to each other about the abysmal state of modern culture. The following passage, written by Berenson in response to Hapgood's request for a "virila" letter, clearly attests the extent to which, in Berenson's mind, political, social, and artistic changes mingled to form a vague, yet apocalyptic, vision of a civilization whose only hope for rescue from certain ruin was the reinstatement of the traditional values of his class.

> I believe more and more in culture and the hideous setback first harbingered by the tam-tam nonsense of a Gertrude Stein, followed by the anarchically solipsistic lingo of Joyce, and triumphant with futurists and surrealists, prophesizing not intentionally but the more effectively confusion, Bolshevism, Fascism and Nazism.

The hideous setback does not discourage me. It makes
me uncomfortable to remain almost isolated as I do, and
unhappy to have emancipation of the average man from
all the trammels of culture. It is naturally disappointing
how little the featherless biped has been humanized,
how little culture has affected him. I see that the way
is going to be harder, and narrower, and ever and ever
so much longer than we imagined and believed in our
youth. But this same biped will either degenerate into
a real ape, in which case he simply would not interest
the likes of me, or after all rebellion of every totalitarian
species against culture, he will laboriously return to our
position.[23]

Berenson's polemic against modern art and culture cannot be understood simply as a defense of representational art or classical humanism; it was, for all intents and purposes, a plea for the survival of his
way of life.

The ideological implications of Berenson's rejection of modern
culture were much discussed after his death and are in no small measure responsible for the suspicion with which he has been viewed
by subsequent generations. During his lifetime, however, Berenson's
allegiance to bourgeois cultural values was not a major issue; in the
last decades of his life he was lionized by the popular and art press
alike as the last surviving humanist, the "Sage of Settignano," who
stood for a coherent set of values in the face of chaos.[24] The first two
of his post–World War II publications, *Sketch for a Self-Portrait* and
Aesthetics and History in the Visual Arts, were widely and, in the
main, favorably, reviewed. According to Kenneth Clark, the 1952 edition of *The Italian Painters of the Renaissance* instantly sold 60,000
copies.[25]

In a 1955 tribute to Berenson on the occasion of his ninetieth birthday, Francis H. Taylor went so far as to suggest that Berenson's broad
humanism, as expressed in philosophical writings published since
World War II, rather than his expertise as a connoisseur would be

his most enduring legacy. He applauded Berenson for "exposing" the dehumanization of abstract art and for his ability to resist the fads of modern scholarship, which in their pseudoscience reduced art to what can be quantitatively measured. In Taylor's view, Berenson was heir to the critical tradition of Charles Eliot Norton and John Ruskin, with a like ability to see beyond the object to the life and impulse that created it. This insistence on Berenson's humanistic approach to the study of art is evidence of the extent to which popular opinion had disengaged him from the empirical spirit he had a large hand in creating.[26]

The myth of Berenson the sage, watching the sun setting on the Western world from the ivory tower of Settignano, had an irresistible appeal to his admirers and detractors alike.[27] Articles written about him in the final decades of his life, and those written immediately following his death in 1959, stressed Berenson's ability to remove himself from the sordid realities of twentieth-century life as, alternately, his principal virtue or his most alarming shortcoming. The popular press, which expected the least of him, was content to report periodically on his miraculous survival in an age that was both alien and hostile to his worldview. *Time* magazine's 1960 review of *One Year's Reading for Fun: 1942*, an account of what Berenson read while in hiding during the war, spoke not of the substance of his reading but instead of the image this diary furnished of the "civilized use of enforced leisure, the serene play of the mind amid 20th century bustle and terror." The reviewer added that "Bernard Berenson had burnished his insights too long over the magnificence of Renaissance Italy to find the modern age other than trifling and tawdry."[28]

Berenson's last years were devoted to sustaining his polemic against the evils of modern art, amid efforts on the part of the popular press to preserve him as the last humanist and a living anachronism. This combination led to the growing feeling on the part of an increasingly disenchanted professional readership that Berenson's wholesale condemnation of contemporary culture was a regrettable abuse of his authority for which he should be held accountable. If the ideas in his last books were not to be taken seriously, which seemed to be the opinion of many art professionals, his insistence on issuing them as authoritative proclamations and superior moral positions was.

Many reviews of these books, often written as personal favors for Berenson by grateful colleagues, tended to plead for tolerance in view of his advanced age or to argue for the enduring relevance of his humanism even in the face of his clearly dated aesthetic principles. But for the others who recognized Berenson's importance to the historiography of art and criticism (and had little to fear in incurring his wrath), this "God's-eye" view of the present was disappointing and irresponsible. Meyer Schapiro's groundbreaking essay of 1961, the first genuinely critical study of Berenson's career, was certainly written in this spirit.[29]

The campaign against modern art kept Berenson in the public eye and, in so doing, became a major protagonist in his crusade for the survival of Western classicism and the preservation of culture as an aristocratic privilege. Berenson's harshest critics in his last years and since his death have frequently been those who took him most seriously and therefore expected better from him than the seemingly indiscriminate and self-serving rejection of a half-century of art that he chose not to understand.

Aesthetics and History in the Visual Arts

The first of Berenson's publications after World War II, *Aesthetics and History in the Visual Arts,* was written as the introduction to his major study, "Decline and Recovery in the Figure Arts." This was to have been a systematic explanation of the decline of classical form under Constantine and its gradual recovery during the Middle Ages, culminating in the standards of excellence achieved during the Italian Renaissance. *The Arch of Constantine; or, The Decline of Form,* published as a single volume in 1954, was the first chapter. Berenson worked on this study for over three decades and developed his library to pursue research, but he was never able to concentrate his findings into a completed manuscript. He referred to the project often in correspondence, always in anticipation of bringing out a "big book" that would function both as a sweeping historical study and as a comprehensive statement of his aesthetic theories.

Kenneth Clark claimed that this study seemed especially suited to Berenson's unique gifts: "His learning, his memory, his unrivalled power of relating incidents remote from one another and of drawing analogies—in a word his historical wisdom—could all have been united and controlled by his aesthetic principles." [30] Clark attributed Berenson's inability to complete the book to the fact that Berenson's powers over the years were increasingly governed by his immediate response to works of art, which militated against the development of a protracted study. Instead of forging a coherent treatise on art and aesthetics from his vast historical learning and experience, Berenson played with his knowledge and ideas, Clark said, "as the bards treated legend and poetic imagery, as part of an inexhaustible reservoir to be drawn upon for the delight of his audience; and he had a half conscious feeling that to fix facts and ideas on a printed page was to deprive them of their life." [31]

This eloquent apology for the shallowness of Berenson's thought was characteristic of many admirers who had difficulty reconciling his vast learning with his obvious incapacity for sustained logical argument. In retrospect, it appears that the big book was never written because Berenson simply could not come to terms with the possibility that his theory of decline was wrong.[32] It was predicated on the belief that the corruption of classicism in the fourth century resulted from incompetence and lack of proper training, and in no way represented purposive innovation. Berenson's whole approach to art was threatened by the alternative thesis, that such art signaled an intentional departure from classicism rather than a decline. Contemplating this issue in the context of the critical legitimation of modernist art as indicative of a similarly profitable rejection of traditional artistic values, Berenson chose to abandon the writing of a systematic history. He thereby shifted attention from what was a clearly vulnerable thesis to the universality of these values as axiomatic.

The problems surrounding the completion of this study are discussed extensively by Samuels, who points out that to address the central issue Berenson was required to reexamine his definition of art and his approach to art history, the former under assault by modernism, the latter by the followers of Panofsky. In the process, as Samuels explains, the issues became confused.

> His discursive essays trespassed on each other each time he returned to his desk. Thus the discussion of the Arch of Constantine as the paradigm of development with which he began the first essay gave way to a discussion of "aesthetics, ethics and history" that was to preoccupy him until late 1941. He had turned aside to that discussion, he afterward wrote, with the idea of writing "little more than a preface to a book on 'Decline and Recovery in the Figure Arts,'" but the thing ran away with his impatient thoughts and the preface became a book.[33]

In the introduction to *Aesthetics and History,* Berenson stressed that his intention was to explain the assumptions and convictions that had governed a lifetime devoted to the study of art. That this did not result in a systematic theory of aesthetics, he was well aware. He warned his readers that the pages were filled with remarks of the sort that came out in conversation, here shared with a broader public without access to his "table-talk." Berenson expressed regret at his inability to overcome the aphoristic writing style for which he was so well known, but he explained, "I am not a dialectician; I have no gift for developing an argument with abundance of words and instances. So what I have done is to put down whatever happened to come into my head as I meditated on art theory and art history."[34] For the most part this consisted of a restatement, in a somewhat expanded form, of the critical and aesthetic principles established in his early books, intermingled with discursive passages on the disciplinary priorities of art history and the humanistic function of art.[35]

A half-century after their initial formulation in the essays on Italian Renaissance painting, Berenson's artistic essentials remained virtually unchanged. What had once seemed a radically new approach to the study and criticism of art assumes, in this context, a distinctly reactionary tone. Berenson stubbornly insisted, in the face of drastic upheavals of early twentieth-century art, that standards of judgment with respect to painting are timeless and that art should still be esteemed to the extent that it generates ideated sensations of touch, movement, and space in the viewer.

His explanation of these principles and the attendant theory of life-enhancement is more elaborate, but the assumptions remain essentially the same. The sole evidence of concession to more recent ideas in this system of thought is an occasional use of terminology that developed after the publication of his first books. His discussion of tactile values, for example, demonstrates awareness of the theoretical writings of both Clive Bell and Roger Fry, which, as Berenson well knew, were in themselves heavily indebted to his own. In *Aesthetics and History* Berenson discusses form as an aesthetic quality that conveys something beyond human cognizance that, when fully realized, transmits a sense of life directly. Mindful of the extent to which the work of these British critics rested on his own, he states that in his books form means tactile values and that the " 'significant form' of which some of us speak means just that." [36]

Berenson again reminds his readers that only representational art can hope to stimulate ideated sensations, and then only when the qualities of tactile values, movement, and so on, are not exaggerated or distorted. The human spectator cannot identify with a cube any more than with the anatomical geometry of the Italian mannerists, whom he calls the "cubists of yesterday." [37] Furthermore, Berenson insists that to be life-enhancing, these ideated sensations must also be pleasant; the communication of nausea, for example, is not artistic.

In *Aesthetics and History* Berenson made an effort to bring together and to articulate many things that had remained only implied in the earlier essays. Though Berenson continued to insist on the universality of his principles, owing to their reliance on the psychophysical makeup of the human organism, he was careful to point out that they were developed specifically to explain the enjoyment of figurative art in the Western classical tradition. This he believed to be the superior, but not the only, form of visual expression. As a number of reviewers noted, the breadth of his familiarity with art that exists outside of this tradition was impressive.

Berenson considered himself broad-minded in comparison to narrow classicists who recognized as legitimate only art directly descendent from the antique.[38] By way of contrast, he claimed he could enjoy anything that stimulated ideated sensations, including Eastern and even "primitive ethnographic" objects. But the fact remained that, at least for him, the art which most consistently and satisfactorily achieved this end was Western figurative art. This, he urged his readers, should be their primary interest.

One of the seeming inconsistencies of Berenson's early writing on aesthetics had been his tendency to isolate the appreciation of art from the whole of human experience while simultaneously insisting on its humanistic function. This resulted from the sharp distinction he made between "decoration" and "illustration," or, as he says in *Aesthetics and History,* form and content. A central concern of this later treatise was to clarify the meaning of illustration and to establish its role in the process of appreciation. As early as 1916, in the essay on Leonardo da Vinci, Berenson pointed out that the public misunderstood his intentions in making an issue of this distinction. Here again he regrets the ensuing perception that he despised illustration and all consideration of subject and blames the general public's tendency to remember only what shocked them. He supposed that this was to be expected but believed that his professional readership should have known better.

> It is less easy to understand that serious students should have written of me as if I were an apostle of "mere visibility" in the work of art. . . . I have always maintained that the same work of art had a prodigious number of things to tell us . . . I simply insisted that the work of art itself should tell it.[39]

Berenson continued to maintain that for purposes of study art should be split into form and content. He admitted, however, that this was a convenience that did not correspond to actual experience because the spectator was left with an impression of the work as a whole. This bifurcation was necessary to understand art as a separate and unique undertaking, the autonomy of which depended upon its claiming for itself a set of singular concerns independent of other forms of expression. Herein lies the essence of Berenson's early formalism: Unless priority was given to visual evidence, in terms of both understanding and appreciation, art was in danger of being reduced to a plaything for the intellect. In upholding this dichotomy a half-century after he began his career, Berenson demonstrated an ongoing connection to the development of both professional art history and formalist criticism in the post–World War II world.[40]

The actual existence of subject matter was not the focus of this polemic but rather abuses of interpretation. To his mind, many historians, philosophers, and critics who turned their attention to art were guilty of the same thing: undue preoccupation with the nature of the representation at the expense of considerations of form. Berenson believed that the two must be held in balance. Most aesthetic treatises, he claimed, were born not of experience but of reading and cognition. Their main interest was in how a work of art could be placed in the service of a system of thought. Critics who worried about artist's intentions and historians who viewed art strictly as a document of civilization were similarly blameworthy. For all such writers "the work of art is not an object to be enjoyed, loved, and consumed, an enrichment for ever, but an occasion offered to professional thinkers for delighting in their own acumen, their own subtlety and dialectical skill."[41] The end result is that the reader attends to the written text at the expense of the work, thus obstructing the probability of attaining a genuinely aesthetic experience, which is what art alone can provide.

Having explained the need for this distinction between form and content, Berenson went on to say that illustration required further definition, lest it should be understood simply as the literal reproduction of ideas or narrative. His original definition of illustration had been narrow and negative; by saying that it was everything in art that was not decoration, he felt he had implied that illustration was indifferent or opposed to the truly artistic. Here, Berenson argued that illustration was synonymous with representation and that it was as essential to the aesthetic experience as form itself.

In this context, he also made claims for the autonomy of illustration, again seizing this as an opportunity to berate those who would assign what he had once called "over-meanings" to a work. Illustration should not depend for its merits on information or interpretations furnished by an interested spectator. In keeping with his position that the work should be allowed to speak for itself, Berenson insisted that "nothing should be read into the illustration that is not manifestly there" and that "we do not want to know some story, or some doctrine, which may have excited the artist but which his art could not express. What he could bring off is all that interests us." [42]

One of the most important assumptions underlying Berenson's work, here reiterated in the introductory chapter, is that the theory, criticism, and history of art should be concerned with the object itself and its effect on the viewer, not with the artist's intention or the process of creativity in the abstract. In a statement that resonates with his dislike for aesthetic philosophers such as Benedetto Croce, Berenson asserted that "the work of art is the *product* of the mind's activity, but not that activity itself." [43] Berenson conceived of the artist's job in terms of the ability to fix a vision, given personal skill and mastery of available traditions. He did not think it was useful to inquire about what went on in the mind of an artist at the moment of creation, primarily because artists themselves, he claimed, were not conscious of these things.

Artists, in his view, are prisoners of their habits, both of visualizing and executing. At any given moment they are chiefly occupied with matters of technique and problem-solving. Although Berenson admitted that the outcome of their work would be influenced by their life experiences, because this was not a situation unique to art, he did not deem such factors worthy of consideration. As he stated in the introduction to this treatise, when he spoke of artists he meant the creative energy that produced art, not the personality of an individual. The art object was the highest reality, and what interested him was not how it came to be, which he felt was in fact a rather simple matter, but how it affects the viewer.

It is in the context of how the object speaks to the spectator that illustration, like decoration, assumes its role as an artistic essential. In order to preserve its life-enhancing function, art must necessarily traffic only in the representation of ideals and aspirations. Berenson claimed that the words "beauty" and "ugliness" had no place in discussions of decoration, which is by its very nature indifferent to subject. Good form could vitalize any representation, no matter how repellent the subject. This explained the appeal of artists such as Henri de Toulouse-Lautrec, whose subjects were often distasteful. Illustration, on the other hand, is more circumscribed by the demands of life-enhancement. In essence, Berenson argues here that life-enhancement through art depends on both good form and ennobling subject matter, pointing out that, with respect to the aesthetic experience, "the veto power that distaste, loathing, or obstinate indifference can exert is considerable."[44]

Berenson realized that his recent plea for the essential role of illustration in humanistic art required a good deal of explanation, and in this book he was at great pains to furnish it. On the one hand, he recognized the power of art to affect human behavior; on the other, while he insisted that art could not help influencing conduct, it should not seek to incite action or stir extreme emotion. There is an inherent contradiction in Berenson's contention that the goal of appreciation is disinterested ecstacy, while its purpose is to inspire a striving toward a specific set of lofty ideals. In this argument, the Victorian aesthete seems at cross purposes with the classical humanist.

The conflict between the two was resolved in Berenson's insistence that art could best fulfill both its aesthetic and its didactic function when it represented, not specific incidents or emotions, but the distillation of ideals and material essence, or, as he had written in the

1890s, material and spiritual significance. This can only be accomplished through the judicious choice of subject presented in significant form. Berenson realized that art could show human beings at their best or worst and charged that the artist's responsibility is to extol the former and ignore the latter.

Although Berenson advocated the personal experience of the work of art unobstructed by cognition and preconception, his career rested on the assumption that the viewing public required a great deal of guidance. Given the sheer magnitude of human history and the number of material objects produced in its course of development, he urged historians to be selective about how they spend their time. In the modern world, he complained, it had become taboo to talk about standards of value, as if there were value in everything and anything.

Berenson perceived a state of anarchy in the cultural arena that threatened to undermine the privileged status of Western civilization and in *Aesthetics and History* he offered his normative critical standards as its antidote. His personal despair over the increased acceptance of modern art and popular culture, so much in evidence in the diaries and letters, is less conspicuous in *Aesthetics and History,* wherein the strategy was to reassert the universality of his aesthetic principles. This was not lost on his reviewers, for the most frequently discussed passages were those dealing with the need for a coherent set of values in the face of chaos. It was in these pages, and in those devoted to the disciplinary priorities of art history, that Berenson wrote with greatest confidence, aware that these were the arenas in which his influence would be greatest.

Berenson blamed the historical practices of classical archaeology for the current indifference to value in works of art. Archaeologists were trained in philology, not art appreciation, and from the profession's earliest days its interest in objects had been limited to their use in shedding light on known classical texts. Winckelmann had attended to standards of artistic value, and had established canons of plastic beauty that, until the twentieth century, remained inviolate.

Early in the present century, Berenson argued, archaeologists lost faith both in these canons and in their own methodology. As objects that could neither be measured by Winckelmann's canons nor mined for insight into classical texts were unearthed from all over the world, archaeologists threw up their hands and decided everything from the past was interesting and relevant. This was coincident with a crisis in the profession of art. Overwhelmed by a market saturated with these ethnographic objects, a similar abandonment of standards among artists ensued. The process of leveling threatened to eliminate the distinction between fine and minor art, or between real art and objects of curiosity. The archaeologist's indiscriminate admiration for all objects of material culture and the modern artist's worship of the "primitive" have worked in tandem to encourage the public to celebrate what they can never understand for the sake of mere novelty or "otherness."

In Berenson's view, to correct for this deterioration of standards, the critic's primary responsibility is to direct the public toward art that is life-enhancing; it is the job of the historian to chart the developmental course of such art. Neither should be distracted by objects that are not worth their time. Both in practice and in theory, as Berenson described them, art history and art criticism are two sides of the same coin. If his authority in the realm of criticism was seriously undermined by the legitimation of modern art, his influence in shaping the disciplinary priorities of art history was and has remained considerable.

"Art History Specifically," the final chapter of *Aesthetics and History,* reads like a procedures manual for formalist art history.[45] In this chapter Berenson contends that it is the business of the art historian to describe and interpret objects that have distinguished themselves from mere artifacts by virtue of their authentically artistic values. Historians and critics should concern themselves with masterpieces, turning the rest of material culture over to anthropologists. They should not succumb to fads but instead should be taught to appreciate art for its intrinsic merits and "value in a humanistic scheme of life."[46] Most important, art history is the history of significant changes in style, which Berenson defined as formal models representing ways of seeing, not the history of artists or thought. According to

Berenson, the purpose of art history is to study the kinds of artistic objects that have been made in the course of civilization, how people felt about them, whether they are enjoyed by subsequent generations, and if so, for what reasons. Finally, once the object is fully understood in terms of its own development and history, the art historian may venture a guess as to the kind of world that spawned its creation and thus contribute to our understanding of the aspirations and ideas of a given historical period.[47]

Berenson had always been a little uneasy with the role of art as a document in the history of civilization, given as he was to indulging in the pleasure of the aesthetic moment at the expense of more systematic thought. This ambivalence echoes through *Aesthetics and History,* wherein he makes an effort to establish the parameters within which art can contribute to the writing of general history. What troubled Berenson was not the suggestion that art reflects the spirit of a given age, but rather the insinuation that that is all it does and, worse still, that it is a complete and adequate expression of this age. As Berenson understood it, art is a selective view of aristocratic taste and, as such, it can not speak for an entire civilization. Within limits, art could be used to understand human history, provided conclusions were drawn on what is self-evident in the work and not based on the wishful thinking of historians whose primary concern is to mold art to fit into a given methodological or ideological scheme.

This insistence that art history should be separate from the rest of human history is entirely consistent with Berenson's desire to see the work of art preserved as an object of rare and almost mystical significance, not to mention high market value. But in a very real sense, it is also an act of self-preservation that continues to reverberate through the discipline. Justifying his life's work required that the autonomy of both art and art history be protected.

> We should stick to art, and not run off the track into cultural, economical, sociological, religious, and literary fields—at all events without knowing what we

> are doing. We should do so only while gathering ma-
> terials with which to illuminate and interpret great
> masterpieces and specific masterpieces.[48]

According to Berenson, the relationship of art to the whole of civilization should not be explored until one had first penetrated the work for all that it had to offer. One could then draw meaningful conclusions by reading around the object, a practice that Berenson himself, given his extraordinary erudition, found immensely rewarding.

Berenson understood that the best way to facilitate the survival of Western hegemony is to ensure the continued dominance of cultural values dependent upon it. Thus, there was no room in this model of art historical practice for the comprehensive study of non-Western cultures, although he did acknowledge that there were other areas of the world with "civilized histories." For European (and by extension American) culture, the history of the Mediterranean was all that mattered, and then only what was recognized as part of the mainstream. Berenson felt that it was futile to attempt to understand cultures whose language, thought, and history were alien to our own. In history, as well as art, the "selective principle of value remains in watchful control."[49] Historians should not waste their time on curiosities that cannot contribute to the understanding of their own history, nor should they lose sight of the fact that "history should lead us to recapture the past at those points that we most gladly recall and enjoy."[50] Written history, in other words, should also be life-enhancing.

"Decline and Recovery in the Figure Arts"

Given the fact that *Aesthetics and History* was to have been the introductory chapter of a major treatise on the decline and recovery of the figure arts, which necessarily would have dealt in detail with a plethora of life-diminishing art forms, Berenson's sermon on the obligations of the Western art historian seems a little hypocritical. Clearly, he felt that his own interest in the so-called pathology of art was worthwhile as long as the practical results would be to warn about the growth of such aberrations in the present. The historical account of decline that Berenson outlined in *Aesthetics and History* and later in *The Arch of Constantine* served as the empirical component of his humanistic theory of aesthetics. He furnished this data as evidence that declining artistic form was symptomatic of a deteriorating civilization and that the latter could recover only when the classical culture and its attendant life-enhancing forms were reinstated. As such, it functioned as a provocative metaphor for his despair over the state of art in the modern world.

Central to Berenson's theory of decline was the phenomenon he referred to as the "originality of incompetence." He used this expression to account for the deterioration of drawing that seemed to result when generations of artists mechanically copied existing artistic models rather than attending to the direct observation of form in nature. This principle had its origins in his previous discussions of mannerism and Milanese painting, in which he warned against the danger of unproductive imitation of classical models. In these later books he applies this idea to the works of "provincial" and "peripheral" or "marginal" artists who operate outside the mainstream.

Provincial artists, as Berenson described them, are those trained in the dominant tradition at its center of development and then dispatched to work in the provinces, where they slip into mechanical and uninspired copying of the models from which they learned. By contrast, the peripheral (or marginal) artist is one who copies these same standard conventions but without the benefit of formal training. Crude departures from the model result in both cases; what appears to be original form is really just the sign of incompetence brought on by slovenly or untutored draftsmanship.

Peripheral art had the greatest chance of success in a society so barbarized that its members lose the ability to appreciate the original models. They begin to prefer the degenerate art of their indigenous artisans, causing the latter to become self-satisfied and complacently indifferent to standards of value. Real artists then all but disappear, leaving the production of objects to these marginal artisans, whose incompetent originality becomes the new dominant style. Without guidance or proper leadership, form totally deteriorates, as they abandon themselves to their own devices and pander to the debased tastes of their clientele.[51]

The theory of decline was meant to account for the collapse of classical models in the late Roman Empire, but Berenson claimed that it could be applied with equal validity to other periods. He explained the deterioration of artistic form after Constantine, for example, as analogous to that of the present, insofar as it was a function of

> the disappearance of creative artists and the survival
> of mere artisans who, reduced to successive copying,
> and deprived of leadership, sank back to primitive geo-
> metrical patterns, vertical and frontal designs. This
> phenomenon seems to characterize, in our European
> world at least, all moments of serious disintegration,
> as has been the case with us from the beginning of art
> nouveau at the end of the last century to the so-called
> abstract art of to-day.[52]

In drawing these parallels, Berenson hastened to point out that the decline witnessed at the end of the ancient world was gradual, genuine, and, to his mind, inevitable, whereas that in the present appeared to be rapid and self-willed. Furthermore, the artisans who survived the last days of the Roman Empire did the best they could under the circumstances; though they sunk into complacency, they did not expect brilliant careers to result from their incompetent originality, as did, in Berenson's view, their modern counterparts.

Berenson was stimulated to write on the theme of decline in part as a challenge to German scholars such as Alois Riegl and Franz Wickhoff, who advanced the idea that the artists of late antiquity chose to reject classical models in the interest of discovering a new mode of expression. This theory was totally unacceptable to Berenson, both because it went against his concept of stylistic development and because, by extension, it could be used to legitimate modern art. In Berenson's view, artists did not act deliberately when they changed styles: "When there are problems to be solved, taking the technical means at hand, artists settle them in accordance with their gifts of mind, character and hand."[53]

As Berenson explained it, changes in visual models result from the complex interaction of factors in which conscious invention plays a minor role. In certain periods of history, Berenson admitted, artists seem to flounder, either because their circumstances make them lose interest in the dominant style or because they are unprepared to meet the demands made on them.

> They scratch and chip and daub and smear with a vague urge, perhaps, but no patterns in their minds. Accidentally, the less incompetent among them, those that have some natural endowment for their craft, produce something that satisfies their own conceit. They communicate this satisfaction to their literary friends and these seldom fail to persuade the craftsman that his carving or painting is an example of carefully thought-out, purposeful, metaphysically grounded, cosmically priceless newness.[54]

Just as Berenson was unable to consider the possibility that the imaginative designs of an artist such as Sassetta could be productively employed in the twentieth century, he was unwilling to accept the departure from classicism as anything but a symptom of social and artistic pathology.

The crucial difference for Berenson between the decline of form in late antiquity and that of the present was the notion of deliberate rejection of classical models. He stubbornly refused to believe that the schematic, nonnaturalistic reliefs on the Arch of Constantine resulted from anything other than artisanship "feeding on the crumbs fallen from the table of art."[55] As Berenson understood history, these sculptors would never have thought of themselves as pioneers of a new style reflecting a different concept of the world or a different mentality, because that is simply not how art works. The artists of the Arch of Constantine did not reject classical models, they unconsciously corrupted them by resorting to crude, infantile shapes better suited to their limited talents and more accessible to their simplistic feeling than art based on intellectual training. Only in the present world, he averred, have artists been so arrogant as to presume that they can turn their backs on this training and on the past. As far as Berenson was concerned, even if the German historians were correct in their assumptions of intellectual awareness, it did not make this art any better. If anything, it was more disconcerting to know that such horrors were executed with intention.

Although Berenson denied exact parallels between the decline of art in the ancient and modern worlds, his reference to their curious resemblance is essential to understanding the fundamentally moral and ethical nature of his aesthetic theory as it was articulated in the late books. He wrote in *Aesthetics and History* that "what counts in actual experience is the kind of representation—grace it with the name of vision, or exalt it by calling it a revelation—the kind of world which is offered to our eyes by means of graphic design."[56] He did not have to look very carefully at modern art to be repelled by the world it offered to his eyes, and it was on the basis of this vision that he spurned it.

Berenson's rejection of modern art embodies a tacit judgment of the cultural and social conditions that had nurtured its development. Effectively, it was a comment on the modernist zeitgeist. It is worth noting that the conclusions he drew with respect to the twentieth century required precisely the kind of reasoning that he had discouraged in the study of historical art. When Berenson emphasized such things as a crisis within the profession and the lack of aesthetic discrimination on the part of the viewing public he avoided stating explicitly what was implicit in this comparison: Artistic decadence went hand in hand with moral decadence.

In his essays on Italian Renaissance painting, Berenson directed

viewers to be aware of those qualities that yielded purely artistic pleasure, secure in the knowledge that the values and aspirations of their
respective cultures could be taken for granted. But formalism was
a luxury he could ill afford when confronted with modern art. His
metaphorical theory of decline was intended to alert readers to the
pathology of an entire culture, of which decadent art was a highly
revelatory symptom.

Aesthetics and History in the Visual Arts was widely reviewed,
and Samuels notes that Berenson was gratified by the attention it received. For the most part, it was taken as a very personal statement
that would appeal to general readers, to the extent that they shared
Berenson's humanistic outlook and his aesthetic bias toward classicism. Mutual intolerance of contemporary art was the most decisive
factor for supportive reviewers who welcomed Berenson's insistence
on standards of value as a cleansing agent in a world fraught with
disillusionment and aesthetic confusion. Those who agreed with the
premises of the book applauded Berenson for remaining faithful to
his earliest intuitions; those opposed accused him of failure to grow.[57]

It is instructive to compare reviews by Kenneth Clark, Clement
Greenberg, and Meyer Schapiro. Each brought vastly different interests and backgrounds to the task, but each also held the common
conviction that Berenson did not always practice what he preached.
Clark, who shared Berenson's social and cultural values if not his aesthetic prejudices, emphasized Berenson's humanism and the nature
of his criticism as distilled from personal experience: "The lasting
impression of this book is of wisdom and tolerance raised only to
indignation by the encroachment of barbarism, or contempt by the
eager welcome recent guardians of civilization have extended to the
barbarian invasion."

Clark warned the reader that there would be many points of potential disagreement due to Berenson's insistence on inappropriately applying standards of value derived from the art of ancient Greece and
Renaissance Florence to objects that could not be evaluated in those
terms. But he also pointed out that Berenson's theories were very
limited in comparison to his actual experience and that Berenson's
classicism was not as pure as he would have his readers believe.[58]

Greenberg similarly observed that as proud as Berenson was of his classical bias, it was more professed than felt and that Berenson had proved himself capable of showing a discriminating appreciation of past art of all kinds. He faulted Berenson for "a peevish misapprehension of the art of his own age," but he acknowledged that Berenson's insistence on the priority of the experience of art, rather than knowledge of it, was something art writers would do well to heed. Later, in his review of *The Arch of Constantine,* Greenberg pointed out that despite Berenson's declaration of intention to describe the phenomenon of decline in strictly formal terms, he did enter into ethical judgments in drawing his conclusions.[59]

Greenberg did not think much of Berenson as a theorist, but he admired his critical acumen and was basically sympathetic to Berenson's methodological priorities. This was not the case for Meyer Schapiro, who in many ways was Berenson's antithesis. Schapiro feigned amusement at Berenson's narrow "contractionism" with respect to judgments of artistic value but was careful to remind his readers that Berenson's excoriation of modern art and his resolute commitment to the moral and ethical superiority of figurative art in the classical tradition placed him in very bad company.

> Amidst the general decline of our age, three power-
> ful, ruthless men, Stalin, Mussolini, and Hitler, have
> repudiated modern art and its unhealthy exoticism
> and have restored the perennial tactile values through
> heroic, frontal, erect, nude figures. There they stand, in
> the Parks of Culture and Rest, in the great stadia and
> palaces of glass, those magnificent, sturdy, naked figures
> which teach the Russian, German, and Italian people
> how to stand and how to carry themselves as perfect
> Communists, Nazis and Fascists.[60]

Like Greenberg and Clark, Schapiro also questioned the nature of Berenson's classicism, noting that Berenson's intense aestheticism was subjective rather than rational.

Schapiro, along with the other two, conceded the essential value of

Berenson's experiential criticism, but he was suspicious of Berenson's narrow concept of humanity and was unsympathetic to his method- ological bias. Schapiro was one of the first of an increasingly vocal group of art professionals who when writing on Berenson cast as- persions on the kind of art history and the concept of culture for which he stood: "His capricious judgments of what springs from an outlook other than his own betray the limitations of his idea of the life-enhancing and humanizing. He wants art and man to be beauti- ful and to overcome the irrational, animal nature; but he is unaware, or insufficiently aware, of the depths of the human struggle towards self-mastery, freedom, and creativeness, its innumerable secret ties with institutions, events, and everyday life, and of the presence of the human, in its good sense, in vulgar experience and in the life and arts of the less civilized peoples."[61]

The Performing Monkey

> I have had and am still having my own world. When it
> was in the making I was proudly delighted with being
> too good for all but the happy few. Now I am grieved
> to be of the few and not at all happy. Is it because I feel
> that I have been tried and thrown over, abandoned? Is
> that my real grievance, rather than what appears on
> the surface, my distress over the disruptive politics, the
> drivelling verse, the anti-art of most visual artifacts of
> the day?[62]

Evidence of Berenson's relentless crusade against modern art and the constant self-examination that accompanied it is scattered through- out his diaries. From the standpoint of his public, it did not appear to require much explanation; the central argument of *Aesthetics and History* had come as no surprise to many readers who had long since forgotten, if they had ever known about, his youthful enthusiasm for modern art. In part this can be explained by Berenson's habit of referring to the "art of our own time" in late nineteenth-century terms as if there had been no art in the twentieth century, which was essentially what he believed to be the case—at least none since World War I. After a half-century spent in the study of Italian Renaissance art and in the company of aristocrats and millionaires, Berenson's contempt for modern culture seemed perfectly logical.

Recent writers have tended to treat Berenson's diatribes against the critical acceptance of modernism as a matter of economic expedience. It was not that simple. When the late books came out, with their barely disguised polemic, most reviewers understood his inexorable hostility toward the new as a consequence of his advanced age and his perception that Western humanism was on the brink of collapse. The fragmented and disorderly imagery of modernist painting, taken by many to be symptomatic of social instability, seemed reason enough for a dedicated classicist of Berenson's generation to loath the intrusion of modern chaos on the serenity of the kingdom of art. Also, abstract art appeared to some writers as clearly incompatible with Berenson's aesthetic theories. They reasoned that Berenson, on a purely professional level, would not welcome art against which he could not test his theory of life-enhancement through ideated sensations. Nor was there an easy way for him to fit abstraction into his historical frame of reference, which, though considerable, was strictly occupied with figurative art.

Except by those who noted that Berenson's expertise as a connoisseur of Italian painting would be of little help to him in appraising a modern, especially an abstract, work, the seeming logic of his disapproval of modern art was almost never explained in terms that suggest he made considered judgments based on visible evidence. The strength of Berenson's early analysis of Renaissance painting had rested on his extraordinary sensibility to the nuances of visual detail. In the late books his formalism is reduced to a myopic view of visual expression, understood as internal development in a single direction. To him modern art was a phenomenon, and he no longer seemed to consider it important to distinguish between individual works or even artists.

Berenson appears to have lumped the entire history of twentieth-century art after cubism into the category of what he called "unkunst" from which he then pulled out "isms" at will, mainly to serve the purposes of a general argument that did not require discriminating knowledge of particular forms. The often repeated axiom that Berenson's criticism grew out of actual experience of the work did not seem to have had much relevance when it came to recent painting and reviewers rarely called upon him to justify his conclusions by furnishing examples. *Aesthetics and History* and *The Arch of Constantine* are replete with references to specific works drawn from Berenson's vast knowledge of historical art, but modernism in these books is rarely more than a vague concept that does not readily attach itself to actual images.[63]

Berenson typically referred to twentieth-century painting in terms of his perception of a profession in a state of crisis or in terms of the undermining of humanistic values in art. The vocabulary he used to describe modern artists consists primarily of pejoratives revealing more about his personal frustration than about the individuals he meant to characterize: distortionist, deformist, deflationist, contortionist, inflationist, and so on. After his death, Elizabeth Hardwick pointed out that Berenson seemed to look upon the art of the twentieth-century "with painful distaste and something like hurt feelings"; his discussions of it are informed with no small measure of resentment that a pictorial language he found hermetic, cryptic, and largely inaccessible had emerged in spite of him.[64]

As a young man Berenson took great pride in an aesthetic sensibility that set him apart from the philistine majority, but in old age he began to talk about the general public as if he were one of them. In the 1954 essay "For Whom Art?" he bemoans the fact that this new art is produced in absolute defiance of public expectations. "We, the public, exist only to pay with our purses and to bleat in the chorus of praise, gratitude and worship that the artist, always a genius, now expects from our humility."[65] Speaking as a member of this forgotten public, he calls for a rebellion against this unapproachable art on the grounds that historically art has existed for the viewer, whose requirements in terms of comprehension should not be ignored as they are today.

Berenson was clearly indignant that after a lifetime devoted to art he could understand neither the new painting nor the criticism written in its defense. He was almost ninety when he wrote this essay, but he rarely hid behind his age; he was, in fact, inclined to bolster his arguments by stressing his six decades of experience. The wisdom of old age was enlisted to convince his readership (and perhaps himself) that if there was substance to this new work, he certainly would be able to identify it.

To the many reasons for Berenson's disproportionate anger about the ascendence of modernism should be added his personal disappointment at not becoming, as he once hoped, the Winckelmann of his generation. Berenson had played a formidable role in molding the aesthetic interests of collectors and viewers at the turn of the century, and he would like to have done the same for artists. But his understanding of art assumed the existence of a meaningful and mutually beneficial relationship between the artist and the viewing public that could no longer be taken for granted.

Berenson had shown a vital interest in the most progressive art of his youth and no doubt expected to remain engaged with its subsequent development. If anything, his contribution to early twentieth-century aesthetics had been to create a milieu in which this "unkunst" could flourish and it pained him to be so far at odds with the result.[66] In his great frustration at being dealt out of a scenario in which he had expected to play a major role, his only recourse was to call for a redirection of art toward a set of standards that would not disallow the continuation of his participation and influence.

Disappointment of this sort probably accounts for his lifelong uneasiness in the company of artists who did not agree with him and for his contempt for what he regarded as their pretensions to genius.[67] A recurring theme of his late books is that of the contemporary painter who has rejected past traditions to save himself the trouble of mastering them and who then uses the urge to express the self as justification to do whatever he pleases. His disgust at this syndrome was fueled by the suspicion, pronounced in old age, that these artists were insincere. He often fell back on the cliché that modern artists were opportunists who relied on friendly critics to convince the buying public of the superiority of their endeavors.

Berenson clearly took this very personally. He made frequent reference to the modern artist's great bitterness toward critics who insisted on holding recent work to the same standards as they apply to the art of past. Rather than acknowledge that many artists questioned the validity of these standards, he chose to believe that they feared exposure of their ineptitude.

In addition to listing artists' personal laziness, opportunism, and insincerity as causes of the crisis in the profession, Berenson also blamed current practices in art education. He was especially critical of the growing tendency in the Anglo-American world toward the college-educated painter, one which he held responsible for a confusion of verbal and visual gifts. Berenson was convinced that the making of great art and the writing of theory were basically incompatible. He thought Roger Fry was a competent theorist but questioned whether he had ever created a masterpiece. In keeping with his insistence on the separation of these realms, Berenson repeatedly entreated Walter Pach to stick to writing and give up painting. This advice was based on Berenson's admiration for Pach's criticism, but it reflects an implicit judgment about his painting, of which in fact he knew little.[68]

As his late books demonstrate, Berenson was attached to the idea of the classical artist struggling with the demands of a job and doing his best to tame unruly materials.[69] For him artistic creation was a matter of work and thought, the practical application of training to the solution of artistic problems. There was no place in this nostalgic model for the notions of spontaneous or instantaneous creation that stood behind a good deal of modern art. Artists who indulged in these travesties were, in Berenson's view, egocentric individualists who did not want to work. He confided to the American painter

George Biddle his doubts that painting and sculpture could be rejuvenated without returning to the apprentice system. Berenson even suggested that a modern form of monasticism might be the perfect vehicle to rescue the arts from the new "Dark Ages."[70]

Related to his despair over current professional practices was the increased tendency he had observed in modern critics and historians to confuse considerations of technique and materials with the study of art. Berenson was inclined to dismiss what he did not like or did not understand as invention on the level of technique or materials; he made a sharp distinction between newness of vision and newness of what he called "notation."

This objection to exaggerated emphasis on technique and materials was raised frequently in the context of complaints about modern criticism and can be understood as a protest against the kind of formal analysis used to evaluate modern art. Berenson believed that criticism of this kind (which he had practically invented), when employed in discussions of modern art, tended to ignore the human content in favor of intricate descriptions of composition and formal detail, as if they were a self-sufficient goal. It was of course the seeming absence of such content in the work itself that stimulated this kind of criticism, and it is significant that he so often mentioned this with reference to Roger Fry. Berenson's early work on Italian painting was an essential model for Fry, who would later apply both his mentor's critical method and his notions of artistic essentials to the study of modern art.

For Berenson this confusion of fresh notation with newness of vision explained the sudden and, to his mind, unjustified interest in Caravaggio and his followers.[71] To Berenson, Caravaggio was the paradigm of the cult figure whose eccentricity of technique and personality promised an easy way out from under the discipline and hard work required of art. His sensational chiaroscuro superseded the need for competent drawing, and his outrageous behavior captured for him a place in the popular imagination. Berenson held that Caravaggio's historical reputation depended on a prurient interest in his sordid life, encouraged by "German-minded" scholars who made exaggerated claims about the access to Caravaggio's life history and personality through his images. He explained Caravaggio's "incongruity" as the simple desire to "épater le bourgeois," enlisting the very expression that had prompted him to write in defense of Matisse when similarly accused a half-century earlier.[72] Berenson set himself in deliberate opposition to the current understanding of Caravaggio both because he disliked the artist's work and because he held in absolute contempt the historical and critical apparatus that had elevated Caravaggio to the status of an artistic prophet.

When it came to the popularization and critical legitimation of challenging artists, Berenson was always on the offensive. A similar spirit of skepticism hovers over his book on Piero della Francesca. In the opening pages he asserts that the current fascination with this quattrocento painter stems not from belated recognition of his merits but from the desire to find a historical precedent for Cézanne. Berenson is prompt to point out that although modern viewers see many formal similarities in the works of Cézanne and Piero, "they do not attribute the spiritual religious sentimental qualities [to Cézanne] which they seem to discover in Piero."[73] Both Piero and Cézanne possess the quality of "ineloquence" (reticence in terms of emotional expression), which Berenson admired, but the distinction here suggests that he found Cézanne's work lacking in spiritual significance or that Cézanne emerges as a lesser genius because he is understood as a strict formalist by modern viewers.

Spiritual content was not the same thing as emotional expression, which Berenson associated with representations of specific situations rather than of ideals or potential in the abstract. He disliked emotionally suggestive art, believing the business of art is to express essence and character, something best achieved by adherence to certain formal models. Where the canons of classicism were upheld, expressionism had no place. It was his conviction that overexpression was a German, not Mediterranean, characteristic.

> Its appeal is to the insensitive, the inattentive, who must
> be shouted at before they will hear, hit in the eye before
> they will see, shaken and kicked before they will feel.

"Expressionism" appeals to barbarians, aspiring barbarians perhaps, but barbarians as are the Surrealists, to
lost sheep who dare not bleat according to their ovine
nature, to abstract artists, to anaesthetic geometers.[74]

This statement about the appeal of inexpressive art incorporates
a recurring theme that is of paramount importance to understanding Berenson's intellectual posture toward modernism in the final
decades of his life: the fusion of barbarism, geometry, and abstract
art. The scenario Berenson proposed for the twentieth-century was
one of deliberate descent into barbarism that resulted in reduction
of artistic form to essential and exaggerated geometry and, finally,
in a total disintegration into abstraction. He claimed that the decline
witnessed in the fourth century might also have eventuated in abstraction were the artists not required to fulfill requirements in the
realm of illustration. Berenson was harsh in judging early art that did
not meet his standards, but he typically forgave the artists as prisoners of circumstance. When it came to recent art, however, he was
implacable. Modernism represented not simply a failure to measure
up but also a failure to conform, and it was the latter transgression
that incurred his greatest wrath.

Berenson made it quite clear, in *Aesthetics and History* and elsewhere, that he blamed the recent success of decadent art on an excessive and misguided fascination with exotic art, by which he meant
not Oriental but "primitive" tribal objects. One of the anecdotes
most often repeated in the late books was his recollection of a pre–
World War I visit to an exhibition of "Negro Art" at the Grand Palais
in Paris.

As we were leaving I remarked that it was the beginning
of a renaissance of savagery, of primitive infantilism, as
the Italian Renaissance had been of Antiquity. I had no
idea, however, how soon it would happen, how far it
would go, and how it would carry almost all practicing
artists and positively all writers with it.[75]

Berenson's intense dislike of cubism was due at least in part to its seeming affinity with the schematic and reductive geometry of tribal objects. In 1918 he wrote Mary Berenson from Paris that he had been coaxed into seeing a small exhibition of Matisse, Picasso, and their "nigger insperars," which he affirmed were not for him.[76]

As I have pointed out, for an artist to replace the canons of classicism with formal models produced by what Berenson viewed as a primitive and unspeakably barbaric culture was for him an alarming setback in the process of humanization. Humans had risen from the primitive state through the use of intelligence, and art had been an important catalyst in this transformation from beast to civilized being. To Berenson the return to the primitive in art was indicative of a resurgence of the animal nature that humanism had sought to overcome; a deliberate reversion of this process was simply unimaginable.

Berenson understood this fixation on tribal objects to be the successful enactment of a plan by ingenious art dealers to flood the market with exotica and to convince an aesthetically apathetic public of their intrinsic merits.[77] In an essay titled "Exhibitionitis" he explained his conviction that the bringing together of large numbers of disparate objects was a disservice to the public and was especially damaging when these were the products of barbarism.[78] Because ordinary viewers were like archaeologists, insofar as they lacked training in art appreciation and thus did not hold strong visual convictions, these large exhibitions could only confuse the general public about standards of value. People were easily convinced that tribal objects had real merit, and they were therefore not alarmed when the formal qualities of these objects began to appear in contemporary art.

In Berenson's view, the acceptance of abstraction could also be explained by a departure from normal visualization resultant from this inundation with exotic objects. Their distorted form corrupted the viewer's faith in the requirement that art be dependent on objective reality and thus opened the door for pure abstraction. As evidence of this phenomenon, he pointed out that in Italy, where the "infantile incunabulistic products of barbarous and savage lands" were not widely exhibited, there had been less damage and he upheld that Italian artists would not have taken to abstraction were they not susceptible to the influence of Paris.

The formal characteristic of tribal sculpture that had led Berenson to equate modern art with decadence was reductive geometry in the representation of human anatomy, a feature that he had observed in the late reliefs of the Arch of Constantine. This tendency toward geometry was also evident in cubism, where it was connected in Berenson's mind both with Western decadence and with tribal art. In its most extreme manifestation this tendency resulted in geometric abstraction, a form of expression that was wholly conceptual and that approximated the appearance of machinery. Berenson alternately discussed abstraction in terms of the "daub and smear" variety (the fruit of ineptitude and excessive individualism), and in terms of "anaesthetic geometry," which he associated with intellectualism and machinery. Neither in his view had explicit meaning or purpose as art, but both were fair game for critics who mined them in search of encapsulated private insight that could then be verbally articulated.

Berenson's fixation on geometry is multidimensional and his writing on the subject is confusing, when not wholly contradictory. On one hand, he associated geometric schematization in art with decadence of form and behavior. On the other, his rejection of geometric art was part of a larger discomfort with anything mathematical that was beyond his comprehension. He was not unsympathetic to the tendency toward geometry in art when it involved a proper compromise with representation, as is evident in his attraction to artists such as Mantegna, Piero della Francesca, and Cézanne. But he could not abide a reduction of art to geometric pattern, for the latter, as far as he was concerned, was reminiscent of pure mathematics and, as such, the kind of abstract thought that for him had always been alien.

The inaccessibility of pure mathematics to the average human mind, a major source of its appeal to Bertrand Russell, who admired math as sublimely nonhuman or above the human, was a primary reason for Berenson's hatred of everything smacking of geometry. Dislike of machinery is a secondary theme in Berenson's discussions of geometricization because the technology that made machinery possible was the product of science, which he also associated with abstract thought and, ultimately, with mathematics.[79] Like many intellectuals of his generation, Berenson believed human beings were in danger of becoming depersonalized through machinery, a fear that makes itself heard in myriad forms between the world wars.[80]

Science, technology, and geometric abstraction coalesced in Berenson's mind to form an apocalyptic image of a future world ruled by mathematicians in which he would be utterly helpless.

> I try to get some idea of what contemporary science is up to and find myself balked by its being ever more and more mathematical and I am without mathematics. . . . I never approach these matters without a feeling that the experts in these things will govern us, forming an elite with abstract ideals, more arrogantly entertained than by any previous *governing* clan in the whole of history.[81]

Berenson perceived the twentieth-century as an age dominated by abstraction, in art and in thought, and he felt this was to blame for the cruelty and inhumanity that he had witnessed. He was equally uncomfortable with the forces that seemed to drive the many progressive factions mobilized to change art and to challenge existing social hierarchies. In his old age, what Berenson feared most were the tyranny of abstraction and the tyranny of the masses. He could find no way to relate to either except through negation.

The Geometricization of the Individual: Humanism at Risk

> What has happened in Russia? A "geometricization" of individuals, a greater coarsening than that which is noticeable in other countries; the death of a ruling class and the blossoming of the masses, to whom images,

> myths and projects which make sense to them are di-
> rectly addressed. . . . The geometricization first revealed
> itself in art with Cubism, then in life, then in politics; it
> is a descent into barbarism.[82]

The rhetoric of humanism under siege, so dominant in Berenson's late publications, was informed by an understanding of modern society as drifting toward purely technological and egalitarian interests. In his use of the term "geometricization" Berenson meant to suggest both the disindividualization that he viewed as the inevitable conse-quence of a modern state increasingly occupied with the welfare of the masses and the depersonalization of human beings in a machine-dominated world.

In *Aesthetics and History,* he defined culture as "the effort to build a House of Life where man will be able to attain the highest devel-opment that his animal nature will permit." [83] Berenson understood humanism as the determination to shape a world in which this re-mains the highest priority: "Humanism consists in the belief that something worthwhile can be made of life on this planet; that man-kind can be humanized, that it is happiness to work towards that goal." [84] Anything that undermined the individual's capacity to pur-sue this goal or threatened to dislodge it was an enemy of human-ism. Medieval Christianity had been a threat to humanism insofar as it required the shunning of earthly life. Humanism, however, faced its most formidable enemy in the modern totalitarian state, which sought to satisfy the lowest human appetites at the expense of culture and to crush individual freedom in the interest of the common good.

Although Berenson's belief in culture and its seminal function as a civilizing agent was sincere, in its practical application his cam-paign to save humanism functioned as an intellectual justification for ignoring the political and economic realities of the twentieth century. When his wartime diaries were published as *Rumor and Reflection,* a reviewer for the *New Republic* noted that Berenson was incredibly naive about politics and ill-prepared to penetrate the troubling conditions of modern life: "He retains a constitutional incapacity to look facts in the face, except when they have, or can be given, an esthetic patina." [85]

Although Berenson considered himself an enemy of totalitarianism in all its forms (he was an outspoken anti-Fascist), it is no secret that he did not have a highly developed social conscience. Meyer Schapiro was among the first to note that as a young immigrant Berenson adopted the social and cultural values of the class he aspired to join in Boston and he did not look back. Berenson viewed culture as both the privilege and the responsibility of an elite. It was to them and on their behalf that his remarks were primarily addressed. As Schapiro observed, Berenson's faith in humanism must be understood in terms that recognize the extent to which he accepted social hierarchy as permanent. [86]

In addition to the prejudices of his adopted social class, Berenson's intense aestheticism was in itself an obstacle to the development of a social conscience. His social and political development were impeded by a seemingly willful failure to disengage from the aesthetic culture of his youth. If, as has been suggested, he insisted on giving reality an aesthetic patina, he could aestheticize only what was good, ideal, and pleasing. When he said of modern art, "this is not art," he might easily have said, "this is not life," or at least not life as he wanted to know it. His humanism depended on a painfully restricted conception of both. [87]

In similar fashion, Berenson's faith in Greek classicism presupposed the separation of art from the squalid realities of actual existence.

> I know that their art, their literature, their written history even, offer no picture of Greek actuality. How sordid and foul, malignant and wicked it was I know from many sources, but chiefly from Jacob Burckhardt's cruel *History of Greek Civilization*. All the more admirable that they could aspire to a way of being so radiant, so beautiful, so vitally and deeply human. [88]

He explained in *Aesthetics and History* that by Hellenism he had in mind not a specific historical society but rather an attitude and approach to life, "a path, a way, a reaching out towards a humanity that is as remote from chaos as it can succeed in soaring above and beyond 'nature.' "[89] So great was Berenson's belief in the ennobling potential of classical art that he seems to have viewed the unpleasantness of actual life in ancient Greece as a requisite condition for its achievements. Berenson proposed that the lesson to be learned from the Greeks is that art can provide what is absent from life; the misery of ancient life was a powerful stimulant for their longing toward an ideal mode of existence that could be expressed in art.

One of the prospects Berenson found most unsettling in the modern age was that social efforts to alleviate the misery of humanity would be a death blow to culture as he understood it. He remarked to Umberto Morra that "if individual well-being was going to have to lead to the destruction of civilization through the form of Communism, I would prefer that the individuals perish rather than the civilization."[90] For Berenson, and for many other members of his generation and his social class, fear for humanism was inseparable from fear of Communism. A vision of a Communist-dominated Europe reverberates through his conversation, correspondence, and diaries in the last three decades of his life.

But when discussing the threat to humanism posed by mass social movements and totalitarianism, he was not always specific and tended to use Communist Russia, Nazi Germany, and Fascist Italy interchangeably. Berenson's fear of the tyranny of the masses and his conviction that the flourishing of civilization depended on the preservation of culture by an elite protectorate suggest that his hostility was directed toward social leveling and populism in the abstract, rather than toward a specific political system. His perception of twentieth-century barbarism and decadence was informed by the historical concept of "bread and circuses."[91]

In *Aesthetics and History* Berenson described the mechanism whereby a mass social movement could seriously undermine the interests of humanism. Ordinary people, he explained, find the burden of humanization too much to bear and are easily convinced that it is a waste to strive for so remote an ideal. They are quick to give into the animal side of nature that humanism seeks to control and thus are vulnerable to promises of satisfaction and freedom from responsibility.

He went on to say that the prospect of a society in which everything is decided and directed from cradle to grave is the dream of average human beings who wish for nothing so much as the exemption from serious thought. Those who want to use their minds in such a society dedicate themselves to problems of organization and mass production, in other words, the facilitation of a technico-industrial civilization. Berenson could not conceive of a world in which humanism and the modern technological state could coexist: "To us humanists they can offer no terms; our ideals are irreconcilably opposed. Between them and us there can be no peace nor truce. Our opposed policies cannot be neighbors on this small planet." [92]

Berenson's concept of the masses, or the "crowd-minded majority," recalls that of José Ortega y Gasset, insofar as it implies psychological type rather than class membership. He made a point of stating that the promise to satisfy animal impulses "appeals irresistibly to this average or sub-average person in all grades of society from the highest to the lowest." [93] Patrick Brantlinger, who discusses the concepts of modern classicism advocated by writers such as Ortega y Gasset and T. S. Eliot in the context of their contempt for mass culture, observed that Ortega y Gasset's authority on the masses was not Karl Marx but Oswald Spengler. A similar assumption could be made for Berenson who, on completing *The Decline of the West*, wrote to Ivins that Spengler "told me little I did not know and less I hadn't thought; but he reminded me of so much I had forgotten." [94]

As Brantlinger suggests, average human beings are Spengler's barbarians; they lack respect for tradition, social order, and the elite genteel circle that tends the culture of the past, the circle to which Berenson felt the strongest allegiance. Ortega y Gasset, like Berenson, believed that science and technology were responsible for the transformation of "man" into "mass-man," and he was especially harsh on the tendency away from general culture toward overspecialization. Traditional culture was vulnerable to an invasion from within when it was left in the hands of individuals who lacked both the knowledge and the desire to nurture its development. Brantlinger could be describing Berenson's theory of decline when he states, "Ortega's 'revolt' is a metaphor for a degenerative process or disease that is attacking society on all levels—it is almost a metaphor for modernity." [95]

It is worth recalling that before the threat of a mass society became a practical reality to Berenson, his contempt had been reserved for the bourgeois philistine. He shared the prejudice of the educated, cultured elite of the late nineteenth century against the intellectually average and, more important, the aesthetically insensitive. Remy Saisselin, who has made the most extensive study of Berenson's cultural ideology, points out that Berenson played a pivotal role in reinforcing the tendency, increasingly evident in capitalist democracies such as the United States, to make class distinction a matter of aesthetic interests and education rather than mere wealth. [96] Berenson's early work on Italian art stood on the premise that an aesthetic elite guided by his principles of appreciation could exist apart from wealth and possession. Saisselin explains that when Berenson made the act or moment of appreciation the center of the aesthetic experience (rather than the object itself), he kept the aesthetic at a safe distance from the realm of property and legal ownership.

This distinction between cultural elitism and class as defined by wealth was very much in evidence when Berenson discussed the aesthetic interests of the "grand bourgeois" in the United States. It amused him, for example, to note in a catalog of a Picasso exhibition how many paintings were lent by members of the "American plutocracy;" and he wondered what possible meaning these pictures could have for them. He expressed similar sentiments about the many works of Toulouse-Lautrec in American private collections.

> What do these publicly respected grand bourgeois have
> to do with this art? Surely not the purely pictorial quali-

ties, which despite repugnance of subject matter appeal
to me. . . . Do the owners of these paintings ever look
at them to ask what they mean? Perhaps it is enough
satisfaction that they could afford to buy them, and to
be on a level with others, a trifle their social superiors,
who bought them first.[97]

It was precisely this gap between true appreciation and private
ownership that Berenson had promised to bridge as a connoisseur.
Through his expertise and his theory of appreciation, he offered a
way for the grand bourgeois to rise above their vulgar mercantile
interests and to enter the realm of high ideals. They could be taught to
admire Toulouse-Lautrec for the right reasons, and, thus, the gesture
to purchase would become a testament to a refined aesthetic sensibility rather than a function of the bourgeois desire for property.[98]

The problematic aspect of Berenson's theory of appreciation,
when it is considered in the context of his elitist view of culture,
is that, in principle, it was inherently democratic. Life-enhancement
through ideated sensations is a viewer response theory whose universal application, by Berenson's own admission, rested on its vital connection to the psycho-physiological constitution of human beings.
As a critical tradition, it was far more accessible than systems that
presupposed an extensive background in literature, history, or philosophy as essential to art appreciation. But, as Saisselin points out,
neither Berenson nor Vernon Lee, whose theories were similarly empathetic, intended to imply that true appreciation was open to the
masses. They both thought of responsiveness to art as an elitist privilege reserved for those who were willing and able to put themselves
into a state of readiness.

Berenson (and Lee) protected the elitist nature of art appreciation
by insisting on the need for aesthetic training on the part of the viewer.
The erudition once assumed as a requisite for access to the rarified
pleasures of art was displaced by cultivation of aesthetic sensibility.
Busy American industrialists who could not spare the time for aesthetic training could, Saisselin argues, bypass this stage by relying on

advice from Berenson, who was both a connoisseur and an expert on the nature of the aesthetic experience. For the collector who bought a painting recommended by an expert who was also an aesthete, entry into the privileged class of the cultured was direct and automatic.[99]

Berenson's insistence on separating fine art from artifacts and his claims for the superiority of artistic traditions that were historically aristocratic clearly reinforced the premise that the existence of "high" culture was dependent on the preservation of class distinctions. That his inherently egalitarian theory of aesthetics might threaten to undermine the present social hierarchy became evident to Berenson as he witnessed his principles of artistic essentials enlisted in the critical evaluation of modernism. As Saisselin points out, when Roger Fry "tried to apply Berenson's theory of tactile values to the understanding and experience of modern art," he quickly learned the extent to which aesthetic sensibility was the domain of privilege.[100]

In the 1920 essay "Retrospect," Fry recalled that many of his own readers found the defense of post-impressionism inconsistent with his previous admiration for works of the Italian Renaissance. The cultured public did not welcome this new art, and Fry claimed that its most vigorous opponents were often those who had been most sympathetic to his past critical efforts on behalf of quattrocento painting. Although he referred to the public in general terms, Fry's account of this situation directly implicates Berenson.

> These people felt instinctively that their special culture was one of their social assets. That to be able to speak glibly of Tang and Ming, of Amico di Sandro and [Alesso] Baldovinetti, gave them a social standing and distinctive cachet. This showed me that we had all along been laboring under a mutual misunderstanding, i.e., that we admired the Italian primitives for quite different reasons. It was felt that one could only appreciate Amico di Sandro when one had acquired a certain considerable mass of erudition and given a great deal of time and attention, but to admire a Matisse required only a certain

> sensibility. One could feel fairly sure that one's maid
> could not rival one in the former case, but might by a
> mere haphazard gift of Providence surpass one in the
> second.[101]

The reference in this passage to Matisse in the same breath with that of Amico di Sandro, an artistic personality invented by Berenson to give a temporary identity to a group of unattributed paintings, is highly significant in light of Berenson's personal relationship with Fry. Fry began to take a serious interest in modern art at approximately the same time that Berenson went to work for Duveen. This coincided with Berenson's defense of Matisse for *The Nation*. Berenson and Fry's relationship had begun to deteriorate before then, but in seeking a reason for their eventual estrangement we need go no further than the above passage.

Fry, who more than any other of Berenson's contemporaries, took him on as an intellectual rival, recognized early what eventually became evident to only the more astute of Berenson's observers: that Berenson's opposition to modern art was a posture rather than a carefully considered aesthetic judgment. What is more, Fry was quick to grasp the limitations of Berenson's formalism—as Fry had demonstrated in his review of Berenson's *The North Italian Painters,*— and the nature of its exaggerated disregard for the requirements of illustration. The misunderstanding of which Fry speaks in the essay "Retrospect" refers to the realization that Berenson, whom he assumed had admired certain works of art strictly on the basis of their formal qualities, was hostile to modernism because of a moral, ethical, and social bias toward historical art, which Fry himself did not share. Fry perceived the extension of Berenson's criteria to modern painting as logical and consistent with his work on Italian art; that Berenson himself did not was evidence that the two of them had indeed admired the art of the past for very different reasons.

Implicit in Berenson's concept of civilization was the notion of culture as aristocratic privilege. The survival of culture, and ultimately of civilization, depended on the guarantee of this privilege within a stratified society. Berenson's chief preoccupation was with the results of social leveling because, like T. S. Eliot, he thought of true culture and mass society as mutually exclusive. In an effort to give the reactionary tenor of Berenson's late books an appropriate context, reviewers compared him to Ortega y Gasset, Spengler, and even to the American writer Dwight McDonald. It is also true, however, that Berenson had a good deal in common with Eliot. Despite Berenson's expressed dislike for Eliot's poetry and cult status, he could not have disagreed with the proposition that egalitarian culture is equivalent to no culture because it is by its very nature barbaric.[102]

Berenson's theory of decline, his lack of generosity toward the masses, and his unfailing belief in the superiority of classical culture made him a paradigm of what Brantlinger has called the "negative classicist." His dislike of modern art was inseparable from the assumption that it represented a descent from a superior form of civilization that has served history as an ideal model. Like others who subscribed to the myth of negative classicism, Berenson perceived the success of egalitarian social movements as a threat from within to an already weakened civilization, the consequences of which would be the subversion of cultural ideals historically associated with privilege. In his mind, the dilution of these values could only result in decadence, as it had in the original era of bread and circuses. Although he entertained the possibility of a future society without prestige values, he was not interested in exploring the terms in which art and culture would be redefined to accommodate its impulses toward creative expression.

Seeing and Knowing

> The term "abstract art," like such contradiction in terms
> as a wet dryness, an icy heat, or a soft hardness, may
> be conceivable to the mind but scarcely to the senses.
> For many thousands of years visual art has been based
> on ideated sensations, on a compromise between what

one knows and what one sees and between what one
sees and what one can reproduce for others. It therefore
would seem to correspond to a continuous need or desire
or demand of human nature, of man who is matter and
spirit, body as well as mind.[103]

Although most of Berenson's late books can be understood as facets
of his polemic against modern culture, only one is explicitly concerned with the history and development of modern art. *Seeing and
Knowing,* written in 1948 and published in 1953, is Berenson's attempt to explain his favorite aphorism: Abstract art is a contradiction
in terms. Berenson suggested the importance of representation in art
in his diaries and discursive essays, but here he has given it center
stage as the core of an argument against the claims of abstraction to
legitimacy as artistic expression.

His previous defenses of illustration had already established that
the appreciation of art depends upon recognizable subject matter.
Also, as he noted frequently, the further art moves away from representation, the harder it is to discover anything to which artistic
quality can adhere. Neither Berenson's critical standards nor his
theory of appreciation were of any use when confronted with abstraction. Because he defined art strictly in those terms he reasoned
that abstraction is not art.

To make a case for the necessity of representation, Berenson shifts
the emphasis in *Seeing and Knowing* from art as life-enhancement
to art as communication. As a strict formalist, he had studiously
avoided using the notion of communication in his theoretical writing,
probably because it typically connotes awareness of artist's intentions, which he did not consider essential to appreciation. Berenson's
recognition of the importance of communication in art, however,
does not necessarily indicate a capitulation to the priorities of expressionist criticism. He understood communication as a dimension
of coherence or intelligibility, rather than of emotional expression or
intention.

Seeing and Knowing opens with an account of Berenson's experience at the Siena Palio. He claimed to have perceived an image consisting of color patches, which he instantly recognized as a crowd of people (rather than a mass of flowers) because he was aware that the square was filling with spectators. In other words, he matched what he saw with what he knew. Seeing, as Berenson explained it, is essentially a utilitarian practice that grows out of the need to recognize in the environment what it is expeditious to approach or avoid. When seeing is not utilitarian, it is representational. Berenson, who was consistently anti-philosophical in his interests, did not speculate on the nature of representational seeing. He simply took it for granted as a basic human impulse. What occupied him was the nature of artistic convention—which he understood as a manner of representational seeing that became common practice—and its function in the development of visual art.

Conventions of all sorts, whether directed toward practical or representational ends, exist to facilitate communication, making their preservation and continued development necessary to the human race. In the modern world, representational conventions in art were under siege. Because he would not recognize the new set of artistic conventions evolving to displace the old Berenson upheld that modern art results in a regression to the private universe of the individual, which cannot be shared in any meaningful way. Art without representational conventions thus loses its ability to communicate and ceases to be a worthwhile human endeavor.

Essential to Berenson's understanding of convention is the notion of historically sanctioned artistic tradition; for him, classical figurative art was the perfect reconciliation between observation and concept, between seeing and knowing. His call for the reinstatement of this tradition was prompted not only by the "occultation" of classical form but also by the offensive nature of modern representation. Communication alone is not enough; as he had so clearly stated elsewhere, art must be life-enhancing through its decoration and illustration, combined. Berenson's discussion of modern art in *Seeing and*

Knowing centers on these two requisite conditions: that the subject reveal itself without effort and that, once revealed, it be pleasant and uplifting.

Perhaps because he was writing explicitly about modern art, as opposed to dealing with it on the level of analogy or metaphor, Berenson made an uncharacteristic effort to contextualize its more disturbing aspects to the turmoil of the twentieth century.

> The idolized poets, painters, sculptors and critics after
> the first world war gave vent to the feeling of despair
> regarding the future by expressing their contempt for
> everything in the social order, in politics, and in all the
> arts that had brought them to that pass.[104]

According to Berenson, this state of mind manifested itself in a loathing of anything that smacked of academicism or standardized conventions of form and space. It was accompanied by the current conviction that "the squalid, the sordid, the violent, the bestial, the misshapen, in short that low life, was the only 'reality.' "[105] The latter premise was not based on seeing or observing, but stemmed instead from exasperation and from certain preconceptions about human nature.

Berenson further suggested that these distortions might have eventuated in a return to sanity or even a rejuvenation of the classical tradition had leadership appeared to direct the future course of development. Instead, these artists sought inspiration in historical figures, who similarly unleashed their fury against decorum and classicism. In the absence of productive genius, abstraction took root, and seeing was now in danger of being eclipsed by knowing.

What interests artists of the twentieth century, Berenson contended, are things that are known to exist but cannot be given visible shape, "visceral, intestinal and meaningless cerebral activities," rather than the "sensible, sensuous, sensual world of the eye."[106] His greatest contempt was reserved for geometric abstraction, a complete desertion of visible nature for the streamlined perfection of technology. Berenson believed that the enjoyment of both kinds of abstraction (originating in surrealist fantasy and in the utopian aesthetics of the 1920s, though not identified as such) is intellectual rather than aesthetic. The genuinely aesthetic experience, which for centuries turned on this struggle to reconcile seeing with knowing, had been forsaken for the "Nirvana of abstraction." [107]

Of all the late books, *Seeing and Knowing* most betrays the extent of Berenson's ignorance with respect to the origins and development of modern art. In his scenario, corruption of form and content has simply spiraled downward into abstraction. Nowhere does Berenson attempt to come to terms with the range of expression exemplified by twentieth-century painting or with the complexity of its formal models. For purposes of argument, Berenson renders virtually interchangeable the images of distorted human anatomy, cerebral and visceral activity, and geometric shapes; in his view they signify nothing in particular but are understood in terms of what they are not. German expressionism, cubism, abstract surrealism, and the work of the Bauhaus are to art what communism, fascism and nazism are to society: diversions from an ideal and threats to civilization.

There is no logic in the contention that recognition of squalor and violence in daily life eventuated in abstract artistic form. Nor does it seem even remotely possible for the artists of the twentieth century to return to Berenson's conception of the moral and ethical mandate of art to glorify humanity and celebrate classical ideals. The sole principles operational in *Seeing and Knowing* seem to have been Berenson's intuitive dislike for art existing outside the realm of his personal experience and his disappointment with the fact that time did not stand still in deference to his values.[108]

In the main, reviews of *Seeing and Knowing* were negative, even on the part of those who otherwise admired Berenson's achievements. The book was recognized by most thoughtful readers as a deliberate assault on modern art by a critic who was well out of his métier, and as such it was thought to do him little credit.[109] Serge Hughes, writing for *Commonweal*, objected more to Berenson's presumptuousness than to the essay's central theme and remarked, "It would have been far better to have written a short article bustling with cultured aphorisms, revealing that there is a lot of nonsense going on in contemporary art." [110] This sentiment was expressed by other reviewers, who noted that one did not have to be happy with the direction of modern art to realize that Berenson's conclusions stemmed from an innate lack of sympathy for, as well as understanding of, recent art. [111]

Reactions to *Seeing and Knowing* ranged from benign dismissal as completely unimportant in light of Berenson's advanced age and outdated cultural values to angry resentment at the abuse of his authority. Belle Krasne, writing for the *College Art Journal,* conveyed what must have been the sentiment of much of its professional readership: that the book was little more than a vehicle to air Berenson's prejudices, a clear reflection of his fin de siècle aestheticism, worthless to scholars and misleading for the general public. She also took issue with his narrow conception of art history and of stylistic development as retreat or progress in relation to a classical ideal. The tenor of Krasne's review approached hysteria, suggesting that despite her insistence that the book was totally without merit, she feared it might still have influence with a public in awe of Berenson's reputation. [112]

Negative criticism of *Seeing and Knowing* turned largely on the issue of Berenson's competence. The general consensus was that he had ventured too far out of his proper orbit to be taken seriously. Berenson was fond of parading his years of experience before the reader, and reviewers of his late books often used that as a point of departure. But in the case of *Seeing and Knowing* his lack of expertise seemed a far more salient issue. The observation that "the author regards our present situation with a God's-eye view justified by his long and conscientious experience," while it may have been wholly appropriate to *Aesthetics and History,* cannot be enlisted with the same conviction for *Seeing and Knowing.* [113]

The former was a guide to Berenson's critical and methodological priorities, which, by way of comparison, made passing reference to the deterioration of classicism in the twentieth century. It was understood as a defense of humanism and, within this context, Berenson's contempt for modernism seemed perfectly consistent and rational. But when he focused his attention on the phenomenon of modern art specifically, he was ill-equipped to come to terms with a body of work that had long departed from the values he so assiduously upheld. By lapsing into clichés and vituperative rhetoric, Berenson cast in sharp relief the limitations of his aesthetic principles and his willful ignorance of the cultural realities that had driven the century in which he spent over half his life.[114]

*   *   *

As long as Berenson could take the ennobling potential of art for granted, he felt no need to make his aesthetic theory dependent upon it. In the wake of what he liked to call the "manquake" of the twentieth century, however, he was driven to restate this as an axiom, which current wisdom had done its best to overturn. For Berenson, the purpose of art was not to comment on the human condition or to provide an expressive vehicle for the inner life, but to guide them, and this required representational subject matter. As he explained in *Aesthetics and History,* for the average viewer, the work of art speaks on the level of subject before it reveals the power of its form, and if this is what is to be carried away, then it stands to reason that through representation art fulfills its mission to humanize. Whereas he once expressed contempt for the kind of viewer insensitive to genuinely aesthetic qualities, in old age he was prepared to content himself with the hope that the moral and ethical appeal of art would at least survive.

Again, one senses in Berenson's pleading a lingering feeling that he shared a measure of responsibility for the state of modern art. When he discussed the concept of significance in art in *Aesthetics and History,* he confessed that a half-century ago he had been too eager to believe in the separation of the material and the spiritual. By material significance he intended the rendering of object qualities in terms of artistic essentials, a position that informs a good deal of modern art. Spiritual significance, on the other hand, like illustration, was subject to very specific expectations about the life of the spirit, and it simply did not occur to Berenson in the 1890s that a work of art could embody a spirit of despair or nihilism.

Conclusion

There was a polemical reason for
writing my books; not so much the
need to oppose Ruskin, who was a
genius, but to oppose the followers
of Ruskin—those who judged a
picture according to its abstract
subject. For this reason I tried to
exaggerate the importance of the
hitherto neglected pictorial
qualities, with the result that
whoever has read me has, in his
turn, exaggerated my intentions,
and from my moderate disapproval

of the "illustrative" quality of painting, has derived a cubist aesthetic.

1931

By a Philistine we mean an active minded man who cannot conceive another outlook upon society, another standard of values than his own.

1950

Taste is exercised by innocently re-experimenting with what is beautiful in its own account in works already admired. It cannot be exercised freely on new things; too much of our personal future enters into anything which is in the formative stages—our desires and doubts, hopes and fears. Interests converge which are not aesthetic, from which we cannot separate ourselves. If we are honest, and clearsighted, we have to admit that there is no comment one can make on the new products of the day.[1]

In 1900 Mary Berenson recorded a conversation with her husband on the nature of the picturesque. Remarking that it had taken him nearly two decades to appreciate this kind of beauty, one to which the art student acquaintances of his youth had been particularly sensitive, Berenson then "questioned if it were not pure snobbishness and the weight of authority backing up the pleasures more difficult of attainment that makes us feel what we call art superior." She reminded him that a Greek statue as a fully realized work of art is so much more suggestive than a landscape in that it acts as a stimulus to the best human ideals. Berenson replied, "Then it is an ethical and not an aesthetical question."[2]

The young Berenson was eager to disengage aesthetics from ethics and morality. His early theoretical writings, with their emphases on the recognition of artistic essentials and the uniqueness of the aesthetic experience, earned him distinction as the apostle of "pure visibility." As both a critic and a connoisseur, Berenson stood for the priority of formal elements in the evaluation and appreciation of painting, a position that, at the time, required the devaluation of subject matter as the primary signifier in a work of art.

By encouraging the viewer to be responsive to artistic form itself as the vehicle through which significance is expressed, Berenson sought to deflect attention from the interpretation of subject. He opposed, not the representational nature of art, but rather an excessive interest in meaning at the expense of what he regarded as properly artistic qualities. For Berenson, painting provides a singular opportunity to experience life-enhancement through artistic form, but one that is accessible only to those capable of apprehending its "decorative" as well as its "illustrative" qualities.

Berenson's theory of life-enhancement was predicated on the belief that art acts in a direct, concrete way on the spectator; he reasoned that certain visual qualities can induce an empathetic response. In his criticism, he sought to isolate those formal elements through which the goal of intensified life could be achieved. But as twentieth-century artists began to experiment with the possibility that these qualities could be presented in the abstract, Berenson was forced to modify his position by insisting that ideated sensations of tactile values, movement, and space composition are inseparable from representation. In his last years, Berenson argued that art fulfills its life-enhancing function as much through the illustrative as through the decorative qualities. The imperative to humanize, to build the House of Life, superseded the potential to enhance the individual life, and the moral purpose of art was fully reinstated.

Although Berenson had worked hard to disengage the literal meaning of subject from the process of appreciation, he never intended to suggest that art has no meaning outside its formal relationships or that its sole purpose is to delight the senses. Berenson argued in the final decades of his life that the moral implications of his aesthetic theory were undervalued by those chiefly attracted to the originality of his critical method. He had set himself against conventional concepts of morality, such as the Ruskinian notion that art should embody good Christian virtue. Instead, Berenson suggested that the moral purpose of art is intrinsic to form itself. Good form is the embodiment of good morality; responsiveness to art promises greater fulfillment in life.

It is precisely this need to justify aesthetic pleasure that separates Berenson from more stringent formalists such as Clement Greenberg, who regarded Berenson's insistence on the life-enhancing function of art as philosophically naive. Greenberg upheld what Berenson had admitted to his wife in 1900: that the valuation of art on the basis of its didactic potential is not an aesthetic judgment. By describing

Berenson's dislike of modern art as a posture, Greenberg implied that it was a conscious decision not a theoretical deduction. Even those who were basically sympathetic to Berenson's humanistic theory of art, and thus shared his contempt for abstract painting, reasoned that Berenson simply did not like modern art and opposed it for personal rather than theoretical reasons.

Berenson's outspoken campaign to discredit modern art was driven in large part by events and circumstances external to his aesthetic sense, but his dislike of this art was in no small measure simply a matter of taste.[3] It is often observed that Berenson's aesthetic theories served primarily to justify his taste, a trap many believe even Greenberg, for all his philosophical sophistication, could not himself entirely avoid. For even though Berenson's theory of formal values experienced as ideated sensations was developed to explain the superiority of Italian Renaissance painting, it was not, as has been demonstrated, incompatible with the interests of many twentieth-century painters.

The rejection of modern art on the basis of stylistic preference rather than theoretical bias was characteristic of other critics who shared Berenson's elitist view of culture and his veneration of the Western classical tradition. In her study of American aesthetic theory in the early twentieth century, Virginia Mecklenburg concluded that conservative critics were often aligned by their taste rather than by the similarity of their theoretical principles. She points out that American critics such as Kenyon Cox, Frank Jewett Mather, and Royal Cortissoz, all of whom were Berenson's close acquaintances, banded together to present a united front against modernism, even though they held very different views about the nature and function of art.[4]

Dedicated classicists such as Cox (and to a certain extent Berenson) maintained that all art is governed by a set of internal principles and, accordingly, placed great emphasis on the relationship of formal elements in their criticism. Cortissoz, on the other hand, was an expressionist critic, one for whom a work of art is the embodiment of the artist's individual feeling. Both of these proclivities, one toward form and one toward personal expression, have counterparts among apologists for the avant-garde. Willard Huntington Wright may be considered an example of the former and the painter-critic Max Weber of the latter. According to Mecklenburg, the critical priorities of these two sets of writers were quite similar, although applied to very different kinds of art. But rather than employ their principles to assess a form of expression that offended their personal taste and cultural values, Cox and Cortissoz set aside their theoretical differences to present a unanimous vote in favor of traditional artistic form.

Berenson's posture toward modern art can be understood in similar terms. He came to the eventual conclusion that it was not for him and refused to take it seriously except as a symptom of decay. What impeded Berenson's appreciation of recent art, as he told Morra, was the intervention of subjective interests that were not aesthetic, something he scrupulously avoided in his work as a connoisseur of Italian painting. It is of course arguable that Berenson's attributions were highly subjective insofar as they had direct bearing on his financial well-being, but only the most jaded of his critics have denied Berenson's stature as the exemplary practitioner of modern connoisseurship in his chosen area of expertise.[5]

Long before his judgment toward modern painting hardened, Berenson had become dissatisfied with what he viewed as the inadequacies and aridness of connoisseurship. Perhaps stimulated by Morelli's suggestion that connoisseurship should become the basis for a new history of art divested of extraneous literary and philosophical interests, Berenson aspired to be a critical historian and an aesthetic theorist, to enlist his expertise as a connoisseur in the elucidation of certain general ideas. But rather than affecting such presumed detachment in the evaluation of modern art, as did Roger Fry and, later, Alfred Barr, Berenson chose to define himself by his opposition to what he perceived as its essential decadence.

Berenson learned as he grew older that connoisseurship would never replace interpretive historical approaches, which went further toward providing a broad understanding of art as a meaningful human activity. In the face of his declining influence in professional circles, Berenson concentrated his efforts on the mechanism of appreciation and the way it facilitated the humanistic function of art. Although he understood perhaps better than any member of his generation the satisfaction to be derived from self-identification with a work of figurative art, in terms of appreciation, Berenson was an instrument, not a vehicle.

Unconvinced that he could make people feel what he felt and faced with the kind of figural distortion that would become common currency among avant-garde painters, Berenson fell back on discussions of humanism to prop up his guidelines for appreciation. He never became the theorist that he had envisioned in his youth, and he was not content to be a critic and connoisseur. So Berenson tried to be a sage, a moral leader to an age that had outgrown his sense of morality and that had little tolerance for his narrow concepts of humanity and art.

Berenson's efforts to distance himself from early radical positions cast him in an unfortunate light during his last years. As he struggled to come to terms with the consequences of these ideas, he found himself in an uneasy alliance with reactionary factions determined to undermine the interests of progressive art for reasons he could hardly have admired. When he opposed modern art in the early part of the century, he was in the honorable company of Edith Wharton, Royal Cortissoz, and George Santayana, writers he esteemed for their professional accomplishments and general level of culture. But Berenson had lost many of his contemporaries by the outbreak of World War II, and subsequent kindred spirits were of a very different variety.

An example of the sort of figure who viewed modern art in much the same way as Berenson is the American critic Thomas Craven, an outspoken champion of the American regionalist painters during the 1930s. Craven's opposition to European modernism was informed by extreme nationalism bordering on xenophobia and by hatred of what he perceived as artistic elitism in the dominant spheres of American culture. While Craven clearly admired Berenson's books on Italian Renaissance painting, he also held that an excessive preoccupation with formal structure at the expense of human values was responsible for the success of modernism. In his 1931 book, *Men of Art,* Craven describes the process whereby the critical panorama mapped out by figures such as Berenson eventuated in the frame of mind that made modern art possible.

Craven's own writing on Renaissance art relies heavily on Berenson's theory of tactile values. He describes Masaccio as a master of pure form and three-dimensional illusion but goes on to say that the pursuit of pure form should not be the end of art. The latter was an error, he believed, made by the many modern artists who admire the plasticity of quattrocento Florentine painting but fail to recognize its broad humanism. Such artists tend to forget that "great painting, over and above technical necessaries[sic], is animated by a profound human purpose," a statement with which Berenson surely would have agreed.[6]

In the chapter devoted to recent art, Craven argues that modernism owes its success to a critical climate made sympathetic by "aesthetic thoroughbreds" and "aristocrats of art" who strove to divorce art from its human context. As he describes the situation, the concept of "pure aesthetics," a "critical attitude propped up by the tenets of an unstable psychology," has been enlisted to defend an art completely void of human values.

> It consisted in restricting the significant factors in the production and appreciation of art to those whose understanding rested upon special training or unusual experience. Thus technique, essentially a matter for painters and a few specialists, became the whole of art, a field completely isolated from vulgar understanding. Into this exclusive field the thoroughbreds dragged the values belonging to the profoundest art and annexed them to minor technical issues. . . . The "purification of painting" was a fine name given to this dehumanizing tendency, and to be looked upon as in the know, one was forced to subscribe to the high sounding chatter about abstraction, empathy, significant form, dynamic relationships, and so forth![7]

For Craven, the decisive factor in the development of modern art was the isolation of formal values divorced from literal meaning and then brought to bear on the aesthetic experience. His account of this situation clearly owes a great deal to his understanding of Roger Fry, Clive Bell, and Vernon Lee, all of whom were widely read in American critical circles in the decades after the Armory Show. But he has in mind a critical outlook that descends directly from Berenson, one he holds largely responsible for the triumph of modern art. Craven also viewed this notion of pure aesthetics as foreign and had harsh words for the "merchants and esoteric idealists" who promoted a view of art and culture that he considered antithetical to an American way of life. The implication here is not that Berenson is personally responsible but rather the approach to art and aesthetics which he popularized at the turn of the century in tandem with his efforts to elevate the taste of the American public.[8]

It is hard to imagine that Berenson, with his elitist view of culture and bias toward the European, would have been comfortable in the company of an avowed American nationalist like Craven, but their statements about modern art were remarkably similar. Echoing through Craven's criticism are the same clichés found in Berenson's frequent references to modern painting in his late books: it is needlessly theoretical, it is a hoax perpetrated on the public by opportunistic critics and dealers, it demonstrates contemptuousness of its public, it is stripped of human values and reduced to concepts that could only interest scientists and mathematicians, and it is understood in terms of metaphysical speculation and self-expression. Similarly, Craven failed to see in Picasso any more than a clever, inventive personality whose reputation rested not on superior achievements but on his influence as a technical innovator. Berenson would probably not have disagreed with Craven's contention that "Picasso is generally credited with having a mighty intellect. I find no evidence to support this opinion. Mighty intellects do not exhaust themselves playing with trifles."[9]

Craven reasoned that because the capacity to experience aesthetic emotion was pronounced in those who love art more than life, it was a characteristic that eventuated in a shriveled condition of receptivity responsive only to abstraction. This observation is particularly interesting when it is remembered that Berenson himself believed his general ideas had facilitated the development of abstract painting. In his late books he sought to rescue the notion of aesthetic emotion from this kind of deceptive reductionism. Berenson was determined to demonstrate that the concept of aesthetic emotion itself is not to blame, but rather the kind of art that, of late, is said to arouse it.

*   *   *

Insofar as formalism is understood as a methodological approach to the study of art or an attitude toward art appreciation originating in the careful scrutiny and disinterested judgment of modern connoisseurship, Berenson rightfully assumes a pivotal role in its historical development, especially in the context of Anglo-American art criticism and scholarship. If, on the other hand, the concept of aesthetic formalism is broadened, as it has been in the twentieth century, to encompass art that is presumed to be self-critical or wholly occupied with the internal relationship of formal elements, Berenson can be considered no more than a transitional figure. As Craven implied, and as intuitively understood by Berenson himself, Berenson contributed to the creation of an environment in which formalism could be converted from a critical mentality to an aesthetic imperative.

It is important to remember that Berenson's radical formalism originated in his dissatisfaction with the practice of criticism, not with the state of art. He had always believed that criticism was the crux of the problem and simply wanted people to admire art for the right reasons. Berenson regarded late nineteenth-century French painting as equivalent in vigor and excellence to that of historical periods that represented to him high points in Western culture. Although he came to the eventual conclusion that Degas's major failing was in the area of composition, he was originally sympathetic to the need for reaction against exhausted artistic formulas. Apropos of Degas, he told the British painter William Rothenstein in 1900: "Reaction is our means of preserving what was good in the past, which we are in danger of losing. That is why when people come to me and deplore the Classical Reaction, I am not distressed." [10] This comment, as well as most of Berenson's early theoretical writing, predates the rejection of representational conventions that so alarmed Berenson and led him to turn his back on modern art.

Although his aesthetic principles are clearly informed by admiration for qualities he discovered in the progressive art of his youth, as a theorist Berenson chiefly addressed himself to reconsideration of the aesthetic experience in light of a new set of critical priorities. This is in sharp contrast to later formalists such as Roger Fry and Clive Bell, who became apologists for modernism. Fry's criticism in particular was directed as much toward understanding the principles underlying modern painting as it was toward the nature of the aesthetic response. While Berenson sought chiefly to justify formalist criticism, Fry and Bell were also concerned with the justification of formalist art. [11]

There can be no doubt that Roger Fry was at liberty to address himself to the legitimation of early modern art in no small measure because of the critical outlook popularized by Berenson, and, although Fry's formalism was far more deliberate and philosophically sophisticated, his debt to Berenson was considerable. Most often Berenson's influence on Fry is discussed in the context of the connoisseurship of Italian painting, and it is certainly in this arena that their personal rivalry was acute. [12] But as Fry's biographer Francis Spalding, and Kenneth Clark, among others, observed, Fry's aesthetic theories were also dependent upon Berenson's general ideas as articulated in the early essays on Italian Renaissance painting. [13]

The concept that had the most direct bearing on Fry's aesthetic theories is Berenson's principle of "ideated sensations," which forms the basis of what Fry would later refer to as the "emotional elements of design." [14] Historians of formalism recognize that the notion of ideated sensations was crucial to its development, but it is sometimes suggested that because of the concept's multiple origins, there is no certainty that Fry depended on Berenson, who had himself leaned on Hildebrand, James, and Goethe. There is truth to the observation that this concept grew out of the climate of psychological aesthetics in which both Berenson's and Fry's ideas were formed. But it is unreasonable to assume that Fry was more influenced by his reading of these texts than by his contact with Berenson, who was, for all intents and purposes, his mentor.[15]

Fry first discusses the emotional elements of design in his 1909 *New Quarterly* article, "An Essay on Aesthetics," now regarded as a central document in the history of modern formalism.[16] In this essay Fry is very specific about the formal qualities he considers to be appropriate vehicles for the communication of aesthetic emotion. For contributions to his thinking on aesthetics Fry did admit a debt to Denman Ross, whose work on the study of design he refers to by name, as well as to Tolstoy, but the unacknowledged spirit of Berenson's early books on Italian painting also hovers over this essay.[17]

Francis Spalding points out that, of all the authors Fry had read, it was Berenson who placed the greatest emphasis on artistic form as the purveyor of significance, a principle that would become the mainstay of Fry's criticism. "An Essay on Aesthetics" is a polemic for this new critical attitude. Better written, more self-consciously philosophical, it concentrates into a lucid theoretical statement many ideas scattered through Berenson's writings, where they are obscured by the context of his critical remarks made with reference to specific artists or where they are buried under Berenson's often difficult prose.

In *The Florentine Painters of the Renaissance* Berenson distinguishes between the response to artistic form and form as we experience it in nature. He argues that only when an object is separated from the interest we take in its bearing on actual existence can we respond to it aesthetically. Fry makes a similar distinction in identifying the "imaginative life," which differs from actual life by its freedom from the need for responsive action. The imaginative life, Fry claims, is distinguished by the possibility to perceive with greater clarity and purity. Art is its chief stimulus because "it is only when an object exists in our lives for no other purpose than to be seen that we really look at it." [18]

Fry was interested in the means whereby painting moved beyond gratification of the need to see in an orderly fashion to the actual arousal of emotional states. This occurs when certain values are translated into emotional elements of design that are "connected with the essential conditions of our physical existence." To Berenson's categories of tactile values, movement, and space composition, here described as mass, rhythm of line, and space, Fry adds color, the pictorial rendering of light and shade, and what he calls the "inclination to the eye of the plane." [19] He notes that when these elements are rendered in the abstract, the emotion communicated is not strong, but when they are concentrated in a representational image, the effect is intensified, especially if the human figure is involved.

Fry was aware that by linking the efficacy of these emotional elements of design with the presentation of natural appearances, he was in a sense undermining the challenge raised by many artists and critics of his generation to the mimetic nature of art. Having raised the question that also preoccupied Berenson, he wondered: if these elements are extracted from objects by artists for the purpose of arousing aesthetic emotion and then restored to the object in the form of a representational image, why is the experience of nature different from that of art? His reply was that nature in its indifference to the needs of the imaginative life cannot guarantee that "the emotional elements will be combined appropriately." This idea echoes Berenson's earlier contention that nature does not furnish accentuated values of movement and mass and that the business of art is to create conventions through which they may be transmitted.[20]

The ensuing discussion of the relationship between art and nature relies heavily on Kant's principles of disinterested contemplation as a feature of the imaginative life of art. But Fry in his conclusion returns once again to Berenson's original concept of ideated sensations aroused by giving specific values to retinal impressions.

> When the artist passes from pure sensations to emotions
> aroused by means of sensations, he uses natural forms
> which, in themselves, are calculated to move our emo-
> tions, and he presents these in such a manner that the
> forms themselves generate in us emotional states, based
> upon the fundamental necessities of our physical and
> physiological nature.[21]

Fry concludes that the nature of the representation is wholly determined by the kind of emotion sought by the artist. It may be extremely realistic or it may be highly simplified, relying entirely on
the "force and intensity of the emotional elements" to achieve the
desired effects. For Fry, as well as for Berenson, likeness to nature is
an inadequate measure of artistic quality. The viewer need consider
only "whether the emotional elements inherent in natural form are
adequately discovered," or, as Berenson would have put it, the significance of the object is effectively communicated by means of ideated
sensations.[22]

In the final sentence of "An Essay in Aesthetics," Fry alludes to
one of the central issues that will later separate his criticism from
Berenson's. After pointing out that similarity to nature is of little
consequence, Fry adds "unless, indeed, the emotional idea depends
at any point upon likeness, or completeness of representation."[23] For
Berenson, the ideas embodied in art were unquestionably dependent
on legible representation. But, as Fry later explained, his own contact with modern painting inspired him to reconsider this aspect of
aesthetic emotion. In the essay "Retrospect," published in 1920, Fry
recounts his discovery that although post-impressionist artists were
moved by formal relations in works of art, they did not think in terms
of the emotions he supposed them to convey. He thus came to the
conclusion that "since it was impossible in these cases to doubt the
genuineness of the aesthetic reaction it became evident that I had
not pushed the analysis of works of art far enough, had not distinguished the purely aesthetic elements from certain accompanying
accessories."[24]

At this juncture Fry began writing criticism that would serve as justification of modernist art, and he was willing at least to consider the possibility that significant form could be disengaged from naturalistic representation. It is this line of reasoning, he explains in "Retrospect," that led his friend Clive Bell to conclude that representation is wholly irrelevant. Fry was not entirely comfortable with this position, although he believed that it stimulated important discussion of the need to isolate the experience of the purely aesthetic from the many other ways in which art effects us. Berenson, of course, had addressed this issue in the 1890s, but, unlike Fry or Bell, he was not interested in entirely disengaging the aesthetic elements from their accessories. For Berenson the emotional idea is inextricable from representation; life-enhancement depends on recognizable human and natural form.

Another essential difference between Fry and Berenson lies in their respective explanations as to the value of aesthetic experience. Berenson believed that art empowers the sensitive viewer to experience a sense of heightened capacity and intensified life. The concept of life-enhancement furnishes aesthetic pleasure with a moral justification. This became even more important as Berenson began to understand the life-enhancing function of art as a mandate to humanize.

Fry, on the other hand, was far less specific about the value of aesthetic pleasure. In "An Essay on Aesthetics" he, like Berenson, was intent on separating aesthetic pleasure from conventional morality; but beyond this he offered little more than recognition of this experience as a desirable thing. He remains noncommittal in "Retrospect," reiterating that aesthetic emotion is removed from ethical values as Tolstoy understood them and that it is remote from actual life, but as for its intrinsic value, "one can only say that those who experience it feel it to have a peculiar quality of 'reality' which makes it a matter of infinite importance in their lives." [25]

That Fry regarded the aesthetic experience as a self-sufficient goal not requiring justification enabled him to assess modern painting in terms of its structural unity rather than its moral value. It did not, however, resolve for him the essential relationship between formal significance and representation and to the end of his life Fry remained uncertain about this. In comparison, Berenson's insistence that art fulfilled its purpose by advancing humanistic values, a position that necessitated in his mind the complete rejection of formalist art, had the effect of clarifying this relationship and equipped him to explain it. Notwithstanding Fry's statement in "Retrospect" about the need to disengage pure aesthetic elements from their representational accessories, the historian Beverly Twitchell maintains that Fry was never sure if this could actually be done, and it made him perpetually uncomfortable with the relationship between form and content.

The problem that plagued Fry, as numerous writers have pointed out, was one that complicated any strictly formalist view of representational painting: how to analyze the abstract value of form without taking into account the nature of the representation. Bell's solution was to render representation irrelevant, a position he would later modify and one that Fry always regarded as too extreme. In "Retrospect" Fry admits that the person so occupied with form as to be blind to associative meaning is rare. "Nearly everyone, even if highly sensitive to purely plastic and spatial appearances, will inevitably entertain some of those thoughts and feelings which are conveyed by implication and by reference back to life."[26] He concludes that it is probably impossible to fuse aesthetic emotions with those aroused by dramatic content into a single artistic unity; the viewer will always be more sensitive to one than to the other. Berenson, on the other hand, upheld that in a fully realized work of art they had to work together. Form conveyed humanizing content by accentuating certain aspects of the representation.

Fry's inability to reconcile form and content was also complicated by his insistence on mass as the essence of art. As he states in "Retrospect," "even the slightest suggestion of the third dimension in a picture must be due to some element of representation."[27] Fry, like Berenson, did not really believe that mass could be rendered in the abstract; his admiration for Cézanne turned on the assumption that tension between two-dimensional surface pattern and the illusion of depth is an essential component of pictorial design. Without this tension, the emotional elements of design lose their force. Thus, despite his more fully developed formalism, Fry remained close to Berenson's original position that representational form is the most effective vehicle to stimulate aesthetic emotions.

Ultimately, what separated the two was Fry's willingness to see in modern art the same formal principles operational in historical art. In this way, Fry was able to understand modernism, in its striving for formal unity and balance, as a continuation of classicism. Unlike Berenson, he did not require explicitly humanistic content to insinuate a link with the classical past. To Berenson, the concept of classicism was more directly tied to antiquity and the uninterrupted development of Western civilization, prompting him to conclude that the omission of human values in painting was tantamount to anti-humanism.[28]

*   *   *

Although it is fitting to think of Berenson as a paradigmatic modernist aesthete, turned paradigmatic reactionary philistine, it is perhaps more appropriate to define his historical role in terms of his one consuming passion. Richard Wollheim has aptly noted that

> Berenson was not a sage, nor a great thinker; nor much
> of a theorist. He was a man obsessed by painting and
> tied to it by the most obvious and direct of all links: the
> visual. Indeed, I can think of no better way of charac-
> terizing the true (as opposed to the legendary) relation
> in which he stood to the arts than by using the famous
> words uttered by Cézanne of Monet: Il n'est qu'un oeil,
> mais, mon Dieu, quel oeil![29]

Berenson was a great eye, aspiring to the achievements of a great mind; his ambition was to define the terms in which art can be said to enhance life. That this infamous eye refused to enter into a genuinely critical relationship with a modernist painting was indicative, at least in part, of the extent to which Berenson realized that his early theoretical positions had inadvertently contributed to the eventual collapse of what he held most sacred.

When Berenson began writing criticism in the 1890s, he took certain things for granted. He developed a theory of aesthetics based on ordinary human sensibility, but he could not envision a world in which art disengaged from historical tradition and social privilege. He argued that subject, ethics, and morality had no bearing on appreciation because he could not imagine an art that did not glorify man. When it became evident that his ideas could be placed in the service of an aesthetic elite that set itself in opposition to both the social values and the artistic traditions he admired, he retreated. Berenson's last years were spent trying to undermine the rising tides of populism and modernism; he could best accomplish this by advocating elitism and classicism and by becoming what he had once despised: a critic more concerned with the moral purpose of art than its aesthetic qualities.

Had Berenson wished to apply himself seriously to the study of twentieth-century art, he might have been one of its most perceptive critics. To do so would have required that he bring to it the same discerning judgment that made him one of the most distinctive voices in early modern criticism. But subjectivity is the enemy of the connoisseur, and with respect to the art of his own age, Berenson was a prisoner of his personal prejudices, his taste, and, ultimately, his ambition.

Notes

Introduction

1. Bernard Berenson, "Decline and Recovery in the Figure Arts," in *Studies in Art and Literature for Belle da Costa Greene*, ed. Dorothy Miner (Princeton: Princeton University Press, 1954), 25–26. Berenson's treatise on decline was never completed. The theme occupied him from the end of World War I until his death and in large part shaped the contents of his personal library. In addition to this foreword, the introductory chapter was published in 1948 as *Aesthetics and History in the Visual Arts* and the first chapter was issued as a separate volume in 1954, under the title *The Arch of Constantine; or, The Decline of Form.*

2. See Paul Barolsky, "Walter Pater and Bernard Berenson," *New Criterion* 2 (April 1984): 47–57; and Sydney Freedberg, "Berenson, Connoisseurship, and the History of Art," *New Criterion* 7 (February 1989): 7–16.

3. Robert Hughes, "Only in America," rev. of *Bernard Berenson: The Making of a Connoisseur*, by Ernest Samuels, and *Being Bernard Berenson*, by Meryle Secrest, *New York Review*, 20 December 1979, 19.

Ernest Samuels's two-volume biography remains the standard reference on Berenson's life and work. See Samuels, *Bernard Berenson: The Making of a Connoisseur* (Cambridge: Harvard University Press, 1979), and *Bernard Berenson: The Making of a Legend* (Cambridge: Harvard University Press, 1987). For further biographical information on Berenson see Sylvia Sprigge, *Berenson: A Biography* (Boston: Houghton Mifflin, 1960); and Meryle Secrest, *Being Bernard Berenson* (New York: Holt, Rinehart and Winston, 1979). There is virtually nothing in either of the last two works that is not covered with greater thoroughness and accuracy in Samuels.

4. See especially chap. 7, "I Tatti; or, Sublimating Sales," in Remy Saisselin, *The Bourgeois and the Bibelot* (New Brunswick, N.J.: Rutgers University Press, 1984).

5. Bernard Berenson, *Rumor and Reflection, 1941–1944* (London: Constable; New York: Simon and Schuster, 1952), 206.

6. Bernard Berenson, *Sunset and Twilight* (New York: Harcourt, Brace and World, 1963), 102.

7. Berenson, *Rumor and Reflection*, 245.

8. The observation that Berenson's dislike of modern art was rooted in an exaggerated fear for his way of life is not new. In a 1961 essay for *Encounter*, which remains the most important discussion of Berenson's relationship to modern culture, Meyer Schapiro suggests a number of ways in which the purity of Berenson's aesthetic vision, including his opinion of recent art, was corrupted by the desire for wealth and social acceptance. See Meyer Schapiro, "Mr. Berenson's Values," *Encounter* 16 (January 1961): 57–65.

Robert Hughes, for whom Schapiro was a point of departure in his own assessment of Berenson, states unequivocally that "Berenson's asp-like hostility to the culture of his own day ran deeper than ordinary fear of the unfamiliar. Berenson experienced modernism as a direct threat to his own values, livelihood and well being. He took its rhetoric of destruction, the stock in trade of Futurism, Dada, Surrealism, at face value." Hughes, "Only in America," 28.

9. Mary Smith Costelloe married Bernard Berenson on 27 December 1900. In this study she will be referred to as Mary Costelloe (or simply Costelloe) from the time of her first meeting with Berenson and as Mary Berenson after their marriage.

10. Although Berenson's understanding of the word "decorative" was idiosyncratic, in other respects his application of critical nomenclature was perfectly consistent with contemporary usage. Especially noteworthy for this study are his references to the "primitive" and "Oriental." In keeping with late nineteenth-century Western cultural values, the word "primitive" typically described tribal cultures while "Oriental" referred collectively to cultures east and southeast of the Mediterranean. These terms, which have their origins in the semantic categories constructed to distinguish Europe from other parts of the world, were used throughout the nineteenth century to assert the cultural hegemony of the West, and it is in this spirit that Berenson invoked them. Although he had catholic taste and held many forms of non-Western expression in high esteem, he never wavered from his belief in the superiority of Western cultural traditions.

Chapter I

1. Corrado Pavolini, *Cubismo, Futurismo, Espressionismo* (Bologna: Nicola Zanichelli, 1926), 23–25, 60–61.

2. "B.B.," *Time*, 10 April 1939, 58.

3. Frank Getlein, "The Legendary Berenson," *New Republic*, 26 October 1959, 21–22.

4. Sidney Alexander, "The Last Aesthete?" rev. of *The Bernard Berenson Treasury*, ed. Hanna Kiel, *Reporter*, 18 July 1963, 56.

5. Meyer Schapiro, "Mr. Berenson's Values," *Encounter* 16 (January 1961): 62. Reiterating Schapiro's grudging concession to Berenson, Marianne Martin, who investigated the origins of abstraction in early twentieth-century American criticism and art theory, came to a similar conclusion: "There is no question that the views and actions not only of Fry and Bell, cited by Schapiro, but of a great many other American and European artists and critics were deeply stirred by Berenson's authoritative version of formalism. Indeed, his followers helped very much in turning the tide of modernism." Marianne Martin, "Some American Contributions to Early 20th Century Abstraction," *Arts* 54 (June 1980): 163.

6. Linda Nochlin, "The Realist Criminal and the Abstract Law," *Art in America* 61 (September–October 1973): 60.

7. Paul Barolsky, "Walter Pater and Bernard Berenson," *New Criterion* 2 (April 1984): 47–57. See also Barbara Reise, "Greenberg and the Group: A Retrospective View," *Studio International* 175 (May–June 1968), pt. 1, 254–57; pt. 2, 314–16.

8. Bernard Berenson, *Sunset and Twilight* (New York: Harcourt, Brace and World, 1963), 375.

9. Kenneth Clark had the following to say about Berenson's aspirations toward theory: "Berenson was not a philosopher in the limited or professional sense of the word. His thoughts were not controlled by logic; his mind, which could accommodate such a multitude of concrete impressions, was hostile to abstractions; and he had a corresponding mistrust of systems." Kenneth Clark, "Bernard Berenson," *Burlington Magazine* 102 (September 1960): 385. See also John Walker, *Self-Portrait with Donors* (Boston: Little, Brown, 1974), 97.

10. Clement Greenberg, "Greenberg on Berenson," rev. of *Piero della Francesca; or, The Ineloquent in Art* and *The Arch of Constantine; or, The Decline of Form, Perspectives USA* 1 (Spring 1955): 150–54. This appraisal is consistent with the views of Meyer Schapiro and Sydney Freedberg, both of whom make a strong case for Berenson's seminal contribution to the study of Renaissance art, but are very specific about his limitations. See Meyer Schapiro, "The Last Aesthete," rev. of *Aesthetics and History in the Visual Arts* and *Sketch for a Self-Portrait, Commentary* 8 (December 1949): 616; and Sydney Freedberg, "Berenson, Connoisseurship, and the History of Art," *New Criterion* 7 (February 1989): 9.

11. Eleanor Clark, "Berenson's Last Years," rev. of *Sunset and Twilight,* and *The Selected Letters of Bernard Berenson,* ed. A. K. McComb, *New York Review,* 5 March 1964, 4.

12. Bernard Berenson, *Rumor and Reflection, 1941–1944* (London: Constable; New York: Simon and Schuster, 1952), 206.

13. Andrew Brink contends that this feeling was not mutual; as evidence

he points out Russell's failure to honor Berenson with more than perfunctory mention in his autobiographical writings, a gesture Brink understood as Russell's implicit judgment of Berenson's intellectual importance. Nor is it difficult to agree with Carl Spadoni's observation that Berenson's opposition to metaphysics placed him at a disadvantage in gaining Russell's intellectual respect. Andrew Brink, "The Russell-Berenson Connection," rev. of *Bernard Berenson: The Making of a Connoisseur,* by Ernest Samuels, *Russell* 35–36 (Autumn–Winter 1979–80): 45; and Carl Spadoni, "Bertrand Russell on Aesthetics," *Russell,* n.s. 4 (Summer 1984): 59.

14. For an account of Russell's objections to Berenson's aesthetic theories, see Ernest Samuels, *Bernard Berenson: The Making of a Connoisseur* (Cambridge: Harvard University Press, 1979), 229–33 (hereafter cited as Samuels, *Connoisseur*); and Spadoni, "Russell on Aesthetics," 62–65. Russell's skepticism worried his sister-in-law, but Berenson, who at the time felt he was drowning in advice, failed to do anything about it.

15. Spadoni points out that aesthetics was one of the few branches of philosophy that Russell failed to treat systematically. Russell told Berenson that though he believed in art intellectually, in terms of feeling it he was a "good British Philistine." Spadoni, "Russell on Aesthetics," 50–51.

16. Santayana to Mrs. Frederick Winslow, 6 December 1912, in *The Letters of George Santayana,* ed. Daniel Cory (New York: Charles Scribner's Sons, 1955), 121. "I Tatti" is the name of Berenson's estate in the village of Seltignano outside Florence.

17. A central theme of Schapiro's essay, "Mr. Berenson's Values," is that Berenson's need to deny the side of himself involved in art dealing and to maintain his image led him to retreat from the vital intellectual currents of his day and diminished him as a thinker. See Meyer Schapiro, "Mr. Berenson's Values," 59, 65, and "The Last Aesthete," 616.

Similarly, Robert Hughes remarked that Berenson's dependence on art dealing caused him to ossify as a critic and thinker. Hughes, "Only in America," rev. of Samuels, *Connoisseur,* and *Being Bernard Berenson,* by Meryle Secrest, *New York Review,* 20 December 1979, 25.

18. Bernard Berenson, *Sketch for a Self-Portrait* (London: Constable; New York: Pantheon, 1949), 62–63.

19. Mary Berenson to Alys Russell, 26 May 1930, in *Mary Berenson: A Self-Portrait from Her Letters and Diaries,* ed. Barbara Strachey and Jayne Samuels (New York: W. W. Norton, 1983), 279–80.

20. Vernon Lee (Violet Paget) had also tried to convince Berenson that he could not write, and then she proceeded to publish at length on the subject of psychological aesthetics. The Berensons believed that she had made generous use of ideas acquired from her conversations with him. For a de-

tailed account of the altercation with Vernon Lee, see Samuels, *Connoisseur*, 283–90; and René Wellek, "Vernon Lee, Bernard Berenson and Aesthetics," in *Friendship's Garland: Essays in Honor of Mario Praz on His Seventieth Birthday*, ed. Vittorio Gabrieli (Rome: Edizioini di storia e letteratura, 1966), 233–51.

Both Clark and Freedberg point out that in the autobiographical books written after World War II (and, significantly, after the death of his many literary critics), when his intention was to communicate and not to preach, Berenson's style was better and often quite good. The unhappy reality of Berenson's writing was that he was at his worst in those works he viewed as most important: the essays on aesthetics and art theory.

In retrospect, it would appear that Sydney Freedberg is correct in his assertion that what contemporary readers object to in Berenson's writing is a style and tone that is characteristic of his generation and his cultural milieu. Freedberg reminds us that Berenson's early books were admired by their first readers, although, even with Berenson's wife's frequent intervention to correct his prose, they could not be saved from an "air, unwelcome to us now, of didactic condescension—of preaching, on occasion—or the episodes of stiff-jointed, starchy prose, or the strained, self-conscious Paterisms." Freedberg, "Berenson, Connoisseurship, and the History of Art," 8.

21. Berenson diary entry, *The Bernard Berenson Treasury, 1887–1958*, ed. Hanna Kiel (New York: Simon and Schuster, 1962), 295.

22. Berenson to Mary Costelloe, 7 November 1890, in ibid., 46.

23. Mary Costelloe to Robert Pearsall Smith, 24 November 1893, in Strachey and Samuels, *Mary Berenson*, 54–55.

24. Portions of the correspondence between Mary Costelloe Berenson and Hermann Obrist can be found in the Berenson Archive, Harvard University Center for Italian Renaissance Studies, Villa I Tatti, Florence, Italy (hereafter referred to as I Tatti), and in the H. W. Smith Papers, Lilly Library, Indiana University, Bloomington, Indiana (hereafter referred to as Indiana). There are also excerpts in Strachey and Samuels, *Mary Berenson*.

25. Mary Costelloe to Hermann Obrist, 6 June 1895, Indiana.

26. "I know well, from having worked all spring with BB, the hard, sweating intellectual labor it takes to simplify the thing and get at the bottom. . . . What happiness for me, who cannot originate, but can take pleasure in real thinking." Mary Costelloe to Hermann Obrist, 24 June 1895, in Strachey and Samuels, *Mary Berenson*, 64–65.

27. Freedberg expressed the consensus that "it was the conjunction in him of the finest, searching sensibility and the most precise weighing, measuring and referential intelligence that made Berenson so extraordinary. In the history of art, such a conjunction of qualities defines a connoisseur, and *that*,

as we have always recognized (although Berenson himself recognized it only with reluctance) was the most substantial part of his wide accomplishment, and the most influential." Freedberg, "Berenson, Connoisseurship, and the History of Art," 9.

28. David Brown, *Berenson and the Connoisseurship of Italian Painting* (Washington, D.C.: National Gallery of Art, 1979), 39.

29. Greenberg, "Greenberg on Berenson," 152. Donald Kuspit pointed out that Greenberg's own efforts to establish a philosophical basis for art criticism can, in part, be understood in terms of his desire to avoid Berenson's shortcomings. Donald Kuspit, *Clement Greenberg* (Madison: University of Wisconsin Press, 1979), 12–13.

30. Quoted in Samuels, *Bernard Berenson: The Making of a Legend*, 61.

31. Creighton Gilbert, "The Classics: Berenson . . . How Can We Use Him?" *Arts* 34 (June 1960): 15.

32. Greenberg used the word "posture" to describe Berenson's attitude toward modern art in my interview with him, April 1989.

Chapter 2

1. Ernest Samuels has done an extraordinary job of giving shape and order to Berenson's life and career. The following discussion of Berenson's early books relies heavily on Samuels not only for the events of Berenson's life but also for the substance and origins of his thought. Unless otherwise noted, all biographical information on these years comes from Samuels. Specific sources will be cited only when the inclusion or interpretation of information obtained from archival sources differs substantially from that of Samuels. See Ernest Samuels, *Bernard Berenson: The Making of a Connoisseur* (Cambridge: Harvard University Press, 1979); and Samuels, *Bernard Berenson: The Making of a Legend* (Cambridge: Harvard University Press, 1987) (hereafter cited as Samuels, *Connoisseur,* and Samuels, *Legend,* respectively.).

2. In recent years a number of important studies have been undertaken on the history of formalism. Collectively they furnish an excellent account of late nineteenth-century art criticism. For an understanding of Berenson, the most pertinent are those that deal with Anglo-American criticism, specifically the writings of Roger Fry, who was a close associate of Berenson's and who wrote for essentially the same audience. See Jacqueline Falkenheim, *Roger Fry and the Beginnings of Formalist Criticism* (Ann Arbor: UMI Research Press, 1980); and Beverly Twitchell, *Cézanne and Formalism in Bloomsbury* (Ann Arbor: UMI Research Press, 1987). These studies consider Fry's writings in the context of contemporary English-language criticism and also

discuss the impact of German psychological theories of aesthetics, which inform the works of both Fry and Berenson.

3. On Walter Pater and modern criticism see Richard Stein, *The Ritual of Interpretation: Fine Arts as Literature* (Cambridge: Harvard University Press, 1975); F. C. McGrath, *The Sensible Spirit: Walter Pater and the Modernist Paradigm* (Tampa: University of South Florida Press, 1986); and Paul Barolsky, *Walter Pater's Renaissance* (University Park, Pa.: Pennsylvania State University Press, 1987).

For discussions of Berenson's debt to Pater see Paul Barolsky, "Walter Pater and Bernard Berenson," *New Criterion* 2 (April 1984): 47–57; and Franklin E. Court, "The Matter of Pater's 'Influence' on Bernard Berenson: Setting the Record Straight," *English Literature in Transition* 26 (1983): 16–22.

4. See especially David Brown, *Berenson and the Connoisseurship of Italian Painting* (Washington, D.C.: National Gallery of Art, 1979); and Carol Gibson-Wood, *Studies in the Theory of Connoisseurship from Vasari to Morelli* (New York: Garland, 1988).

5. Remy Saisselin succinctly describes Berenson's view of art as "Bostonian in its Italian and Japanese orientation, Anglo-American in its emphasis on the Renaissance, Germanic in assuming a pure, disinterested aesthetic experience and its pretensions to scientific expertise," and Victorian in its Hellenism, in that it was characterized by its opposition not to barbarism but to philistinism. For the most part, these values will remain unchanged throughout his long life, excepting that barbarism will eventually replace philistinism as the locus of his fears for the survival of Hellenism. Remy Saisselin, *The Bourgeois and the Bibelot* (New Brunswick, N.J.: Rutgers University Press, 1984), 142.

Marianne Martin also makes a connection between Berenson's formalism and the aesthetics of Boston orientalists such as Ernest Fenollosa. See Marianne Martin, "Some American Contributions to Early 20th Century Abstraction," *Arts* 54 (June 1980): 162–63.

6. Among the numerous references in the literature to the probable influence of German aesthetics on Berenson's general ideas and critical method see especially, Samuels, *Connoisseur;* Edgar Wind, *Art and Anarchy* (New York: Alfred A. Knopf, 1964); and Alan Robinson, *Symbol to Vortex: Painting, Poetry and Ideas, 1885–1914* (New York: St. Martin's Press, 1985). This is also discussed by Twitchell (*Cézanne and Formalism*) and Falkenheim (*Roger Fry*), who note a similar debt on the part of Roger Fry, and in the literature on Vernon Lee (pseudonym for Violet Paget), whose aesthetic theories were so close to Berenson's that Berenson suspected her of having plagiarized him from their numerous informal conversations on art

in Florence. The parallels between the thinking of Lee and Berenson have been extensively examined elsewhere and will not be considered in detail here. See especially Peter Gumm, *Vernon Lee: Violet Paget* (London: Oxford University Press, 1964); René Welleck, "Vernon Lee, Bernard Berenson and Aesthetics," in *Friendship's Garland: Essays in Honor of Mario Praz on His Seventieth Birthday*, ed. Vittorio Gabrieli (Rome: Edizioni di storia e letteratura, 1966), 233–51; and Samuels, *Connoisseur.*

7. Later in his life Berenson did acknowledge a debt to Wölfflin for his "masterpiece on classical art" as one of a list of writers who prepared him in the only way possible, by "putting him into a state of eager and zestful anticipation." Bernard Berenson, *Aesthetics and History in the Visual Arts* (New York: Pantheon, 1948), 104–5.

It is often said, not only with respect to Berenson but also to Vernon Lee and Roger Fry, that these ideas were in the air; psychological aesthetics was an important part of the intellectual fabric of the late nineteenth-century, and art criticism reflects these principles in varying degrees. Perhaps more significant in considering Berenson's modernity was, as Schapiro pointed out, that he continued to adhere to them long after they were considered obsolete by philosophers and psychologists.

8. Falkenheim, *Roger Fry,* 50–51. See also E. H. Gombrich, *Art and Illusion* (Princeton: Princeton University Press, 1956), 16–17.

9. Mary Costelloe to Alys Smith Russell, 3 September 1891, in the collection of the H. W. Smith Papers, Lilly Library, Indiana University, Bloomington, Indiana (hereafter Indiana).

10. Mary Costelloe to her family, 19 September 1891, Indiana.

11. Mary Costelloe to her family, 13 November 1891, Indiana.

12. Mary Costelloe to her family, 15 June 1892, Indiana.

13. Falkenheim suggested 1895 as the year in which this audience awakened to contemporary French art and asserted that as late as 1905 the majority continued to be hostile to the purely painterly, sensate concerns of impressionism. She identified R.A.M. Stevenson's book on Diego Velázquez, published in 1895, as the first aesthetic defense of impressionism insofar as it pleaded for its acceptance on technical and formal grounds. Falkenheim, *Roger Fry.* Berenson made a similar case in both *The Venetian Painters of the Renaissance* (New York: G. P. Putnam's Sons, 1894) and *Lorenzo Lotto: An Essay in Constructive Art Criticism* (New York: G. P. Putnam's Sons, 1895; rev. ed., London: George Bell and Sons, 1901; hereafter referred to as *Lorenzo Lotto;* quotations from the 1901 edition).

14. In a letter to her family, Costelloe wrote of her inability to describe the sentiment of Raphael's Sistine Madonna because she "found the picture so absolutely beautiful or sane that it is impossible—or almost impossible—

to feel any sentiment about it whatever," and, "I don't care to criticize the picture that way—it is a perfect beauty as it is." 25 August 1891, Indiana.

15. Mary Costelloe to her family, 22 August 1891, and 6 September 1891, Indiana.

16. Mary Costelloe to Hannah Smith, 3 September 1892, Indiana.

17. From an 1892 Berenson notebook, in Bernard Berenson, *The Bernard Berenson Treasury, 1887–1958*, ed. Hanna Kiel (New York: Simon and Schuster, 1962), 61–62.

18. Bernard Berenson to Senda Berenson, 28 August 1892, in the collection of the Berenson Archive, Harvard University Center for Italian Renaissance Studies, Villa I Tatti, Florence, Italy (hereafter I Tatti). Burke bought works by Degas, Paul Albert Besnard, Eugene Boudin, and Pissarro.

19. Berenson to Senda Berenson, 17 October 1892, I Tatti.

20. Bernard Berenson, *The Venetian Painters of the Renaissance*, 1894 (hereafter referred to as *The Venetian Painters*), 8. All quotations from the texts of these four essays are taken from the 1952 Phaidon Press edition of *The Italian Painters of the Renaissance*. They were first consolidated into a single volume in 1930 by Clarendon Press, which also published the lists in a separate volume in 1932 under the title *Italian Pictures of the Renaissance*.

21. Ibid., 8.

22. Ibid., 26.

23. Ibid., 35.

24. Berenson to Senda Berenson, 17 October 1892, I Tatti.

25. Kenneth Clark, *Moments of Vision* (New York: Harper and Row, 1981), 115. In the 1956 edition of *Lorenzo Lotto*, Berenson admitted that his insistence on Alvise Vivarini as a major influence on Lotto and all of fifteenth-century Venetian painting was mistaken.

26. Kenneth Clark, *Another Part of the Wood* (New York: Harper and Row, 1974), 159.

27. Berenson to Senda Berenson, 18 October 1892, I Tatti.

28. Berenson, *Lorenzo Lotto*, 250.

29. The superiority of the modern is established early in the text, when Berenson notes, for example, that the excellence of Giovanni Bellini in comparison to Vivarini must have been as apparent to cultivated Venetians as impressionist landscape painting is to us now. Berenson thought that Vivarini's greater popularity with the masses was understandable, since Bellini would not have been known to most Venetians any more than an American youth of ten years ago living in Paris would have heard of Degas or Pissarro. Berenson, *Lorenzo Lotto*, 35.

30. Berenson, *The Venetian Painters*, 35.

31. Berenson, *Lorenzo Lotto*, 276.

32. Ibid., 123.

33. Ibid., 124.

34. Ibid., 278.

35. Rev. of *Lorenzo Lotto*, *Spectator*, 28 September 1895, 407.

36. Rev. of *Lorenzo Lotto*, *Quarterly Review* 184 (October 1896): 454–79; *Athenaeum*, 13 April 1895, 481; *Dial*, 1 January 1896, 21; *Critic*, 12 January 1895, 38–39; *Atlantic Monthly* 75 (April 1895): 556–59; *New York Times*, 12 January 1895, 23. See also Samuels, *Connoisseur*.

37. Berenson's preface to the 1901 edition of *Lorenzo Lotto* makes a point of his diminishing interest in the work of art as a document in the history of civilization, observing that such study can result in a confusion between historical and aesthetic standards. A notice on this later edition suggested that Berenson was not likely to undertake another study like this because his interests had clearly changed. The reviewer confirmed that in *Lorenzo Lotto* Berenson moved directly from formal considerations to psychological causes, bypassing the aesthetic value of the works, and he suspected that therein Berenson was least in sympathy with his former attitude. Rev. in *Athenaeum*, 18 April 1903, 503–4.

In this preface Berenson also introduces a discussion of the fundamental difference between technical advances and artistic progress. An interest in the history of technique, he urges, is not to be confused with a love of art, and he cautions against the notion of progress altogether. Berenson is perhaps faulting himself for having been overly impressed by the painterly technique of impressionism and Venetian art. His clear tendency had been to view this change in technique as an advance and, in the face of his later preference for Florentine monumentality, this must have seemed a trivial and misguided judgment.

This discussion of technique represents one of the earliest of Berenson's maneuvers to distance himself from the modernist stance, as he warns his readers to beware of "finding beauty where there is only curiosity," an admonition that will echo through his future denunciations of twentieth-century art. Berenson, *Lorenzo Lotto*, preface to the 1901 edition, ix.

38. Berenson to Senda Berenson, 23 April 1893, I Tatti. Fabbri was born in New York of an Italian immigrant father and an American mother. His uncle and eventual guardian worked for J. P. Morgan. Following the death of his father, Fabbri returned to Italy, where his extended family maintained a home in Florence and a villa in the country. He studied painting in the United States (with J. Alden Weir) and in Florence before moving to Paris in 1896. Fabbri also dabbled in architecture and design, but eventually he decided to devote his energy and sizeable financial resources to support the teaching and performance of the Gregorian chant. He was one of the first collectors

to acquire a significant number of Cézannes, and it is likely that Berenson saw his first Cézannes with Fabbri's encouragement. Berenson's interest in Cézanne will be discussed later in this chapter. See Mabel La Farge, *Egisto Fabbri* (New Haven: privately printed, 1937); Walter Pach, *Queer Thing, Painting* (New York: Harper and Brothers, 1938); and John Rewald, *Cézanne and America: Dealers, Collectors, Artists and Critics* (Princeton: Princeton University Press, 1989).

39. Mary Costelloe diary entry, 11 February 1893, I Tatti. "Doctrine" was what Costelloe, along with Michael Field, called Berenson and his ideas.

40. Costelloe diary entry, 10 April 1894, I Tatti.

41. Hermann Obrist to Mary Costelloe, 10 July 1894, I Tatti.

42. See Peg Weiss, *Kandinsky in Munich: The Formative Jugenstil Years* (Princeton: Princeton University Press, 1979), 28–34.

43. Hermann Obrist to Mary Costelloe, 27 October 1894, I Tatti.

44. Hermann Obrist to Mary Costelloe, 1 November 1894, I Tatti. Obrist was part German and part Scottish and definitely looked upon the vigorous and passionate side of himself as Teutonic. In the 10 July letter, that makes a case for the ability of the uncultured to appreciate art, he also feels compelled to rebuke Costelloe for her inability to truly enjoy life in the inhibiting ambience of overaestheticized Florence. He insists that she could not enjoy a wild country dance to save her life and that Berenson's idea of "enjoying animal life was to take a brisk constitutional walk." Just as he opposed his fiercely subjective engagement with art to Berenson's bloodless objectivity, he claims that when away from Florence he regularly indulges in invigorating activities like a good German. "You 'love' animal life, but you don't do it. It is too vulgar and requires too much strength. But we do it and are not always vulgar at it." This comparison has particular relevance in light of the empathetic response theory then brewing in Berenson's mind. Hermann Obrist to Mary Costelloe, 10 July 1894, I Tatti.

45. Hermann Obrist to Mary Costelloe, 1 November 1894, I Tatti.

46. In measuring himself against Berenson, Obrist felt more alive but slower witted. He clearly resented the ease with which Berenson assimilated, processed, and discarded ideas that he himself had arrived at only after much thought and deliberation. In May 1895 Costelloe requested that Obrist share his thoughts on the issues Berenson had taken up in *The Florentine Painters* by letter, since he could not be there to discuss them. Obrist's response was that he was reluctant to be generous with the hard-won distilled wisdom he had acquired. A month later, after an exchange of letters between them, Costelloe had to reassure Obrist that Berenson would not steal his ideas. She agreed to his suggestion that she write out carefully what she remembered of their previous conversations and show it to him. Hermann Obrist to Mary

Costelloe, 20 May 1895, I Tatti, and Mary Costelloe to Hermann Obrist, 24 June 1895, Indiana.

The whole episode was a prelude to a similar dispute with Vernon Lee in 1897. The jealousy with which these ideas were guarded was a measure of the inflated importance assigned to them by the small and regrettably petty circle of hypersensitive aesthetes who were part of Berenson's life in Florence.

47. Mary Costelloe to Hermann Obrist, 30 April/1 May 1895, Indiana. To my knowledge these notes are not available in any of the repositories consulted for this study.

48. Hermann Obrist to Mary Costelloe, [undated, circa May 1895], I Tatti.

49. Hermann Obrist to Mary Costelloe, 28 April 1895, Indiana.

50. Hermann Obrist to Mary Costelloe, 20 May 1895, I Tatti. This pamphlet was not identified by name. The author is possibly the German aesthetic philosopher Konrad Lange.

51. Mary Costelloe to Hannah Smith, 3 June 1895, Indiana.

52. Mary Costelloe to Hermann Obrist, 6 June 1895, Indiana.

53. Hermann Obrist to Mary Costelloe, letter recorded in her diary 19 October 1895, I Tatti.

54. Costelloe diary entry, 10 April 1894, I Tatti.

55. Mary Costelloe to Hermann Obrist, 4 June 1895, Indiana.

56. The historian Peg Weiss stressed Obrist's radical departure from the traditional conception of monumental sculpture to a kind of fantasy construction based on nature as compelling evidence of his originality. Weiss, *Kandinsky in Munich,* 31–32. Costelloe's comments on the Liszt memorial must be understood as extreme intolerance of any such dalliance when the human figure was concerned. She and Berenson were far more encouraging about Obrist's embroidery designs, because they could appreciate them on a much different level. See Mary Logan [Mary Costelloe], "Herman Obrist's Embroidered Decorations," *The Studio* 9 (1896): 98–105.

57. When Costelloe reassured Obrist that Berenson would not steal his ideas, she stressed that the essay on the Florentines was concerned primarily with the enjoyment of figure painting and only "HINTS" [*sic*] at the appreciation of line. Their residual enthusiasm for Obrist's work was based on admiration for his creative fancy as it manifested itself in the treatment of plant forms and other kinds of ornament. Though they disapproved of his figurative sculpture, Costelloe continued to believe that exposure to Berenson's criticism and ideas had "strengthened the native bent of his [Obrist's] genius which is towards unrepresentative decoration." Costelloe diary entry, 13 July 1895, I Tatti.

In January 1897 Berenson wrote Costelloe during a brief visit of Obrist to Florence that Obrist was now viewed as a *caposcuola* in Germany and was invited to lecture everywhere. Berenson also told her that his own art theories had taken hold of Obrist and had so transformed him that Obrist was barely conscious of their origin. Berenson to Mary Costelloe, 4 January and 5 January 1897, I Tatti.

It is worth repeating here, as Peg Weiss amply demonstrated, that the kind of experimentation with decorative pattern encouraged by Obrist in the milieu of the Jugendstil, as well as his ideas regarding art as the intensification of life, were decisive factors in the development of Munich abstraction.

58. Mary Costelloe to Hermann Obrist, 1 August 1895, Indiana.

59. Hermann Obrist to Mary Costelloe, 6 August 1895, Indiana. Samuels noted Schopenhauer as one of the writers Berenson claimed to have read before the age of nineteen, but references to him as a possible source of Berenson's aesthetic theories are rare. Samuels, *Connoisseur*, 25.

Obrist clearly had in mind Berenson's hypothesis, outlined in *The Florentine Painters,* that art provides a quickened sense of life because the artist is able to isolate certain essential object properties, such as tactile values and movement, and present them in accentuated form, divorced from the context of practical action. The Schopenhauer passage to which Obrist referred as "word for word B.B." is from vol. 1 of *The World as Will and Representation:* "and hence aesthetic pleasure is essentially one and the same, whether it be called forth from a work of art, or directly by the contemplation of nature and of life. The work of art is merely a means of facilitating that knowledge in which this pleasure consists. That the Idea comes to us more easily from the work of art than directly from nature and from reality, arises solely from the fact that the artist, who knew only the Idea and not reality, clearly repeated in his work only the Idea, separated it out from reality, and omitted all disturbing contingencies. The artist lets us peer into the world through his eyes. That he has these eyes, that he knows the essential in things which lies outside all relations, is the gift of genius and is inborn; but that he is able to lend us this gift, to let us see with his eyes, is acquired, and is the technical side of art." Arthur Schopenhauer, *The World as Will and Representation,* trans. E.F.J. Payne (New York: Dover Publications, 1966), 195.

60. Hermann Obrist to Mary Costelloe, [undated, possibly August 1895], Indiana. The references to Lipps in this letter suggests that it was written in response to Costelloe's letter of either 1 August or 8 August 1895 (both in collections at Indiana), but it could have been as late as summer 1896 because Obrist states that he has received *The Florentine Painters.* He could be referring either to the published book or to the as-yet-unpublished manuscript.

61. Lipps's lectures were delivered between 1894 and 1913 at the University of Munich. His principle of empathy was presented in *Raumästhetik und geometrisch-optische Täuschungen* (Leipzig: J. A. Barth, 1897).

62. Late in life Berenson acknowledged that he began to read the work of

Lipps as a young man but was put off by his style of writing and vocabulary. Berenson, *Rumor and Reflection,* 73–74.

63. Mary Costelloe to Hermann Obrist, 8 August 1895, Indiana.

64. Berenson claimed that when he read about art it was mainly to find others who thought as he did; he liked confirmation of his way of thinking even though he was not very interested in the ideas of others. Berenson, *Sunset and Twilight,* 443.

65. Berenson to Senda Berenson, 2 June 1895, I Tatti.

66. E. H. Gombrich, among others, saw in Hildebrand's thesis the origins of Berenson's theory of tactile values. Gombrich, *Art and Illusion,* 16.

67. Berenson to Mary Costelloe, [1893/1894], I Tatti.

68. Costelloe diary entry, 17 February 1896, I Tatti.

69. Mary Costelloe to Hermann Obrist, 8 August 1895, Indiana.

70. Bernard Berenson, *The Florentine Painters of the Renaissance* (New York: G. P. Putnam's Sons, 1896), 40, hereafter referred to as *The Florentine Painters.* (See note 20 regarding source of quotations.)

71. Ibid.

72. This is made clear in an article in defense of Berenson's theories by Mary Costelloe, written for *Atlantic Monthly.* When she reviewed his books, Costelloe often elucidated principles underlying Berenson's critical position that are implied but never clearly explained in the essays themselves. "The Philosophy of Enjoyment of Art," *Atlantic Monthly* 77 (June 1896): 844–88. Samuels attributes this unsigned article to Mary Costelloe.

73. Berenson, *The Florentine Painters,* 41.

74. Costelloe diary entry summarizing Berenson's letter to Reinach, 22 December 1895, I Tatti.

75. Berenson, *The Florentine Painters,* 45.

76. Ibid., 54.

77. Kenneth Clark made this observation in "Bernard Berenson," *Burlington Magazine* 102 (September 1960): 384.

78. Berenson, *The Florentine Painters,* 42.

79. Ibid., 42–43.

80. Both Russell and Obrist objected to Berenson's curious concept of pleasure. Obrist, as has been pointed out, thought it too narrow; Russell's criticism was more severe and troublesome.

81. Costelloe diary entry, 13 May 1895, I Tatti.

82. The difference in their positions is evident when Costelloe's reference to Raphael is compared with Berenson's discussion in *The Florentine Painters* of Giotto and Cimabue. Berenson argues that we exhaust ourselves trying to take in Cimabue because the mass and position of the figures are unclear. Thus we strain more than we would when taking in actual objects, and

our sense of capacity is diminished. Berenson, *The Florentine Painters*, 44.
83. Costelloe diary entry, 16 May 1895, I Tatti.
84. Costelloe diary entry, 26 May 1895, I Tatti. The Degas had been lent to them by a friend in Florence.
85. Berenson to Mary Costelloe, [January 1892; undated, approximate date added by Costelloe], I Tatti. The reference to the Spoleto door recalls an episode Berenson would describe later in life in which the vitalizing potential of decoration was made evident to him: "I recall when it first came to me. I had already published two books. For years I had been inquiring, excavating, dredging my inner self, and searching in my conscious experience for a satisfying test. I needed a test to apply to the artifacts that I thought I admired but could not hypnotize or habituate myself to enjoy with complete abandon, while the worm of doubt kept gnawing at the felicity of the ideal paradise. Then one morning as I was gazing at the leafy scrolls carved on the door jambs of San Pietro outside Spoleto, suddenly stem, tendril, and foliage became alive and, in becoming alive, made me feel as if I had emerged into the light after long groping in the darkness of an initiation. I felt as one illumined, and beheld a world where every outline, every edge, and every surface was in living relation to me and not, as hitherto, in a merely cognitive one." Berenson, *Aesthetics and History*, 72.

Berenson may have erred in recalling the date of this experience. If it had come after the publication of his first two books, it would have occurred no earlier than 1895, and he had already referred to the door in an 1892 letter to Costelloe. Furthermore, Costelloe's diary entry of 21 May 1900 notes that it had been seven years since they had discovered the decoration at Spoleto. This is confirmed by an earlier entry of 3 May 1893, in which she recorded four hours of rapturous enjoyment at Spoleto. Since Costelloe met Obrist in February 1893 and he, on occasion, traveled with them, it is entirely possible that he was present and may have urged them on in their appreciation of linear decoration. Costelloe diary entry, 21 May 1900, I Tatti; Costelloe diary entry, 3 May 1893, I Tatti.

86. The aesthetic effect of space composition, which would be taken up in Berenson's next book, *The Central Italian Painters*, was clearly not connected with his admiration for Degas. Although his enthusiasm for him never waned, in old age Berenson stubbornly upheld that Degas, for all his gifts, was a poor composer. His inability to appreciate the novelty of Degas's compositions and his unique sense of space is indicative of the kind of blind spot that caused Berenson to denounce all modern art that violated his sense of spatial clarity.

87. Berenson, *The Florentine Painters*, 68.
88. Ibid., 68–69.

89. Ibid., 61.

90. In many ways, Berenson was a classic fin de siècle neurasthenic; he complained often that nervous exhaustion kept him from working (although he seems to have been an indefatigable tourist). I am indebted to Sidney Alexander for helpful comments on the compensatory physicality of Berenson's theories. Comments are from my interview with Alexander, July 1989. Vernon Lee, who was very close to Berenson when he was writing about the Florentines, made an issue of this when she reviewed the essay for *Mind*. Although Lee maintained that she did not accept Berenson's definition of pleasure as complete, she understood his chief preoccupation to be the way in which art, through the realization of objects and movement, gives pleasure in an organic or bodily way. Vernon Lee, "New Books," rev. of *The Florentine Painters, Mind*, n.s. 5 (1896): 271.

91. Mary Logan [Mary Costelloe], "The New Art Criticism," *Atlantic Monthly* 76 (August 1895): 263–70.

92. [Mary Costelloe], "The Philosophy of Enjoyment of Art," rev. of *The Florentine Painters, Atlantic Monthly* 77 (June 1896): 847.

93. Berenson, *The Florentine Painters*, 73.

94. Ibid., 74.

95. Ibid., 75.

96. Ibid., 76.

97. Costelloe diary entry, 14 September 1895, I Tatti.

98. Saisselin also makes a case for the satisfaction of desire as the foundation of Berenson's theory of aesthetics, but he connects this with the subtleties of the art trade rather than his professed humanism (the desire for a glorious but possible humanity). He argues that despite the priority given sensual gratification (which served Berenson as a kind of advertising to prompt the purchase of objects) by attaching to it the potential for life-enhancement, Berenson conferred on art an aura of seriousness and spirituality, which safeguarded it from insinuations that the desire fulfilled was primarily for amusement or possession. Saisselin, *The Bourgeois and the Bibelot*, chap. 7, "I Tatti; or, Sublimating Sales."

99. Bernard Berenson, *Sketch for a Self-Portrait* (London: Constable; New York, Pantheon, 1949), 39.

100. More than one author has made reference to the probability that Berenson's acute perceptions as a young critic inhibited his subsequent development. In a review of several late books by Berenson, Clement Greenberg observes that "fifty years ago or more, in his books on the regional schools of Italian Renaissance painting, he laid out a critical panorama that has withstood where it did not anticipate the revisions of judgment occasioned since the effect of modern art on taste." But Greenberg added that Berenson's early

rightness became a liability. Greenberg, "Greenberg on Berenson," rev. of *Piero della Francesca; or, The Ineloquent in Art* and *The Arch of Constantine; or, The Decline of Form*, 151.

Kenneth Clark also praised Berenson's early essays for their great concentration of thought, but he claimed that they said so much in so little space that it was difficult for Berenson to expand them in a more leisurely study without repeating himself. Clark, "Bernard Berenson," 385.

By the time Berenson did attempt a comprehensive statement of these principles, in *Aesthetics and History*, they had become doctrinaire anachronisms, losing the provocative power so much in evidence in their original context. Also, as Meyer Schapiro and others have observed, in old age Berenson would use these principles to condemn everything he did not like, especially modern art.

Even though Berenson did not demonstrate the kind of deepening insight and critical growth one might expect of one who saw so much and lived so long, he did identify the major issues that would occupy the best critical minds of the twentieth century. When he was not a direct influence on subsequent criticism, he was at the very least an extraordinarily perceptive cartographer.

101. Bernard Berenson, *The Central Italian Painters of the Renaissance* (New York: G. P. Putnam's Sons, 1897), 84–85. (See note 20 for source of quotations). Hereafter referred to as *The Central Italian Painters*.

102. Ibid., 85. This distinction between illustration and decoration was crucial to the development of formalist criticism and is still invoked by both its defenders and its detractors, who prefer the words "content" and "form." Donald Kuspit saw in it a direct link to Greenberg's separation of cubist-inspired modernist abstraction from romantic, literary, expressionistic art and to his notion of the purification of art. See Donald Kuspit, *Clement Greenberg* (Madison: University of Wisconsin Press, 1979), 95–96.

Neither Greenberg nor Berenson argued that art was without content, but after realizing the extremity of this distinction and the kind of painting that would seek justification in it (long before Greenberg and abstract expressionism), Berenson modified his definition of illustration. In *Aesthetics and History* he argued that illustration was representation and made it a requirement of all legitimate art. This will be discussed in detail in Chapter 4.

103. Berenson, *The Central Italian Painters*, 84.

104. Ibid., 84.

105. Ibid., 87.

106. Ibid., 120.

107. The relationship between architecture and music was well known as an aesthetic concept, traceable to antiquity and periodically resurfacing in

subsequent texts on classical architecture. When Berenson claimed here that it had never been explained, he probably meant in the specifically psycho-biological manner in which he was attempting to treat the visual arts.

108. Berenson, *The Central Italian Painters*, 121.

109. Samuels connects the principle with Hildebrand, who was an important source for Berenson's theory of tactile values, as well. Samuels, *Connoisseur*, 179.

110. Berenson, *The Central Italian Painters*, 122. Although Berenson connected this concept with religious emotion, Michael Fixler made a case for space composition as evidence of Berenson's subconscious desire to transcend his Jewish self and the constraints of his immigrant, outsider identity. Fixler's fascinating essay is one of the most original and provocative interpretations of Berenson's aesthetic theories. Its relative obscurity is surprising in light of the current interest in psychoanalytic theory and the arts. Michael Fixler, "Bernard Berenson of Butremanz," *Commentary* 36 (August 1963): 135–43.

111. Berenson, *The Central Italian Painters*, 123. It is precisely because of this kind of dialogue between interpretative strategies and formal analysis, which brings to mind the critical discourse of the last two decades, that it is rash to assume Berenson's relevance as a critic has been exhausted. He loathed such decoding of images and extrapolation of meaning and would set himself in vehement opposition to this tendency in American art history, especially as it manifested itself earlier in the century in the work of Erwin Panofsky and his followers.

112. Ibid., 122. It is interesting to compare this passage on landscape painting to his discussion of the same topic in *The Florentine Painters*. There he stated that if giving palpable reality to visible objects were all that mattered in landscape painting, then it would have reached its most perfect form in the hands of Northern Renaissance painters, who render distant objects with great clarity and precision. But here he claimed that the pleasure taken in landscape painting is only to a limited degree a matter of sight and to a greater extent a matter of intense well-being, "The painter's problem, [therefore,] is not merely to render the tactile values of the visible objects, but to convey more rapidly and unfailingly than nature would do, the *consciousness* of an unusually intense degree of well-being." Berenson, *The Florentine Painters*, 62.

113. See Clark, "Bernard Berenson," and Nicolson's response to Meyer Schapiro's essay, "Mr. Berenson's Values." Benedict Nicolson, "Schapiro on Berenson," *Encounter* 16 (April 1961): 60–63.

114. See Schapiro, "Mr. Berenson's Values," and John Rewald, *Cézanne and America: Dealers, Collectors, Artists and Critics* (Princeton: Princeton University Press, 1989).

115. When Schapiro met Berenson in the 1920s, he had ample opportunity to hear the usual diatribes on modern art. Evidently, he had his own notions about how to open up Berenson's mind, because in January 1929 Schapiro sent him the reprint of an essay on modern art that he had written as part of an introduction to contemporary civilization, for use in an undergraduate course at Columbia University. Berenson had asked Schapiro (as was his custom when he met younger scholars) to send copies of any future publications. Schapiro, regretting that his work on the sculpture at Moissac, France, was not ready, sent this instead. In a cover letter, he described it as a work of propaganda not erudition and hoped to have Berenson's favorable response. Meyer Schapiro to Berenson, 27 January 1929, I Tatti. (A copy of this pamphlet is still extant in the Berenson Library at I Tatti, entitled "Art in the Contemporary World," dated 1928.)

To send Berenson such an essay in the 1920s, when he was at the peak of his power and influence and already an outspoken critic of modern culture, was a subversive, even courageous, act on the part of this enormously gifted scholar, who obviously felt he had little to fear from the consequences. Berenson respected Schapiro, but he could be a ruthless enemy when provoked. Also, at the time of their meeting he could have done a great deal to further Schapiro's career, as he did for appreciative disciples such as Kenneth Clark and John Walker. The audacity of Schapiro's decision to identify himself in Berenson's mind with modern art becomes evident when one considers that many visitors to I Tatti would not even discuss contemporary art with Berenson for fear of arousing his ire. The reluctance of Berenson's guests to bring up the subject of modern art in his presence was recalled by John Walker in my interview with Walker in 1989.

116. Nicolson, "Schapiro on Berenson," 62.

117. Hughes, "Only in America," 26.

118. Saisselin, *Bourgeois and the Bibelot*, 143.

119. Even a cursory review of the vast literature dealing with Cézanne criticism furnishes ample evidence that coming to terms with Cézanne's legacy has been an ongoing concern of twentieth-century art history and theory. See, for example, George Heard Hamilton, "Cézanne and His Critics," in *Cézanne: The Late Work* (New York: Museum of Modern Art, 1977), 139–49; and Richard Shiff, *Cézanne and the End of Impressionism* (Chicago: University of Chicago Press, 1984).

120. Objective appraisals of Berenson are hard to come by; Rewald's hostility is especially evident in the epilogue to *Cézanne and America*. That Schapiro also disliked Berenson is no secret. This was probably a decisive factor in shaping Schapiro's brilliant but largely unsympathetic portrait of him for *Encounter*, coming as it did in the wake of a tidal wave of laudatory and naive obituaries of the "sage of Settignano" in the popular press. See

Helen Epstein, "Meyer Schapiro: A Passion to Know and Make Known," *Art News* 82 (1983): 60–85.

121. Rewald, *Cézanne and America,* 20.

122. Ibid., 20.

123. Ibid., 19.

124. Ibid.

125. Costelloe diary entry, 26 April 1896, I Tatti. In fall of the previous year, Costelloe noted another visit from Fabbri, during which they discussed the role of representation in art. Fabbri took the position that no good work of art could resemble nature and Berenson that a work could be good *even if* (emphasis Costelloe's) it resembled nature. Costelloe diary entry, 19 October 1895, I Tatti.

Both of these meetings took place while Berenson was working on *The Central Italian Painters,* and because it was his custom to engage sympathetic minds like Fabbri in an effort to crystallize his thought, one cannot help but wonder to what extent Fabbri and his enthusiasm for Cézanne hangs over this essay.

126. Whereas Berenson usually found himself in tune with Fabbri and his ideas, they did not agree about space composition. In November 1900 Costelloe noted a visit from Fabbri and her suspicion that he lacked all appreciation of space composition because he was indifferent to Raphael and disliked Perugino. Several years later, in March 1904, Berenson wrote his wife from Paris that he was spending time with Fabbri. It was in July of this year that he made a remark (cited by Rewald) about Fabbri's disappointing Cézannes. In December 1904 Berenson and Fabbri were still arguing about space composition. Berenson tried to persuade Fabbri during a visit to I Tatti that space composition was a separate art, independent of form; Fabbri would not concede, but because his opposition was based on Berenson's former insistence on the priority of tactile values, he was somewhat consoled. Fabbri seems to have tried to get Berenson to stick to the artistic essentials he had outlined in *The Florentine Painters,* volume and mass, and it is entirely possible that he cited Cézanne as the very embodiment of these principles. This would explain a remark made by Berenson somewhat earlier that Fabbri was absurd to reduce painting to Cézanne. Costelloe diary entry, 21 November 1900, I Tatti; Berenson to Mary Berenson, 21 March 1904, I Tatti; Berenson to Mary Berenson, 1 July 1904, I Tatti; Berenson to Mary Berenson, 24 December 1904, I Tatti; Berenson to Mary Berenson, 23 November 1899, I Tatti.

127. Berenson to Mary Costelloe, 27 June 1896, I Tatti. This would confirm Rewald's suggestion that Berenson saw his first Cézannes at the Luxembourg Museum, unless of course Fabbri had brought some of his newly acquired paintings with him to Florence that spring.

128. Rewald, *Cézanne and America*, 26, 339.

129. Costelloe diary entry, 27 June 1897, I Tatti. This entry suggests that Berenson connected Cézanne with the quality of impersonality he saw in Piero della Franscesca long before he published his essay on this topic in 1954, *Piero della Francesca; or, the Ineloquent in Art*. It is sometimes assumed that Berenson came to this conclusion only years later, after the Piero revival of the early twentieth century. See Rewald, *Cézanne and America*, 71 and 339–40. The next day was spent seeing more Cézannes at Durand-Ruel and correcting proofs of *The Central Italian Painters*. It would be interesting to know if the reference to Cézanne was in the original manuscript or was added at this time. Costelloe diary entry, 28 June 1897, I Tatti.

130. Berenson was always conservative in his praise of artists who had captured the imagination of a large audience, and in this respect Cézanne was no exception. In *Sunset and Twilight* Berenson remembered feeling lingering doubt in the back of his mind about both Cézanne and Caravaggio, who in the 1950s was riding a wave of popularity. This, of course, did not prevent him from availing himself of such sentiment if he thought it would facilitate the sale of a painting, as Rewald aptly points out. Rewald, *Cézanne and America*, 340.

Berenson would continue to remark on Cézanne in conversation, in letters, and in print for the next half-century and would keep up on what was being published on the artist, as well. But as generations of critics devoted themselves to crawling inside Cézanne's mind, Berenson's appraisal of him was and remained strictly visual. On a number of occasions he compared the landscape vision of Cézanne to that of the quattrocento Italian painter Fra Angelico as "a rendering of nature singularly like my own behold; and they are eyes that see with Cézanne and his contemporaries." Berenson, *Homeless Paintings of the Renaissance*, ed. Hanna Kiel (Bloomington: Indiana University Press, 1969), 226.

In a letter to the American critic Royal Cortissoz, Berenson wrote that Cézanne "fought the brave fight, to make us realize again with almost Romanesque acerbity and even fury, the full weight of a tri-dimensional object," calling him a "great organist with the dripping brush" who painted "chorals of sky-shaping gravity." Berenson to Royal Cortissoz, 26 April 1938, Royal Cortissoz Papers, Beinecke Rare Book and Manuscript Library, Yale University, New Haven, Conn.

The increased sophistication of formalist art criticism gave Berenson a better vocabulary to articulate his observations regarding Cézanne and his plasticity, but it did not substantially alter them. The following remarks, recorded by Umberto Morra, demonstrate that Berenson clearly had incorporated the critical language of writers like Fry, but the substance of his comments remained essentially the same. Comparing him again to Piero della Francesca, he stated: "Cézanne represents that same tradition almost totally transferred to landscape, with his absolutely cubic values of plastic forms affirming themselves in a way which never occurred before, and values of 'form' being transferred from the country to the sky, which until then had been the background and scenario of paintings. Cézanne incorporates the sky with the earth; it forms part of a whole, and is the live interior of a solid." Bernard Berenson, *Conversations with Berenson*, recorded by Umberto Morra, trans. Florence Hammond (Boston: Houghton Mifflin, 1965), 268–69.

This is what Berenson meant when he said that Cézanne gave the sky tactile values. He came to terms with Cézanne as he did every other painter— with his eyes racing way ahead of his mind and pen.

131. See Sandra S. Phillips, "The Art Criticism of Walter Pach," *Art Bulletin* 65 (March 1983): 106–22. Phillips dedicated this article to John Rewald.

132. Rewald, *Cézanne and America*, 135.

133. Mary Berenson diary entry, 6 January 1906. Mary Berenson wrote that she met Roger Fry at Durand-Ruel's and with him saw their private collection of Cézannes and Degas.

134. Rewald, *Cézanne and America*, 153, note 29. Berenson was paranoid and secretive about his ideas, but his distrust of Fry was especially pronounced. Frequent references to it appear in his correspondence with his wife, who stayed on cordial terms with Fry even after his relationship with Berenson had deteriorated. According to John Walker, Roger Fry and his theft of ideas was a favorite tirade of Berenson's in the years he spent at I Tatti as a young man. My interview with John Walker, 1989.

In 1909, in what appears to be the only recorded conversation in which Berenson and Fry did discuss Cézanne, Berenson imagined that Fry expressed admiration for the painter to impress him. He told Mary Berenson in a letter that he ran into Fry at Vollard's gallery, where they looked at things together, and that Fry, like Israel Zangwill, admired all the works that Berenson admired, those of Cézanne for instance, but even more the work of Paul Gauguin. (Berenson used to complain that his friend Zangwill pretended to like whatever he praised.) Berenson to Mary Berenson, 27 October 1909, I Tatti.

135. Berenson claimed that the stock of visual images we acquire through our familarity with a given art form has direct bearing on how we see. "Let anyone give us shapes and colors which we cannot instantly match in our paltry stock of hackneyed forms and tints, and we shake our heads at his failure to reproduce things as we know they certainly are, or we accuse him of insincerity." Berenson, *The Central Italian Painters*, 105–6. According to

Berenson, the derision with which plein air painting was initially met and the inability of many Western viewers to appreciate Asian art could be explained by conflicting habits of visualization.

136. Ibid., 107–8.

137. Ibid., 108.

Chapter 3

1. Kenyon Cox, "Berenson's Florentine Drawings," rev. of *The Drawings of the Florentine Painters, Nation,* 6 August 1903, 117. The debate over the relative merits of Berenson's connoisseurship versus his criticism has been an ongoing concern in the literature, although it is now recognized that the two were inseparable. See especially Walter Pach, "Connoisseurship or Criticism," rev. of *Essays in the Study of Sienese Painting, Dial,* 2 November 1918, 365–66.

2. Mary Logan [Mary Costelloe], "The New Art Criticism," *Atlantic Monthly* 76 (August 1895): 263–70.

3. Ibid., 270.

4. [Mary Costelloe], "The Philosophy of Enjoyment of Art," rev. of *The Florentine Painters, Atlantic Monthly* 77 (June 1896): 848.

5. Bernard Berenson, *The Study and Criticism of Italian Art,* a series of anthologies comprised chiefly of articles by Berenson previously published in various art periodicals, was issued in three volumes: 1901 (London: George Bell and Sons); 1902 (2d ser. London: J. Murray); and 1916 (3d ser. London: George Bell and Sons).

6. Bernard Berenson, "Rudiments of Connoisseurship (a Fragment)," in *The Study and Criticism of Italian Art,* 2d ser., 111–48. This essay is the only protracted discussion of Berenson's method extant.

7. Kenyon Cox, "Books on Painting," rev. of *The Study and Criticism of Italian Art, Nation,* 7 November 1901, 362–63; and Kenyon Cox, "Books on Art," rev. of *The Study and Criticism of Italian Art,* 2d ser., *Nation,* 6 November 1902, 364. See Ernest Samuels, *Bernard Berenson: The Making of a Connoisseur* (Cambridge: Harvard University Press, 1979), for further discussion of period reviews (hereafter cited as Samuels, *Connoisseur*).

8. American critic Royal Cortissoz wrote generally favorable reviews of Berenson's books, but he too was skeptical of the method, especially as it was practiced by Berenson's followers. In a satirical discussion of the problem, written for *Art and Common Sense,* Cortissoz maintained that though modern connoisseurship had added much to the study of Italian art, those

who practiced it were carried away with their own success, and its adherents spent much of their time taking in each other's laundry. Royal Cortissoz, *Art and Common Sense* (New York: Charles Scribner's Sons, 1913), 8.

9. Roger Fry, "Fine Arts," rev. of *The Study and Criticism of Italian Art, Athenaeum,* 16 November 1901, 668–69.

10. Bernard Berenson, *The Drawings of the Florentine Painters.* 2 vols. (London: J. Murray, 1903); expanded and enlarged to 3 volumes in 1938 (Chicago: University of Chicago Press).

11. Cox, "Berenson's Florentine Drawings," 116–17. Sydney Freedberg defined connoisseurship as "the use of expert knowledge of a field (in this case, the history of art) to identify objects in it, determine their quality, and assess their character." Sydney Freedberg, "Berenson, Connoisseurship, and the History of Art," *New Criterion* 7 (February 1989): 10. Berenson's own definition in "Rudiments of Connoisseurship" was "the comparison of works of art with a view to determining their reciprocal relationship." Berenson, *The Study and Criticism of Italian Art,* 2d ser., 113.

12. Although *The Drawings of the Florentine Painters* is widely regarded as Berenson's most important scholarly achievement, it will not be considered extensively here because its theoretical concerns fall outside the scope of the present study.

13. Edgar Wind, *Art and Anarchy* (New York: Alfred A. Knopf, 1964), 42. It was Wind's belief that Berenson's aestheticism was a natural outgrowth of Morellianism, an intensification of the connoisseur's quest for authenticity, and that it was not necessary to assume that he was led to it by Pater, James, or German aestheticians. In the introduction to the English-language edition of Giovanni Morelli's *Italian Painters: Borghese and Dorai Pamfili Galleries in Rome* (London, 1910), A. H. Layard notes that Morelli also studied and documented drawings and had intended a volume on them, which was left unfinished at his death in 1891. Layard states that Morelli's unfinished volume on drawings passed to his disciple Gustavo Frizzoni with hopes that he might finish it.

14. Cox, "Berenson's Florentine Drawings," 116–17; and "Fine Arts," an unsigned review of *The Drawings of the Florentine Painters, Athenaeum,* 12 November 1904, pt. 1, 662–63; 3 December 1904, pt. 2, 769–71.

15. Bernard Berenson, *A Sienese Painter of the Franciscan Legend* (London: J. M. Dent and Sons, 1909), 33. Originally published in *Burlington Magazine* 3 (1903); pt. 1, 3–35; pt. 2, 171–84.

16. It is instructive to recall that these articles preceded Wilhelm Worringer's essay "Abstraction and Empathy" in which a similar distinction is made between the respective tendencies of Occidental and Oriental art.

Wilhelm Worringer, *Abstraction and Empathy*, trans. Michael Bullock (New York: International Universities Press, 1953).

17. Berenson, *A Sienese Painter of the Franciscan Legend*, 15.

18. Ibid., 38.

19. Berenson was again in the United States during the winter of 1903–1904, after these articles were published. He no doubt discussed them with Ross, whom he thought adhered too stubbornly to the priority of decorative pattern and pictorial design, neglecting the more artistic elements of form and movement. Mary Berenson diary entries, 12 November 1903; and 27 November 1903, from the collection of the Berenson Archive, Harvard University Center for Italian Renaissance Studies, Villa I Tatti, Florence, Italy (hereafter cited as I Tatti).

Later Berenson would confide to his wife that Ross was blinded to quality by his "requirements" and could be unintelligible when in a mood to look at everything as if it were a "turkey carpet." Berenson to Mary Berenson, 31 August 1913, I Tatti.

20. Mary Berenson diary entry, 29 January 1907, I Tatti.

21. Kenneth Clark pointed out that even though Berenson's normative standards were extremely exclusionary, in the Sassetta essays he "helped us to recognize precisely those values which his later attitude seems to reject." See Kenneth Clark, "Thoughts of a Great Humanist," rev. of *Aesthetics and History in the Visual Arts*, *Burlington Magazine* 91 (May 1949): 145.

22. Bernard Berenson, *The North Italian Painters of the Renaissance* (New York: G. P. Putnam's Sons, 1907), 144 (see Chapter 2, note 20 for source of quotations; hereafter referred to as *The North Italian Painters*).

23. Ibid., 145.

24. It is worth noting that the concept of the archaic advanced by Berenson in this essay is not incompatible with the rhetoric of classicism, then dominating the critical discourse surrounding artists such as Cézanne, whose death in 1906 is viewed by many historians as a seminal event in the history of early modernism. There are obvious differences, the most important being that Berenson had in mind the development of a very specific and narrowly conceived figurative model. But a similar emphasis on the heroic struggle of the artist to strike a compromise between art and nature (or concept and percept), the quest for rarified artistic essentials in defiance of the demand for associative meaning, and the insistence on the superiority of this art in the face of exaggeration and imperfection, which are inevitable consequences of the process, can be said to echo much of early modernist criticism.

25. It is impossible not to think of Heinrich Wölfflin in this discussion.

26. Berenson, *The North Italian Painters*, 173. In the original text Beren-

son identified the little-known painter Domenico Brusasorci as the first purely pictorial Italian artist; a footnote to the 1938 edition revises this judgment to credit Veronese.

27. Ibid., 173. This discussion of purely pictorial modes of visualizing prompted Schapiro to conclude that in 1907, a crucial year in the history of modernism, Berenson still thought of modern art in nineteenth-century terms. Meyer Schapiro, "Mr. Berenson's Values," *Encounter* 16 (January 1961): 63.

Though there is truth to this observation, it is necessary to remember the historical context of these essays and the extremely small circle of individuals privy to the existence, much less the intentions, of the artistic vanguard. Berenson complained as late as 1912 that he was still meeting people who had just heard of Monet, are confused by Degas, and frightened by the mention of Cézanne's name. Berenson to Mary Berenson, 26 April 1912, I Tatti.

28. David Brown, *Berenson and the Connoisseurship of Italian Painting* (Washington, D.C.: National Gallery of Art, 1979), 14.

29. Berenson, *The North Italian Painters*, 175.

30. Ibid., 184–85.

31. Roger Fry, "The Painters of North Italy," rev. of *The North Italian Painters*, *Burlington Magazine* 12 (March 1908): 347 and 348. That Berenson was capable of employing this sort of method had already been demonstrated in the Sassetta essays.

32. Berenson, "The Decline of Art," in *The North Italian Painters*, 201.

33. Ibid., 202.

34. Ibid., 203.

35. Ibid., 201, 203.

36. Ibid., 203–4.

37. Hermann Obrist to Berenson, 28 November 1907, I Tatti. Obrist no doubt applauded the antiacademic tenor. He also told Berenson in this letter that he was thankful to be at work in the only domain where anything "archaic" was going on—in the arts and crafts movement—where they (artists) were again beginning at the beginning.

38. Fry, "The Painters of North Italy," 349.

39. A number of these articles were collected in the following anthologies: Berenson, *The Study and Criticism of Italian Art*, 3d ser.; Bernard Berenson, *Essays in the Study of Sienese Painting* (New York: Frederick Sherman, 1918); Bernard Berenson, *Three Essays in Method* (Oxford: Clarendon Press, 1926); and Bernard Berenson, *Studies in Medieval Painting* (New Haven: Yale University Press; Oxford: Oxford University Press, 1930). Unless otherwise noted, quotations are from the English versions published in these anthologies.

40. Berenson, "Notes on Tuscan Painters of the Trecento in the Stadel Institute at Frankfurt" (1926), in *Studies in Medieval Painting* (New Haven: Yale University Press; Oxford: Oxford University Press, 1930), 84.

41. Berenson, "Two Twelfth-Century Paintings from Constantinople" (1921), in ibid., 7.

42. Berenson, *Venetian Painting in America: The Fifteenth Century* (New York: Frederick Sherman, 1916), 55. Berenson's diatribe against interpretation at a time when he was elsewhere urging a return to humanistic values in art may, at least in part, be attributable to his desire to assuage the anti-Catholic sentiments of his American clients. Saisselin points out that Berenson's disinterested aesthetics effectively neutralized the otherwise troublesome content of Italian religious painting for Protestant American buyers. See Remy Saisselin, *The Bourgeois and the Bibelot*, (New Brunswick, N.J.: Rutgers University Press, 1984), 145.

43. Berenson, "Leonardo," in *The Study and Criticism of Italian Art*, 3d ser., 1–37.

44. Ibid., 9.

45. Ibid., 13.

46. Ibid., 12.

47. Ibid., 33.

Chapter 4

1. Berenson to William Ivins, 29 August 1935, Ivins Papers in the collection of the Archives of American Art, Washington, D.C.

2. Bernard Berenson, *Rumor and Reflection, 1941–1944* (London: Constable; New York: Simon and Schuster, 1952), 245.

3. Peggy Guggenheim became acquainted with Berenson's early publications through Arman Lowengard, who was Duveen's nephew. She later told Berenson how much his books had meant to her and he wondered why, then, she collected contemporary art. When Guggenheim responded that she could not afford old masters (and that she felt it was one's duty to support the art of one's time) he told her: "You should have come to me, dear, I would have found you bargains." Peggy Guggenheim, *Out of This Century: The Informal Memories of Peggy Guggenheim* (New York: Dial Press, 1949), 329.

4. Interview with Clement Greenberg, April 1989. Helen Frankenthaler and Clement Greenberg visited Berenson at Vallombrosa in September 1953. Berenson mentioned their visit in a letter to Margaret Barr. Berenson to Margaret Scolari Barr, 2 September 1953, in the collection of the Berenson

Archive, Harvard University Center for Italian Renaissance Studies, Villa I Tatti, Florence, Italy (hereafter I Tatti).

5. I am grateful to Rona Roob, archivist of the Museum of Modern Art for this and other pertinent information regarding Berenson's relationship with the Barrs. Margaret Scolari Barr frequently wrote to Berenson about exhibitions at the Museum of Modern Art and sent him articles from American art publications that she thought might interest him. On occasion, he wrote to her with requests for photographs of things he had seen reproduced in the museum's collection catalogs, which he in turn used as illustrations in his books.

6. When planning the exhibition "Fantastic Art, Dada, and Surrealism," the Barrs encountered some difficulty borrowing paintings by Giorgio de Chirico from the Italian collector and writer Mario Broglio, and they called on Berenson to intervene on their behalf. On 14 September 1936 Margaret Barr wrote Berenson asking him to vouch for them as a personal favor, not as an endorsement of the museum or its exhibitions. She told Berenson the museum would also consider buying some of Broglio's pictures, adding that she had already written Brolio, giving him a heavy dose of flattery for *Valori Plastici*, the Italian periodical he founded and ran from 1918 to 1922. Berenson agreed to have his personal secretary, Nicki Mariano, intervene for the Barrs. In a letter of 17 November 1936, sent along with a copy of the catalog, Margaret Barr told Berenson that Mariano's name appeared in the acknowledgments because she had made the actual contact and because they assumed that Berenson probably would not like his name associated with the project. Barr also told Berenson that he might have had many suggestions for the historical part of the exhibition, but she did not ask him because she thought he would not be interested. Margaret Scolari Barr to Berenson, 14 September and 17 November 1936, I Tatti.

7. In 1908 Berenson bought a small landscape from Matisse, which he lent to the historic Post-Impressionist exhibition at Grafton Gallery in 1910. John Walker remembered that the painting was hung somewhere in the library at I Tatti and was visible all the time. Berenson owned the painting until 1938, when he presented it to his good friend Prince Paul of Yugoslavia for the Belgrade Museum. Interview with John Walker, March 1989.

Berenson told Alfred Barr that he never met Matisse when the artist visited Florence in 1907, possibly because he was away at the time. Berenson to Alfred Barr, 23 September and 20 December 1949, Archives of the Museum of Modern Art, Alfred Barr and Margaret Scolari Barr Papers, New York.

Alfred Barr, *Matisse: His Art and His Public* (New York: Museum of Modern Art, 1951), is in the library at I Tatti, with the inscription: "For BB with affection (and some misgivings). Alfred Barr, New York, December 1951."

8. These recollections are from my conversation with Leo Steinberg April 1990; and from Berenson to George Biddle, 20 August 1957, I Tatti. Leo Steinberg later wrote a brief article on Berenson when he reviewed the catalog of Berenson's personal collection for *Harpers*. Leo Steinberg, " 'BB' as Collector," rev. of *The Berenson Collection, Harper's* 230 (March 1965): 154–56.

9. Margaret Scolari Barr to Berenson, [1948], I Tatti.

10. Margaret Scolari Barr to Berenson, 19 January 1937, I Tatti. Margaret Barr may very well be talking about the exhibition catalog, *Cubism and Abstract Art*. It is interesting to note that in a recent article by Susan Platt on this exhibition and the historiography of cubism, Barr's training in Berensonian connoisseurship as an art historical method is cited as a major factor in the largely formalist approach to the history of modernism that underlies this exhibition. See Susan N. Platt, "Modernism, Formalism, and Politics: The Cubism and Abstract Art Exhibition of 1936," *Art Journal* 47 (Winter 1988): 284–95.

Margaret Barr's fears were not unwarranted; a year before meeting Alfred Barr, Berenson wrote to Philip Hofer: "Alfred Barr I do not know. Surely he can have no aesthetic convictions or he would not have written encyclopedically about 'abstract art' and directed an Institooshin [*sic*] whose activity is so effectively anti-humanistic." Berenson to Philip Hofer, 23 January 1947, in A. K. McComb, ed., *The Selected Letters of Bernard Berenson* (Boston: Houghton Mifflin, 1963), 242.

11. Berenson to Margaret Scolari Barr, 21 July 1950, I Tatti. It is worth noting that Berenson was eighty-five years old in 1950.

12. Berenson to Margaret Scolari Barr, 18 January 1954, I Tatti.

13. Berenson to Margaret Scolari Barr, 13 March 1958, I Tatti.

14. Margaret Barr wrote Berenson asking if Dali ever turned up at I Tatti; she told him she would like to know what he thought of Dali and Gala and wondered if Dali had shown Berenson any of his drawings. Several days later Berenson wrote her that Dali did not show up and he did not regret it. Margaret Scolari Barr to Berenson, 22 October 1938, I Tatti; Berenson to Margaret Scolari Barr, 8 November 1938, I Tatti.

15. Bernard Berenson *Conversations with Berenson*, recorded by Umberto Morra and trans. Florence Hammond (Boston: Houghton Mifflin, 1965), 248.

16. Berenson diary entry, 14 May 1949, in Hanna Kiel, ed., *The Bernard Berenson Treasury, 1887–1958*, ed. Hanna Kiel (New York: Simon and Schuster, 1962), 280–81.

17. Ibid., 21 May 1950.

18. Berenson, *Conversations with Berenson*, 238–39.

19. Berenson to Frank Jewett Mather, 12 December 1919, I Tatti. Even

more telling were his remarks in the same year to his Harvard friend Barrett
Wendell, whom he also told of his renewed interest in late medieval art: "It
is all so futile in the light of the hell-soul revealed by so-called humanity
during the last ten months. So let me feast my eyes and enjoy and be silent
for tomorrow it will have disappeared. The new order will prevail with its
gospel, namely the greatest quantity of food for the greatest number of bel-
lies. The war has hastened the triumph of the new rapture by a half century
at least. Thus I shall be overwhelmed by what I expected to come when I
was well out of the way." Berenson to Barrett Wendell, 7 September 1919,
Houghton Library, Harvard University, Cambridge, Mass.

20. Berenson to William Ivins, 19 November 1933, Ivins Papers, Archives
of American Art.

21. Berenson was amused by Hutchins Hapgood's love of the common
man. In 1927 Berenson wrote Ivins of a recent visit from Hapgood, noting
that he and Hapgood made quite a contrast: "He loves booze and harmony
with himself on a lower level and believes in the PEEPEL [sic] to the nth power,
and loves to wallow in their midst and bring away their stink." Berenson
added that despite this the people soon discovered in Hapgood an aristo-
crat and a puritan, putting his Dionysian appetites in conflict with the fact
that they did not find him "Schmutz and Stankfahig." Berenson to Ivins,
12 January 1927, Ivins Papers, Archives of American Art.

22. Mary Berenson to Hutchins Hapgood, 5 October 1931, Hutchins
Hapgood and Neith Hapgood Papers in the collection of the Beinecke Rare
Book and Manuscript Library, Yale University, New Haven, Conn.

23. Bernard Berenson to Hutchins Hapgood, 15 May 1937, Hapgood
Papers, Yale University.

24. Elizabeth Hardwick described the transformation of Berenson's reputation after World War II: "Post-war prosperity meant an unexpected sweet-
ening of his public image. His possessions, his worldliness, his aestheticism
seemed in a frightened, inflationary world, at the least harmless and, at best,
admirably eternal and shrewd. In the depression decade before the war, his
villa, I Tatti, with its splendid library, its pictures—its Sassetta and Domenico Veneziano—might have been thought exorbitantly self-centered." Elizabeth Hardwick, "Living in Italy: Reflections on Bernard Berenson," *Partisan
Review* 27 (Winter 1960): 75.

25. Kenneth Clark, "Bernard Berenson," *The Listener*, 18 February 1971,
196.

26. Francis Henry Taylor, "To Bernard Berenson on his Ninetieth Birthday," *Atlantic Monthly* 196 (June 1955): 30–32.

Some writers were suspicious of Berenson's born-again antiformalism
and impatient with his assertion of standards and values. In his review of
Berenson's *Aesthetics and History* for *The New Republic*, Lincoln Kirstein

contended that "Berenson's influence in maintaining the negotiable value of precious art, in instruction, in scholarship, in taste, has been and still is imperial. . . . If he has not said art exists for the sake of art, he feels its chief aim is hedonistic or aristocratic assimilation." Lincoln Kirstein, "The Autocratic Taste," rev. of *Aesthetics and History in the Visual Arts*, *New Republic*, 10 January 1949, 16–17.

27. Articles on Berenson after his death make frequent reference to his escapism. Remy Saisselin wrote: "Berenson is an Athenian who knows full well that it is best to savor the fruits of civilization and genius in a remote tower, preferably beneath Mediterranean skies." Remy Saisselin, rev. of *Berenson et André Malraux*, by Bernard Halda, *Journal of Aesthetics and Art Criticism* 23 (Summer 1965): 515.

In his review of Berenson's *Sunset and Twilight*, Ralph Edwards noted that "In this preoccupations with his own personality and his restatement of the humanist ideal there is a suggestion of preciosity of a superior person withdrawn in his ivory tower from the base concerns of the vulgar mob." Ralph Edwards, "The Value of Bernard Berenson's Life," rev. of *Sunset and Twilight*, *Connoisseur* 157 (September 1964): 53.

This was a tendency Berenson shared with his good friend Edith Wharton, who, in the 1930s, held a similarly apocalyptic view of modern society. See R.W.B. Lewis, *Edith Wharton* (New York: Harper and Row, 1975), 505–6.

28. "Landscape of the Mind," rev. of *One Year's Reading for Fun*, *Time*, 15 February 1960, 112.

29. Schapiro regretted that so much of Berenson's writing in his final decades was directed against contemporary art: "While this pleased the philistines, official and unofficial, who could call upon his great authority, it was disappointing to his disciples who had learned from him to recognise quality in works of many different styles." Meyer Schapiro, "Mr. Berenson's Values," *Encounter* 16 (January 1961): 61–62.

This reference to officialdom suggests that campaigns conducted against modern art and artists in the early years of the cold war by the likes of Michigan congressman George Dondero may have found justification in some of Berenson's late books. See Jane De Hart Mathews, "Art and Politics in Cold War America," *American Historical Review* 81 (October 1976): 762–87; and William Hauptman, "The Suppression of Art in the McCarthy Decade," *Art Forum* 12 (October 1973): 48–52.

30. Clark, "Bernard Berenson," 385.

31. Ibid., 386. In *Moments of Vision* Clark wondered if Berenson did not finish the book because his whole thesis of decline and recovery was to some extent contrary to his own deepest responses to art and to his hard-won theory of aesthetics. Clark was always quick to point out that Berenson's capacity for appreciation frequently outran his theorizing. Kenneth Clark,

Moments of Vision (New York: Harper and Row, 1981), 128.

32. This has been suggested by Francis Haskell in "Compromises of a Connoisseur," a provocative review of *Bernard Berenson: The Making of Legend*, by Ernest Samuels, and *The Partnership: The Secret Association of Bernard Berenson and Joseph Duveen*, by Colin Simpson, *Times Literary Supplement*, 5 June 1987, 595–96.

33. Ernest Samuels, *Bernard Berenson: The Making of a Legend* (Cambridge: Harvard University Press, 1987), 441. Berenson struggled to come up with a suitable title for *Aesthetics and History in the Visual Arts*. As he explained in the introduction, he had been inclined to personalize it in terms of his own experience. He considered calling the work "My adventures as an art taster, thinker, and writer, as connoisseur, critic, and historian," which would have covered the scope of his professional activities. All his alternative titles included the word "history," and it was clearly the theoretical part of the treatise about which he was ambivalent, for he suggested words such as "enjoyment," "experience," and "appreciation" as possible substitutions for "aesthetics." His final selection reveals more about his intellectual ambition than any strong conviction he held regarding the substance of his thought as it was articulated in the text. Berenson, preface to *Aesthetics and History in the Visual Arts* (New York: Pantheon, 1948), unpaginated (hereafter cited as *Aesthetics and History*).

34. Berenson, *Aesthetics and History*, 24.

35. In reviewing this book, John Walker suggested that readers could obtain nearly all of these ideas from the first four essays on Italian painting and from Berenson's early articles. John Walker, rev. of *Aesthetics and History*, *Gazette des Beaux Arts*, ser. 6, vol. 34 (October 1948): 294–96.

36. Berenson, *Aesthetics and History*, 65.

37. Ibid., 69.

38. What is paradoxical about Berenson is that as an expert and arbiter of taste he became synonymous with a variant of classicism not entirely consistent with his own taste in art, his pronounced aestheticism, or even his theories. In reviewing *Aesthetics and History*, Meyer Schapiro pointed out that austere rationalists objected to empathetic theories of aesthetics as subjectivist and would surely fault Berenson for his neglect of proportion and structure. Also Berenson's choice of connoisseurship as a profession was in a sense indicative of a distinctly modern, if not romantic (as suggested by Wind), sensibility. Meyer Schapiro, "The Last Aesthete," rev. of *Aesthetics and History*, and *Sketch for a Self-Portrait*, *Commentary* 8 (December 1949): 615.

Both Kenneth Clark and Clement Greenberg made similar observations about Berenson's alleged classicism. Greenberg stated that it was more professed than felt, drawing attention to Berenson's eclectic taste by way of refutation. Clark believed that Berenson's neglect of theoretical proportion and contempt for the seemingly mathematical bent of modernist art was inconsistent with his exaltation of the Greeks and symptomatic of greater allegiance to late nineteenth-century writers like William James and Henri Bergson, than to the ancients. Clement Greenberg, "Art and History," rev. of *Aesthetics and History, New York Times Book Review*, 28 November 1948, 16; Kenneth Clark, "Thoughts of a Great Humanist," rev. of *Aesthetics and History, Burlington Magazine* 91 (1949): 145.

39. Berenson, *Aesthetics and History*, 135–36.

40. This is similar to Greenberg's position as stated in "Modernist Painting," *Arts and Literature* 4 (Spring 1965): 193–201.

41. Berenson, *Aesthetics and History*, 106.

42. Ibid., 98–99. In his review of this book, Frank Jewett Mather points out that if we follow Berenson's approach, it should be impossible to gather anything valid about the author's personality from a text of criticism. Mather realized the absurdity of this in a book that is, as Lincoln Kirstein said, a portrait of its compiler, with Berenson's personality on every page. Frank Jewett Mather, rev. of *Aesthetics and History, Magazine of Art* 42 (February 1949): 74; Lincoln Kirstein, "The Autocratic Taste," rev. of *Aesthetics and History, New Republic*, 10 January 1949, 16.

43. Berenson, *Aesthetics and History*, 16.

44. Ibid., 95.

45. Mather called the book a directive for the historian or art critic and cited this section as the most valuable part of the book. Mather, rev. of *Aesthetics and History*, 73.

46. Berenson, *Aesthetics and History*, 213.

47. A period review in the *College Art Journal* demonstrates how perfectly Berenson's vision of art history fit the central concerns that, until recently, have dominated the discipline. Regarding Berenson's standards of value, Shapley claimed: "With these requirements as a touchstone, the critic can recognize among the remains of all ages and all places the productions that have most value for our civilization, and the art historian can classify them and chart their fluctuating appeal to successive generations. He can study, too, the development of styles and the influence of one upon the other, always centering his attention, if he be wise, upon those currents that have contributed most richly to our western civilization." Fern Shapley, rev. of *Aesthetics and History, College Art Journal* 9 (1949–51): 87.

48. Berenson, *Aesthetics and History*, 243. A sermon of this sort also appears in Berenson's brief monograph on Caravaggio, where it is part of a discussion of the destructive influence of German art history: "In the visual

arts (at least) there is an inherent principle of growth and decline, which is little influenced from outside, although its manifestations may coincide with many other contemporary manifestations in other arts, in literature, and in technical thinking. But for German-minded authors a work of art is only a springboard from which to plunge into the turbid depths of the subumbilical subconscience or to rise with leaden wings into an empyrean whence they bring down theories, treatises, pseudo-histories, misinterpretations, romances, gnosticisms, occult theologies, ponderous treatises on the relation of art to class struggle, to plagues and epidemics, to the trade in paint-brushes, in the price of canvas, to the rent of studios, to the kindness of hostesses, to dyspepsia, to the mother-complex, to occupational diseases, etc." Bernard Berenson, *Caravaggio: His Incongruity and His Fame* (London: Chapman and Hall, 1953), 86–87.

Remarks such as these are effective reminders of the extent to which current practices in art history are in a very real sense rejections of Berenson and the methodology for which he stood.

49. Berenson, *Aesthetics and History*, 241.

50. Ibid., 242.

51. Although Berenson's notions of both provincial and peripheral artists were developed to explain the artistic expression of the Middle Ages, they could also be enlisted in the study of early American portrait painting and so-called naive or folk art. It is worth remembering that Berenson grew up in Boston, an important center of colonial art.

52. Berenson, *Aesthetics and History*, 169.

53. Bernard Berenson, *The Arch of Constantine; or, the Decline of Form* (London: Chapman and Hall, 1954), 20 (hereafter cited as *The Arch of Constantine*).

54. Ibid., 20.

55. Ibid., 37.

56. Berenson, *Aesthetics and History*, 225.

57. Many writers agreed with Berenson that intelligibility need not be the cost of artistic freedom or, as Alfred Frankfurter put it, the artist can be free without being irresponsible. Frankfurter, who consistently encouraged Berenson to continue writing and who promoted his late books, was especially generous toward the theory of decline, denying that it was based on a priori judgments or polemics: "The essential fact about this conclusion [that we are in a period of decline] is that it arises not out of the prejudice of a narrow academician but from a constantly searching, almost uniquely sensitive mind which bears evidence right here that its considerations constantly range from the classical through every phase of Western Art." Alfred Frankfurter, "Testament of Daylight," rev. of *Aesthetics and History, Art News* 47 (December 1948): 15.

Though the writer Ray Mortimer regretted the support Berenson's position lent to the most philistine enemies of modern art, he admitted that he was not unsympathetic to the principles behind it. He also found himself increasingly responsive to the content, rather than formal values, of art, a fact he attributed to Berenson's influence and one which attests to the efficacy of his sharp departure from earlier critical positions. Ray Mortimer, "Homage to Bernard Berenson," *Horizon* 20 (October 1949): 260–67.

58. Clark, "Thoughts of a Great Humanist," 144.

59. Greenberg, "Art and History," 14; and Clement Greenberg, "Greenberg on Berenson," rev. of *Piero della Francesca; or, The Ineloquent in Art,* and *The Arch of Constantine; or, The Decline of Form, Perspectives USA* 1 (Spring 1955): 154.

60. Schapiro, "The Last Aesthete," 615.

61. Ibid., 616.

62. Bernard Berenson, *Sunset and Twilight* (New York: Harcourt, Brace and World, 1963), 109.

63. There are some illustrations of modern works in Berenson's late books but only rarely do they seem to have been chosen because they are especially appropriate examples of a point Berenson sought to make. They were more than likely photographs he happened to have had at hand.

64. Elizabeth Hardwick, "Living in Italy: Reflections on Bernard Berenson," *Partisan Review* 27 (Winter 1960): 79. Jocelyne Rotily, who has written on Berenson's dislike of modernism in the context of the crisis of French humanism between the world wars, similarly discusses the grounds for his hostility as almost wholly intellectual and emotional. Jocelyne Rotily, "Bernard Berenson et La France," Ph.D. diss., Faculté de Lettres d'Aix-en-Provence, 1986–87. See especially chap. 2.5, "La crise de l'humanisme: La question de l'art moderne."

65. Berenson, "For Whom Art," in *Essays in Appreciation* (London: Chapman and Hall, 1958), 103.

66. Berenson told Umberto Morra that people shrieked at him when he came out with his theory of tactile values; "and now it is I who get angry with them when they see nothing in painting but tactile values." Berenson, *Conversations with Berenson,* 51.

67. Nicki Mariano recalled that Berenson knew many painters, and he did. But over the years he often spoke of his dislike for their arrogance when they did not agree with him. Nicki Mariano, *Forty Years with Berenson* (New York: Alfred A. Knopf, 1966).

68. Berenson to Walter Pach, 11 August 1924, Walter Pach Papers, Archives of American Art, Washington, D.C., roll 4217, frames 796–99.

69. Rotily notes that Berenson had this in common with the French humanists of his generation. Rotily, "Bernard Berenson et La France."

70. Berenson to George Biddle, 20 January 1956, I Tatti. Late in life, when Berenson visited the Cini Foundation in Venice, he was struck by its functional similarity to early monasteries. He wrote in his diary: "In the new Middle Ages into which we are plunging we again shall need quasi-monastic institutions to save and advance civilization." Berenson diary entry, quoted in Bernard Berenson, *The Passionate Sightseer* (London: Thames; New York: Simon and Schuster, 1960), 41.

71. Berenson's brief monograph *Caravaggio: His Incongruity and His Fame* was written to dispel the popular perception of the artist as a brilliant innovator and the quintessential baroque painter. By "incongruity" Berenson meant both lack of decorum and unexpected formal contrasts. He used the same word in reference to surrealism. In this book Berenson argued that Caravaggio's tenebrism and his untraditional portrayal of religious events and persons was no more than a fresh way to present the "commonplace." Berenson, *Caravaggio*, 66–67.

It is not clear what Berenson intended when he referred to an artistic vision as commonplace. More than likely it implied a vision that did not reflect heroic ideals; but he also used it to describe the routine or unsurprising. At times he referred to the vision of modern artists as commonplace. Basically, the word came to signify an artistic vision that did not teach him anything he wanted to know.

72. In 1908, at the end of a whirlwind tour through the world of avant-garde art, which included several meetings with Matisse, Berenson left Paris for the United States. There he soon encountered an unsympathetic review of the contributions of Matisse to the Salon d'Automne. The writer, Paris correspondent for *The Nation*, had described Matisse's works as a direct insult to the viewers' eyes and understanding, adding that the artist forgets "beholders are not all fools, and that it is not necessary to do differently from all other artists." Berenson promptly wrote a letter to the editor of The *Nation* in which he identified himself as one of the fools Matisse had thoroughly taken in. He drew attention to the reviewer's hackneyed insinuation (made so often in the face of art which is new or unexpected) that the artist was some sort of trickster out to shock the bourgeoisie. "Art," *Nation* 87 (29 October 1908): 422; and Bernard Berenson, "De Gustibus," *Nation* 87 (12 November 1908): 461.

73. Bernard Berenson, *Piero della Francesca; or, The Ineloquent in Art* (London: Chapman and Hall, 1954), 1–2.

74. Ibid., 13. Berenson used the concept of ineloquence in much the same way as the contemporary critic Michael Fried would later use the word "theatricality." Fried argued that great art was not aware of the viewer's presence; it made no appeal for interaction, in other words, it was what Fried

called "anti-theatrical." Michael Fried, "Art and Objecthood," *Artforum* 5 (Summer 1967): 12–23.

75. Berenson, *Sunset and Twilight,* 222.

76. Berenson to Mary Berenson, 8 February 1918, I Tatti.

77. In *Seeing and Knowing* Berenson claimed it would take a Balzac to describe the power of gifted dealers and their influence, bad or good, over the public. He claimed that one could hardly fault dealers such as Durand-Ruel, Wildenstein, and Vollard for all they did to popularize great impressionist works from Manet to Cézanne (or presumedly individuals such as himself for singing the praises of the so-called Italian primitives). But of those who trafficked in tribal objects he said: "Just before the first world war a genius of mercantile propaganda arrived in Paris and settled down on the ground floor of a building close to the Palais Bourbon. There he displayed and showed off Negro wood-carvings of human shapes and ventriloquized about them with phrases that were quickly taken up by the most authoritative art critics in Paris, London, and New York." Berenson, *Seeing and Knowing,* 21.

More than one writer has observed that Berenson had an enviable capacity for self-deception, especially when it involved the trade.

78. Berenson, "Exhibitionitis," in *Essays in Appreciation,* 87–93.

79. Berenson frequently referred to abstract painting as "decalcomania," a term ordinarily used to refer to machine-generated patterns or decals employed in the decoration of ceramics, furniture, and other objects.

80. Berenson wrote in his wartime diary: "Enemy number one is the Machine in whatever form. Not only because of its ugliness as sight, sound, and smell, not only because it reduces entire counties and almost whole countries to sordidness, squalor, and disgusting rubbish heaps. My chief objection to the machine is that it exists only for an end and ignores, must ignore, the means, except in so far as the perfect functioning of the means is necessary to the end. The machine is not only a mechanism, it is a state of mind that existed thousands of years earlier than any but the crudest and simplest mechanism. It is a state of mind which for thousands of years has been aiming at an age like the present, during which the machine will go from triumph to triumph, and end by realizing its millennial endeavor to reduce the individual to a robot." Berenson, *Rumor and Reflection,* 39.

81. Berenson diary entry, 8 March 1950, *The Bernard Berenson Treasury,* 291.

82. Berenson, *Conversations with Berenson,* 122–123.

83. Berenson, *Aesthetics and History,* 126.

84. Ibid., 127.

85. Joseph Frank, "Mostly Rumor," rev. of *Rumor and Reflection, New Republic,* 30 October 1952, 25. Robert Hughes echoed similar sentiments

when he wrote that the ardor of Berenson's aspiration to cultural refinement "saved him from having to think seriously about social organization," adding that his political insights would only make sense to a Boston brahmin of the late nineteenth century. Robert Hughes, "Only in America," rev. of *Bernard Berenson: The Making of a Connoisseur,* by Ernest Samuels; and *Being Bernard Berenson,* by Meryle Secrest, *New York Review,* 20 December 1979, 20. Although it is arguable that a connoisseur of art does not need to think about these things, Berenson's impulse to comment on modern politics and to criticize the deteriorating social order left him open to such attacks.

86. Schapiro, "Mr. Berenson's Values," 64. Meryle Secrest was especially interested in the ideology of Berenson's culture and went so far as to suggest that because of his nonegalitarian views Berenson should not even call himself a humanist. This is only true if, as Secrest claims, humanism is understood as the will to better mankind through the advancement of material welfare. Berenson's humanism, in theory at least, was not especially concerned with material well-being but with the refinement of the human being as defined in opposition to its animal origins. It was predicated on a concern for individual liberty and for the perfection of the intellect, not on economic welfare. Meryle Secrest, *Being Bernard Berenson* (New York: Holt, Rinehart and Winston, 1979), 382. Nonetheless, it is also true that Berenson assumed the very concern for such things was limited to an elite moneyed minority. As he told Walter Lipmann, "Liberty is an aristocratic postulate; the others care only for welfare." Berenson to Walter Lipmann, 1 January 1950, in A. K. McComb, ed., *The Selected Letters of Bernard Berenson* (Boston: Houghton Mifflin, 1963), 264. Finally, to Hutchins Hapgood he wrote, "Our *civilization,* ALL civilization is aristocratic and for the few. The mass feels it as a burden and loves to kick it over." Berenson to Hapgood, 16 December 1940, Hapgood Papers, Yale University.

87. Hapgood maintained that Berenson's love of beauty was almost indecent and that he could never understand how Hapgood's own experience in Italy had helped him to see the aesthetic possibilities of raw life and unhappy situations: "I have realized how the artist goes to work, how he sees in what is called crude life the possibility of symbolically expressing in a plastic form the essences of that crudity. I think that is one of the things that Berenson never saw." Hutchins Hapgood, *A Victorian in the Modern World* (New York: Harcourt, Brace, 1939), 96.

88. Berenson, *Sketch for a Self-Portrait* (London: Constable; New York: Pantheon, 1949), 103.

89. Berenson, *Aesthetics and History,* 244.

90. Berenson, *Conversations with Berenson,* 151. Despite his personal history, Berenson's own view of poverty was essentially romantic. In *Rumor and Reflection* he recalled Henry Adam's suggestion to him that people in

the Middle Ages had a greater zest for life than those in the modern world. Berenson essentially agreed with this contention and ventured to guess that this spirit was still alive among the poor: "What we mean was living keenly, zestfully, relatively free to work as one liked and to loaf when one pleased. It meant not to be the slaves of fixed hours, and of so much output per hour. It meant to run risks, to allow for ups and downs—in short, to leave room for variety, excitement and some sense of adventure. . . . We retain this kind of life in the slums. Cobblers, tinkers, chimney sweeps, plumbers, clothes-menders, small shop-keepers of every kind in these purlieus, can alternate work with play and are not obliged to take either in impalatable, indigestible doses. . . . Though frequently exposed to cold, disease, hunger even, as indeed most city dwellers were in the Middle Ages, may they yet not be happier, more zestful, more eager, in short more amused, than the same number of people in their comfortable well-supplied mansions and country houses." Berenson, *Rumor and Reflection,* 214.

91. As it is described by Patrick Brantlinger, this is a view of mass society whose point of departure is the fall of Rome and the subsequent abdication of high culture and political responsibility for popular entertainment and welfare. The "bread and circuses" analogy has historically been used by theorists of both the Left and the Right to demonstrate the irresponsibility of the common man; it is a concept that transcends ideology. Berenson invoked this analogy often when discussing the theme of decline. Patrick Brantlinger, *Bread and Circuses: Theories of Mass Culture and Social Decay* (Ithaca, N.Y.: Cornell University Press, 1983). See especially chap. 6, "Three Versions of Modern Classicism: Ortega, Eliot, Camus."

92. Berenson, *Aesthetics and History,* 129. Rotily notes that despite Berenson's professed hatred for Communism, his ruminations about a future utopia were not incompatible with Marxism, insofar as they suggest an ideal society in which profit is shared and each member works according to interest and ability. Rotily, "Bernard Berenson et La France," 327.

But it is important to remember that although Berenson was not unsympathetic to the concept of a society in which there would be no forced labor or material deprivation, he could not fathom the idea of living in a world without prestige values. In a lengthy diary entry published in *Rumor and Reflection,* Berenson speculated on the quality of life in such a society. He believed that in the absence of jealousy typically associated with the unequal distribution of wealth, prestige values would not be eliminated, they would simply take another form: "Resentment is unhappily at the bottom of more social discontent than economic difficulties. When these last are overcome, as in the course of time they may be, inequality of physical make-up, of mental and moral gifts, will remain and fester in many natures." Bernard Berenson, *Rumor and Reflection,* 209.

Berenson came to the conclusion that the biggest problem facing the future was how to deal with leisure. The elimination of strife could lead to terminal boredom; nothing to hope for, nothing to fear, nothing to satisfy the craving for adventure. He speculated that the intellectual elite would always have something to do, but in the absence of conflict, "What will the rest of the community do, who have no brains for such occupations, and find no happiness except in a sphere where courage and physical aptitudes count along with brains?" To Berenson, boredom was a much more pressing problem than poverty; what worried him was that "man's last gesture may be a wordless yawn." Berenson, *Rumor and Reflection*, 213, 214. It is worth recalling here Berenson's lifelong interest in the writings of Nietzsche.

93. Berenson, *Aesthetics and History*, 129.

94. Berenson to William Ivins, 15 February 1926, Ivins Papers, Archives of American Art. See Brantlinger on *The Revolt of the Masses*. Brantlinger, *Bread and Circuses*, 186–98. Sidney Alexander pointed out that an essential difference between Berenson and Spengler lies in their respective beliefs about the inevitability of decline. Although Berenson wrote about cycles of artistic decline as if they were inevitable, the fact that he inveighed against the twentieth century was indicative of his belief that decline could be halted if proper measures were taken to prevent collapse at the center of a civilization. Interview with Alexander, July 1989.

95. Brantlinger, *Bread and Circuses*, 187.

96. Remy Saisselin, *The Bourgeois and the Bibelot* (New Brunswick, N.J.: Rutgers University Press, 1984), 160–61.

97. Berenson, *Sunset and Twilight*, 517, 406–7.

98. Saisselin claimed this separation of aesthetic appreciation from legal ownership was a fraud perpetrated by a dealer "posing as a humanist" and that in the real world desire to possess ruled the soul. Berenson's whole career, he maintained, was engineered to support this fraud; it was a "style of life that was a style of selling." Saisselin, *The Bourgeois and the Bibelot*, 161, 166.

99. Berenson's tremendous success is explained by Saisselin as the coincidence of expertise, criticism, and appreciation, working together to elevate the trade value of art. He identified the artistic essentials, he located them in certain specific works, and these became precious because they possessed them. Although this account reduces Berenson to a kind of art racketeer, it correctly describes the practical reality of his career.

100. Saisselin, *The Bourgeois and the Bibelot*, 158.

101. Roger Fry, "Retrospect," in *Vision and Design* (London: Chatto and Windus, 1920), 291.

102. Brantlinger emphasized that Eliot's defense of modern classicism

involved an effort not to define mass culture but to explain the decline of true culture in terms of modern decadence and barbarism. Eliot's approach was perfectly consistent with Berenson's, who in fact did not even believe in the possibility of populist art or culture. Brantlinger, *Bread and Circuses,* 198–210.

In the 1956 essay "Popular Art," Berenson argued that there was no such thing, especially insofar as it was understood as an expression that arose spontaneously from the soul of the masses. So-called "folk art" was simply the kind of thing that resulted from the perpetual and unskilled imitation of traditional models to the point that it "reached the puerile, infantile expression of the mass soul." It was, in his terminology, equivalent to peripheral art. The crude figural distortions characteristic of such art could be explained by the "originality of incompetence" and no more constituted a new way of seeing or expressing than did the reliefs on the Arch of Constantine. Berenson, "Popular Art," in *Essays in Appreciation,* 144.

103. Berenson, *Seeing and Knowing* (London: Chapman and Hall, 1953), 26.

104. Ibid., 22.

105. Ibid., 23.

106. Ibid., 25.

107. Ibid., 29.

108. In an obituary of Berenson for the *Chicago Review,* Alfred Werner aptly characterized this essay as "an old man's admission that time had passed him by." Alfred Werner, "Berenson's Achievement," *Chicago Review* 14 (Summer 1960): 101.

109. Writing for the *College Art Journal,* Belle Krasne best expressed this sentiment: "He is, quite simply, trapped in his own experience, unresponsive to the inexhaustible pleasures of our imaginary museum because of his prejudiced view of art history. . . . If we cannot deny Berenson his prejudices, we can at least recognize *Seeing and Knowing* for what it is: a slight and irresponsible essay by an 89-year-old man who has devoted his life to Italian Renaissance painting, and who has lived, since 1900, in the relative seclusion of a villa near Florence." Belle Krasne, rev. of *Seeing and Knowing, College Art Journal* 12 (Summer 1954): 329. The reference to Berenson's isolation was a gross exaggeration; he traveled extensively until the final years of his life, when ill-health would not allow it.

110. Serge Hughes, "The Outlook of an Olympian," rev. of *Seeing and Knowing, Commonweal,* 16 April 1954, 47.

111. The American painter George Biddle was one of the more generous reviewers. He attempted to find some redeeming quality in Berenson's emphasis on the need to balance observation and conception, a credo he said

was consistent with his own. George Biddle, rev. of *Seeing and Knowing, New York Times Book Review,* 13 January 1954, 7.

112. Krasne claimed that if the book was taken seriously by the general public it would set the arts back fifty years. Krasne, rev. of *Seeing and Knowing,* 329. By the time the second edition of *Seeing and Knowing* was published in the late 1960s, Berenson's reputation had fallen sufficiently to quell this fear and reviews were characterized by sarcastic intolerance. A notice in *Art in America* claimed that "Berenson was 83 and afflicted with hardening of the intellect by the time he got around to recognizing the existence of modern art," and that his remarks on Picasso "would have been embarrassing had they come from the most parochial farmer in Nebraska; coming from a personage of Berenson's experience and putative urbanity, they are appalling." See "Unwelcome Reprise," rev. of *Seeing and Knowing, Art in America* 56 (November–December 1968): 118.

With the publication of this book Berenson's polemic was clearly vulnerable to exploitation by the most reactionary factions of American art. An example of the sort of unfortunate attention he attracted to himself in its wake is to be found in a brief article on Berenson in the conservative art magazine *American Artist*. The painter Frederick Taubes reprinted a letter he had received from Berenson that praised his own recent collection of essays, and Taubes recounted a visit with Berenson in Florence the following year. Berenson emerges from this article as a supreme philistine in collusion with the righteous forces to expose the fraud of modernism to the American people. See Frederick Taubes, "An Afternoon with Bernard Berenson," *American Artist* 20 (November 1956): 56.

113. Margaretta Salinger, "A God's-Eye View," rev. of *Seeing and Knowing, Art Digest,* 1 July 1954, 26.

114. Coming as it did a year after Berenson's death, Schapiro's 1960 essay "On the Humanity of Abstract Painting" is a fitting antidote to *Seeing and Knowing*. Written by one of his most perceptive critics, this essay stands in direct opposition to Berenson's narrow exclusionary concepts of both art and humanism; although he is not named, most of his well-known biases and misconceptions are addressed herein. Berenson and Schapiro stood at opposite ends of the pole in terms of their approach to the study of art. But what separates them most is a fundamentally different conception of humanity. When Schapiro makes the point in this essay that "criticism of abstract art as inhuman arises in part from a tendency to underestimate inner life and the resources of the imagination," he perfectly describes Berenson. For Berenson, humanism was defined strictly in terms of Western classicism; its ideals were timeless and its aspirations were best reflected in the figurative art made in its tradition. Nothing could be further from Berenson's concept of man or

art than Schapiro's proposition that "the notion of humanity in art rests on a norm of the human that has changed in the course of time. . . . Humanity in art is therefore not confined to the image of man. Man shows himself too in his relation to his surroundings, in his artifacts, and in the expressive character of all the signs and marks he produces. These may be noble or ignoble, playful or tragic, passionate or severe. Or they may be sensed as unnameable yet compelling moods." These remarks go straight to the core of Berenson's critical and moral position. He simply did not share this generous a view of humanity, and thus he could be expansive about neither the boundaries of artistic expression nor the quality of the inner life. Meyer Schapiro, "On the Humanity of Abstract Painting," in *Modern Art: 19th and 20th Centuries* (New York: George Braziller, 1978), 232 and 227.

Conclusion

1. Bernard Berenson, *Conversations with Berenson* recorded by Umberto Morra and trans. Florence Hammond (Boston: Houghton Mifflin, 1965), 79.

2. Quoted in Ernest Samuels, *Bernard Berenson: The Making of a Connoisseur* (Cambridge: Harvard University Press, 1979), 345 (hereafter cited as Samuels, *Connoisseur*).

3. In a review of Berenson's anthology *Essays in Appreciation* Cecile Gould observes that the key to Berenson's critical position is the range of his dislikes. Unlike an art historian, who measures a picture according to the aesthetic criteria of its period, Berenson remained a connoisseur "to whom the work of art either speaks or does not." Gould maintains that, in this respect, Berenson's criticism was perfectly consistent and rational; to him the study of art was a question of subjective feeling. Cecile Gould, rev. of *Essays in Appreciation, Apollo* 67 (June 1958): 243.

4. Virginia Mecklenburg, "American Aesthetic Theory, 1908–1917: Issues in Conservative and Avant-Garde Thought," Ph.D. diss., University of Maryland, 1983, 168. See also Susan Noyes Platt, *Modernism in the 1920's: Interpretations of Modern Art in New York from Expressionism to Constructivism* (Ann Arbor: UMI Research Press, 1985).

5. For such a jaded account of Berenson's career see Colin Simpson, *Artful Partners: Bernard Berenson and Joseph Duveen* (New York: Macmillan, 1987); published in England as *The Partnership: Secret Association of Bernard Berenson and Joseph Duveen* (London: Bodley Head, 1987).

6. Thomas Craven, *Men of Art* (1931; New York, Garden City: Halcyon House, 1950), 71. In an undated letter to American artist Thomas Hart Benton, Craven mentions that he has been reading Berenson. Benton Papers

in the collection of the Archives of American Art, Washington, D.C., Roll 2325, frame 103.

I am grateful to Susan Noyes Platt for confirming Craven's interest in Berenson and for bringing this letter to my attention. For further discussion of Craven's criticism see Platt's forthcoming study, "Art Criticism in the 1930's."

7. Craven, *Men of Art*, 502–3.

8. Ibid., 512–13. It is worth noting that when Berenson is viewed as a creator of highbrow culture (rather than a pioneer formalist), the changes that took place over the span of his lengthy career appear far less drastic. If his critical position is understood as an effort to stake out a territory of high culture requiring a specific response, he remained essentially the same, the argument for humanism serving primarily to embellish and reinforce his original intention.

9. Ibid., 498. The question of Picasso's intellect and the nature of his achievements also occupied Leo Stein. Stein, like Craven, believed that Picasso wasted his immense talent on trivialities. But unlike Craven, Stein was neither a bigot nor a philistine. Before moving to Settignano, where he became one of Berenson's neighbors, Stein had been on the frontlines of modernism as one of its most perceptive apologists. His retreat from modern art, so much in evidence in *The New Republic* articles published between 1916 and 1926, bears further investigation, especially within the context of Stein's intellectual debt to Berenson and their mutual discouragement over the critical success of formalist art. See Leo Stein, "Pablo Picasso," *New Republic*, 23 April 1924, 230.

10. Quoted in Samuels, *Connoisseur*, 346.

11. Thomas McLaughlin argued that Bell's initial concern had been to widen the canon of art so as to ensure a place for the kind of work he already admired. Like Fry, Bell's strategy had been to develop a theory that would enable him to explain the concerns of modern painters, and thereby legitimize their art. But unlike Fry, he found it necessary to reject both traditional criticism and the art preferred by those (such as Berenson) who did not share his enthusiasm for the new painting. McLaughlin regarded it as evidence of Bell's growth as a critic that he eventually realized traditional artists with representational intentions were also capable of creating significant form. This, of course was Berenson's position all along. Thomas McLaughlin, "Clive Bell's Aesthetic: Tradition and Significant Form," *Journal of Aesthetics and Art Criticism* 35 (Summer 1977): 433–43.

12. For example, comments such as Berenson's to Leo Stein that Fry was the only one writing decent criticism because he managed to get his ideas straight, or Fry's to Berenson that he dare not read his books "before giving

my present course because I know that what I think I have discovered may be in it," were probably made in reference to solving problems of attribution. Roger Fry to Berenson, November 1901, in Fry, *Letters of Roger Fry*, 2 vols., ed. Denys Sutton (London: Chatto and Windus, 1972), 184. The exchange between Berenson and Leo Stein was recorded by Samuels, in *Connoisseur*, 382.

13. Kenneth Clark, Introduction to *Last Lectures of Roger Fry* (New York: Macmillan, 1939), xiv; and Francis Spalding, *Roger Fry: Art and Life* (Berkeley and Los Angeles: University of California Press, 1980), 62–62.

Historians of formalism tend to minimize both Berenson's contribution to its development as well as the extent of Fry's debt to him. Beverly Twitchell's study *Cézanne and Formalism in Bloomsbury* is especially ungenerous in assessing the degree to which Berenson can be considered a formative influence on Fry. She grants only that the two were mutually opposed to German scholarship and criticism, shared biases toward classical composition and plasticity, and had a tendency to separate form from content. Regarding their similar aesthetic preferences, Twitchell maintains that "much of what they both upheld, however, was characteristic of the art then being created; this is one of the many instances where values of the present are discovered in the works of the past." Beverly Twitchell, *Cézanne and Formalism in Bloomsbury* (Ann Arbor: UMI Research Press, 1987), 46.

Although plasticity and modernity became inseparable for Fry, his aesthetics were informed by an early devotion to Italian painting, which, it must be remembered, he experienced under Berenson's tutelage. In modern painting he sought certain artistic essentials he had come to value in historic art, and Berenson's role in guiding Fry to the conclusion that mass was the essence of art cannot be ignored. Twitchell's remarks were more relevant to Berenson than to Fry, insofar as his critical priorities were shaped by modern and Italian painting simultaneously. By his own admission, Fry was a latecomer to the appreciation of the most progressive artists of his age.

14. Twitchell, *Cézanne and Formalism*, 47.

15. Falkenheim stated that Fry was encouraged by German aesthetics to deal with internal formal structure as the artist's main preoccupation, although she admitted that Fry disliked reading German. Falkenheim, *Roger Fry*.

It is entirely possible that this support came via Berenson, who, through his contact with German theorists such as Hildebrand and Obrist, had at least an intuitive grasp of these principles. Also, Berenson read German with ease, and although he was loath to admit any interest in these treatises on psychological aesthetics, they were more accessible to him than they were to Fry.

Twitchell was at such great pains to establish Fry's independence from Berenson, that, possibly to avoid an unfavorable comparison in which Berenson's thought predates Fry's, she claimed Berenson turned to theory after years of connoisseurship. For examples of Berenson's theoretical principles, she quoted from Berenson's *Aesthetics and History in the Visual Arts*, pointing out that in this late book Berenson begins to sound like Fry. What she fails to note, however, is that *Aesthetics and History* was essentially a recapitulation of ideas that Berenson had formulated and published in the 1890s, when Fry could easily have availed himself of them. Certainly Fry was aware of Berenson's early interest in aesthetic theory. In an 1898 letter to their mutual friend R. C. Trevelyan, Fry writes: "What is wanted now in the way of criticism is someone who will make appreciations as finely and imaginatively conceived [as Walter Pater] and take them into greater details as well. Perhaps Berenson will get to this if he ever gets over his theories." Fry to R. C. Trevelyan, 1 March 1898, in Fry, *Letters*, 171–72.

16. Roger Fry, "An Essay on Aesthetics," in *Vision and Design* (London: Chatto and Windus: 1920), 16–38.

17. Denman Ross, *A Theory of Pure Design: Harmony, Balance, Rhythm* (1907; reprint, New York: Peter Smith, 1933).

18. Fry, "An Essay on Aesthetics," 25.

19. Ibid., 34.

20. Ibid., 36–37.

21. Ibid., 37.

22. Ibid., 38.

23. Ibid.

24. Fry, "Retrospect," in *Vision and Design*, 294–95.

25. Ibid., 302.

26. Ibid., 299.

27. Ibid., 295.

28. In many respects, Berenson can be said to have had more in common with Clive Bell than Roger Fry. Although he frequently spoke out against art for art's sake aestheticism, Bell (like Berenson), was an elitist aesthete, Walter Pater style, whose criticism was more dependent on personal experience and taste than on theoretical deduction. His doctrine of significant form is widely regarded by aesthetic philosophers as inadequately explained and impossibly circular in its argumentation. Berenson and Bell also had in common a fundamental lack of interest in the creative process and the context of art, caring only for coming to terms with their own responses to a work. Finally, Bell's last book, *Civilization*, was remarkably conservative in comparison to his earlier positions. Twitchell reasoned that Bell's late work has been neglected because modern readers have found it to be both insufficiently formalist and

patently offensive in terms of its elitism, thus denying him full development to maturity. This is a fate from which Berenson has also suffered. Twitchell, *Cézanne and Formalism*, 80, 102.

29. Richard Wollheim, "Berenson," rev. of *Berenson: A Biography*, by Sylvia Sprigge, *Spectator*, 25 March 1960, 436.

Bibliography

Primary Sources

Manuscript Collections and Archives
Archives of American Art, Washington, D.C.
    Allyn Cox Papers
    Rene Gimpel Papers
    Abraham Harriton Papers
    William Ivins Papers
    August Jaccaci Papers
    Walter Pach Papers
    Daniel Thompson Papers
Berenson Archive, Harvard University Center for Italian Renaissance
    Studies, Villa I Tatti, Florence, Italy
Columbia University, Avery Architectural and Fine Arts Library, New York,
    N.Y.
    Kenyon Cox Papers
Houghton Library, Harvard University, Cambridge, Mass.
Lilly Library, Indiana University, Bloomington, Ind.
    H. W. Smith Papers
Museum of Modern Art Archives, New York, N.Y.
    Alfred H. Barr, Jr., and Margaret Scolari Barr Papers
Phillips Collection, Washington, D.C.
    Duncan Phillips Papers
Yale Collection of American Literature, Beinecke Rare Book and Manuscript
    Library, Yale University, New Haven, Conn.
    Royal Cortissoz Papers
    Leo Stein Papers
    Hutchins Hapgood and Neith Hapgood Papers

Interviews
Sidney Alexander, July 1989
Giovanni Colacicchi, July 1988
Clement Greenberg, April 1989
Leo Steinberg, March 1990
John Walker, March 1989

Berenson's Published Writings, 1894–1959
Ernest Samuels's two-volume biography contains a complete bibliography of Berenson's published writings. The following entries are for books only. Not included here, but listed chronologically by Samuels, are Berenson's periodical articles.

1894

The Venetian Painters of the Renaissance. New York: G. P. Putnam's Sons, 1894.

1895

Lorenzo Lotto: An Essay in Constructive Art Criticism. New York: G. P. Putnam's Sons, 1895; rev. ed., London: George Bell and Sons, 1901.

Venetian Painting, Chiefly Before Titian, at an Exhibition of Venetian Art, The New Gallery. Preface by H. F. Cook, London: privately printed, 1895.

1896

The Florentine Painters of the Renaissance. New York: G. P. Putnam's Sons, 1896.

1897

The Central Italian Painters of the Renaissance. New York: G. P. Putnam's Sons, 1897.

1901

The Study and Criticism of Italian Art. London: George Bell and Sons, 1901.

1902

The Study and Criticism of Italian Art. 2d ser. London: George Bell and Sons, 1902.

1903

The Drawings of the Florentine Painters. 2 vols. London: J. Murray, 1903.

1907

The North Italian Painters of the Renaissance. New York and London: G. P. Putnam's Sons, 1907.

1909

A Sienese Painter of the Franciscan Legend. London: J. M. Dent and Sons, 1909.

1913

Catalogue of a Collection of Paintings and Some Art Objects. Vol. 1, *Italian Paintings.* Philadelphia: John Graver Johnson, 1913.

1916

Pictures in the Collection of P.A.B. Widener at Lynnewood Hall, Elkins Park,

Pennsylvania. Vol. 3, *Early Italian and Spanish Schools.* Philadelphia: privately printed, 1916.

The Study and Criticism of Italian Art. 3d ser. London: George Bell and Sons, 1916.

Venetian Painting in America: The Fifteenth Century. New York: Frederick Sherman, 1916.

1918

Essays in the Study of Sienese Painting. New York: Frederick Sherman, 1918.

1926

Three Essays in Method. Oxford: Clarendon Press, 1926.

1930

The Italian Painters of the Renaissance. Oxford: Clarendon Press, 1930; new edition, London: Phaidon Press, 1952.

Studies in Medieval Painting. New Haven: Yale University Press; Oxford: Oxford University Press, 1930.

1932

Italian Pictures of the Renaissance. Oxford: Clarendon Press, 1932.

1938

Drawings of the Florentine Painters. 3 vols. Chicago: University of Chicago Press, 1938.

1945

Preface. *Catalogue of the Exhibition of French Paintings in Florence.* Florence: Pitti Palace, 1945.

1948

Aesthetics and History in the Visual Arts. New York: Pantheon, 1948.

1949

Sketch for a Self-Portrait. London: Constable; New York: Pantheon, 1949.

1950

Alberto Sani: An Artist Out of His Time. Florence: Electra, 1950.

1952

Rumor and Reflection, 1941–1944. London: Constable; New York: Simon and Schuster, 1952.

1953

Caravaggio, His Incongruity and His Fame. London: Chapman and Hall, 1953.

Seeing and Knowing. London: Chapman and Hall, 1953.

1954

The Arch of Constantine; or, The Decline of Form. London: Chapman and Hall, 1954.

"Decline and Recovery in the Figure Arts." In *Studies in Art and Literature for Belle da Costa Greene,* ed. Dorothy Miner. Princeton: Princeton University Press, 1954.

Piero della Francesca; or, The Ineloquent in Art. London: Chapman and Hall, 1954.

1957

Italian Pictures of the Renaissance: Venetian School. 2 vols. New York and London: Phaidon Press, 1957.

1958

Essays in Appreciation. London: Chapman and Hall, 1958.

Posthumous Publications of Berenson's Writings

1960

One Year's Reading for Fun: 1942. New York: Alfred A. Knopf, 1960.

The Passionate Sightseer. London: Thames; New York: Simon and Schuster, 1960.

1963

Sunset and Twilight. New York: Harcourt, Brace and World, 1963.

1965

Conversations with Berenson. Recorded by Umberto Morra. Trans. Florence Hammond. Boston: Houghton Mifflin, 1965.

1969

Homeless Paintings of the Renaissance. Ed. Hanna Kiel. Bloomington: Indiana University Press, 1969.

1974

Looking at Pictures with Bernard Berenson. Introduction by Hanna Kiel. Personal reminiscence by J. Carter Brown. New York: Harry N. Abrams, 1974.

Published Correspondence, Bernard and Mary Berenson

Constable, Giles, ed. *The Letters Between Bernard Berenson and Charles Henry Coster.* Florence: Leo S. Olschki, 1993.

Hadley, Rollin V. N., ed. *The Letters of Bernard Berenson and Isabella Stewart Gardner, 1887–1924.* Boston: Northeastern University Press, 1987.

Kiel, Hanna, ed. *The Bernard Berenson Treasury, 1887–1958.* New York: Simon and Schuster, 1962.

Marghieri, Clotilde, ed. *A Matter of Passion: Letters of Bernard Berenson and Clotilde Marghieri.* Berkeley and Los Angeles: University of California Press, 1989.

McComb, A. K., ed. *The Selected Letters of Bernard Berenson.* Boston: Houghton Mifflin, 1963.

Strachey, Barbara, and Jayne Samuels, eds. *Mary Berenson: A Self-Portrait from Her Letters and Diaries.* New York: W. W. Norton, 1983.

Secondary Sources

Books and Manuscripts on Berenson

Bellini, Fiora. *Il Giovane Berenson e la Cultura Italiana.* Tesi di laurea, Universita degli Studi di Siena, 1976–1977.

Brown, David. *Berenson and the Connoisseurship of Italian Painting.* Washington, D.C.: National Gallery of Art, 1979.

Clark, Kenneth. "The Work of Bernard Berenson." Unpublished manuscript of an address to the Fogg Fellows, May 1980, I Tatti, Florence, Italy.

George, Waldemar. *Refutation de Bernard Berenson.* Geneva: Pierre Cailler Editeur, 1955.

Halda, Bernard. *Berenson et André Malraux.* Paris: Lettres Modernes, 1964.

Mariano, Nicki. *The Berenson Archive: An Inventory of Correspondence.* Florence: Villa I Tatti, 1965.

———. *Forty Years with Berenson.* New York: Alfred A. Knopf, 1966.

Mostyn-Owen, William. *Bibliographia di Bernard Berenson.* Milan: Electa Editrice, 1955.

Roberts, Laurence P. *The Bernard Berenson Collection of Oriental Art at Villa I Tatti.* New York: Hudson Hills Press, 1991.

Rotily, Jocelyne. "Bernard Berenson et La France." Ph.D. diss., Faculté des Lettres d'Aix-en-Provence, 1986–87.

Russoli, Franco. Introduction and catalogue to *The Berenson Collection.* Milan: Arte Grafiche Ricordi, 1964.

Samuels, Ernest. *Bernard Berenson: The Making of a Connoisseur.* Cambridge: Harvard University Press, 1979.

———. *Bernard Berenson: The Making of a Legend.* Cambridge: Harvard University Press, 1987.

Secrest, Meryle. *Being Bernard Berenson.* New York: Holt, Rinehart and Winston, 1979.

Simpson, Collin. *Artful Partners: Bernard Berenson and Joseph Duveen.* New York: Macmillan, 1987. Published in England as *The Partnership:*

The Secret Association of Bernard Berenson and Joseph Duveen. London: Bodley Head, 1987.

Sprigge, Sylvia. *Berenson: A Biography.* Boston: Houghton Mifflin, 1960.

Periodical Articles on Berenson (including reviews of his books and of books about him)

The following represents the most extensive bibliography of periodical literature on Berenson compiled to date. Additional references, especially reviews of Berenson's books, can be found in Samuels's endnotes. After Berenson's death, reviews of his biographies increasingly served as a point of departure for discursive essays about his character and his legacy.

1894

Fletcher, Jefferson B. "An Index-Guide to Venetian Painters." Rev. of *The Venetian Painters of the Renaissance, Dial,* 1 May 1894, 268–69.

Rev. of *The Venetian Painters of the Renaissance. Nation,* 12 April 1894, 279.

1895

Cartwright, Julia. "Lorenzo Lotto." Rev. of *Lorenzo Lotto. Art Journal,* n.s. (1895): 233–37.

Curtis, George. "Books and Authors." Rev. of *Lorenzo Lotto. Outlook,* 9 February 1895, 236.

"The Fine Arts." Rev. of *Lorenzo Lotto. Critic,* 12 January 1895, 38–39.

Logan, Mary [Mary Costelloe]. "The New Art Criticism." *Atlantic Monthly* 76 (August 1895): 263–70.

"Lorenzo Lotto." Rev. of *Lorenzo Lotto. Spectator* 28 September 1895, 407.

"Lotto and His Art." Rev. of *Lorenzo Lotto. New York Times,* 12 January 1895, 23.

"Modern Connoisseurship." Rev. of *Lorenzo Lotto. Nation,* 24 January 1895, 76–77.

"Reconstructive Criticism." Rev. of *Lorenzo Lotto. Atlantic Monthly* 75 (April 1895): 556–59.

Rev. of *Lorenzo Lotto. Athenaeum,* 13 April 1895, 481.

1896

"Books on Painting." Rev. of *The Florentine Painters of the Renaissance. Spectator,* 12 September 1896, 339–40.

Cox, Kenyon. "Books on Art." Rev. of *The Florentine Painters of the Renaissance. Nation,* 19 March 1896, 239–40.

[Costelloe, Mary.] "The Philosophy of Enjoyment of Art." Rev. of *The Florentine Painters of the Renaissance. Atlantic Monthly* 77 (June 1896): 844–48.

Lee, Vernon [pseud. of Violet Paget]. "New Books." Rev. of *The Florentine Painters of the Renaissance. Mind* n.s. 5 (1896): 270–72.

"The New Art-Criticism." Rev. of *Venetian Painters of the Renaissance; The Florentine Painters of the Renaissance, and Lorenzo Lotto. Quarterly Review* 184 (October 1896): 454–79.

"Re-writing the History of Italian Painting." Rev. of *Lorenzo Lotto. Dial*, 1 January 1896, 21.

Santayana, George. Rev. of *The Florentine Painters of the Renaissance. Psychological Review* 3 (November 1896): 677–79.

"A Volume of Sound Art Criticism." Rev. of *The Florentine Painters of the Renaissance. Dial*, 1 May 1896, 281.

1897

Cox, Kenyon. Rev. of *The Central Italian Painters of the Renaissance. Nation*, 9 December 1897, 462.

1898

"Art Books." Rev. of *The Venetian Painters of the Renaissance* and *The Central Italian Painters of the Renaissance. Spectator*, 5 March 1898, 349.

Rev. of *The Venetian Painters of the Renaissance. Athenaeum*, 1 October 1898, 458.

1901

Cox, Kenyon. "Books on Painting." Rev. of *The Study and Criticism of Italian Art. Nation*, 7 November 1901, 362–63.

Fry, Roger. "Fine Arts." Rev. of *The Study and Criticism of Italian Art. Athenaeum*, 16 November 1901, 668–69.

Rev. of *The Study and Criticism of Italian Art. Magazine of Art* 26 (December 1901): 94–95.

1902

"Berenson." Rev. of *The Study and Criticism of Italian Art*. 2d ser. *Independent*, 6 November 1902, 2655–56.

Cox, Kenyon. "Books on Art." Rev. of *The Study and Criticism of Italian Art*. 2d ser. *Nation*, 6 November 1902, 864.

1903

Cortissoz, Royal. "New Aspects of Art Study." Rev. of *The Study and Criticism of Italian Art. Atlantic Monthly* 91 (June 1903): 832–42.

Cox, Kenyon. "Berenson's Florentine Drawings." Rev. of *The Drawings of the Florentine Painters. Nation*, 6 August 1903, 116–17.

Rev. of *Lorenzo Lotto*. Rev. ed. *Athenaeum*, 18 April 1903, 503–4.

1904

"Fine Arts." Rev. of *The Drawings of the Florentine Painters. Athenaeum,*
    12 November 1904, pt. 1, 662–63; 3 December 1904, pt. 2, 769–71.
Gropallo, Laura. "Bernhard Berenson." *Nuova Antologia,* 16 October 1904,
    5–33.

1905

Cortissoz, Royal. "Books New and Old." Rev. of *The Drawings of the Floren-
    tine Painters. Atlantic Monthly* 93 (March 1905): 405–7.

1908

Fry, Roger. "The Painters of North Italy." Rev. of *The North Italian Painters
    of the Renaissance. Burlington Magazine* 12 (March 1908): 347–49.

1917

Rev. of *The Study and Criticism of Italian Art.* 3d ser. *Connoisseur* 48 (May
    1917): 46–48.

1918

Pach, Walter. "Connoisseurship or Criticism." Rev. of *Essays in the Study of
    Sienese Painting. Dial,* 2 November 1918, 365–66.
"Sienese Painting." Rev. of *Essays in the Study of Sienese Painting. Times
    Literary Supplement,* 10 October 1918, 480.

1920

Cecchi, Emilio. "Bernard Berenson." *Valori Plastici* 2 (July 1920): 86–88.

1926

Gillet, Louis. "Bernard Berenson." *Living Age* 331 (November 1926): 243–50.

1929

Miklas, Wilhelm. "Bernard Berenson." *Living Age* 336 (June 1929): 265–66.

1933

"Berenson Villa Gift to Harvard." *Art News,* 15 July 1933, 6.

1939

"B.B." *Time,* 10 April 1939, 57–59.

1940

Mayor, A. Hyatt. "Berenson's Revised Book on the Drawings of the Floren-
    tine Painters." Rev. of *The Drawings of the Florentine Painters. Magazine
    of Art* 33 (April 1940): 236–38.

1944

"Vernissage." *Art News* 43 (October 1944): 9.

1948

"Il B.B." *Time*, 5 July 1948, 48.

Breuning, Margaret. "Berenson's Pronouncements." Rev. of *Aesthetics and History in the Visual Arts*. *Art Digest*, 15 November 1948, 48.

Frankfurter, Alfred. "Testament of Daylight." Rev. of *Aesthetics and History in the Visual Arts*. *Art News* 47 (December 1948): 15.

Greenberg, Clement. "Art and History." Rev. of *Aesthetics and History in the Visual Arts*. *New York Times Book Review*, 28 November 1948, 14.

Kazin, Alfred. "From an Italian Journal." *Partisan Review* 15 (May 1948): 550–67.

Rev. of *Aesthetics and History in the Visual Arts*. *Design* 50 (November 1948): 24.

Walker, John. Rev. of *Aesthetics and History in the Visual Arts*. *Gazette des Beaux Arts*, ser. 6, vol. 34 (October 1948): 294–96.

1949

Clark, Kenneth. "Thoughts of a Great Humanist." Rev. of *Aesthetics and History in the Visual Arts*. *Burlington Magazine* 91 (May 1949): 141–45.

Kirstein, Lincoln. "The Autocratic Taste." Rev. of *Aesthetics and History in the Visual Arts*. *New Republic*, 10 January 1949, 16–17.

"Life Calls on Bernard Berenson." *Life*, 11 April 1949, 158.

Mather, Frank Jewett. Rev. of *Aesthetics and History in the Visual Arts*. *Magazine of Art* 42 (February 1949): 73–74.

Mortimer, Ray. "Homage to Bernard Berenson." *Horizon* 20 (October 1949): 260–67.

Preston, Stuart. "Humanists Apologia." Rev. of *Aesthetics and History in the Visual Arts*. *Saturday Review*, 1 January 1949, 17–18.

Schapiro, Meyer. "The Last Aesthete." Rev. of *Aesthetics and History in the Visual Arts* and *Sketch for a Self-Portrait*. *Commentary* 8 (December 1949): 614–16.

Shapley, Fern. Rev. of *Aesthetics and History in the Visual Arts*. *College Art Journal* 9 (1949–51): 85.

Taylor, Francis Henry. "The Essence of 'B.B.' " Rev. of *Sketch for a Self-Portrait*. *Saturday Review*, 18 June 1949, 16.

1950

Gowing, Lawrence. Rev. of *Sketch For a Self-Portrait*. *Burlington Magazine* 92 (February 1950): 56–57.

1951

Behrman, S. N. "The Days of Duveen; Part 4–B.B." *New Yorker*, 20 October 1951, 36–59.

1952

Faison, Jr., S. Lane. "Book of Wisdom." Rev. of *Rumor and Reflection, 1941–1944. Nation*, 25 December 1952, 384.

Frank, Joseph. "Mostly Rumor." Rev. of *Rumor and Reflection, 1941–1944. New Republic*, 30 October 1952, 25–26.

Godfrey, F. M. Rev. of *Rumor and Reflection, 1941–1944. Apollo* 56 (December 1952): 208.

Pick, Robert. "Art and Allies." Rev. of *Rumor and Reflection, 1941–1944. Saturday Review*, 22 November 1952, 26.

1953

Godfery, F. M. Rev. of *Piero della Francesca; or, The Ineloquent in Art.* Italian ed. *Apollo* 57 (March 1953): 149.

"Mr. Berenson and Modern Art." Rev. of *Seeing and Knowing. Times Literary Supplement*, 27 November 1953, 756.

1954

Biddle, George. Rev. of *Seeing and Knowing. New York Times Book Review*, 31 January 1954, 7.

Comstock, Helen. "I Tatti, Bernard Berenson's Villa at Settignano." *Antiques* 66 (December 1954): 472–76.

Hughes, Serge. "The Outlook of an Olympian." Rev. of *Seeing and Knowing. Commonweal*, 16 April 1954, 46–47.

Krasne, Belle. Rev. of *Seeing and Knowing. College Art Journal* 12 (Summer 1954): 328–29.

"A New Debate in Old Venice." *New York Times Magazine*, 21 March 1954, 8.

Pach, Walter. "A Pair of B.B.'s." Rev. of *Caravaggio: His Incongruity and His Fame* and *Seeing and Knowing. Saturday Review*, 3 April 1954, 20–21.

Rev. of *Piero della Francesca; or, The Ineloquent in Art* and *The Arch of Constantine; or, The Decline of Form. Times Literary Supplement*, 15 October 1954, 652.

Rev. of *Seeing and Knowing. Atlantic Monthly* 193 (March 1954): 87.

Rev. of *Seeing and Knowing. Catholic World* 178 (March 1954): 479.

Rev. of *Seeing and Knowing. New Yorker*, 27 February 1954, 117–18.

Salinger, Margaretta. "A God's-Eye View." Rev. of *Seeing and Knowing. Art Digest*, 1 July 1954, 26.

Swift, Emerson H. "Classic Decline." Rev. of *The Arch of Constantine; or, The Decline of Form. Saturday Review*, 4 December 1954, 61–62.

1955

"B.B.: The Last Esthete." *Newsweek*, 4 July 1955, 62–64.

Carver, George A. "A Criticism of a Roman Monument." Rev. of *The Arch of*

Constantine; or, The Decline of Form. Architectural Record 117 (March 1955): 336.

Davis, Frank. "Age Cannot Wither." *Illustrated London News*, 3 September 1955, 392.

"For Bernard Berenson at 90." *Art News* 54 (June 1955): 25.

Friedberg, Judith. "A Day in Berenson's Ninety-First Year." *Reporter*, 22 September 1955, 42–45.

———. "Visit with Berenson." *New York Times Magazine*, 26 June 1955, 47.

Greenberg, Clement. "Greenberg on Berenson." Rev. of *Piero della Francesca; or, The Ineloquent in Art*, and *The Arch of Constantine; or, The Decline of Form. Perspectives USA* 1 (Spring 1955): 150–54.

Nicolson, Benedict. "In Honour of Berenson." *Burlington Magazine* 97 (July 1955): 195–96.

"The Pursuit of 'It.'" *Time*, 25 April 1955, 80–85.

Robertson, Martin. Rev. of *The Arch of Constantine; or, The Decline of Form. Burlington Magazine* 97 (July 1955): 227.

Taylor, Francis Henry. "To Bernard Berenson on His Ninetieth Birthday." *Atlantic Monthly* 196 (June 1955): 30–32.

1956

Taubes, Frederick. "An Afternoon with Bernard Berenson." *American Artist* 20 (November 1956): 56.

1957

Taylor, Henry Fitch. "The Summons of Art." *Atlantic Monthly* 200 (November 1957): 121–28.

1958

"An Expert Outliving His Legend." *Life*, 21 April 1958, 87.

Gould, Cecile. Rev. of *Essays in Appreciation. Apollo* 67 (June 1958): 243.

1959

"Death of a Prince." *Reporter*, 29 October 1959, 4–6.

Fehl, Philip. Rev. of *Essays in Appreciation. Journal of Aesthetics and Art Criticism* 18 (December 1959): 274–75.

Frankfurter, Alfred. "Bernard Berenson, 1865–1959: On the Future of I Tatti." *Art News* 58 (November 1959): 30.

Getlein, Frank. "The Legendary Berenson." *New Republic*, 26 October 1959, 21–22.

"Goodbye to 'B.B.'" *Life*, 19 October 1959, 117–18.

Kaufman, Betty. "Two Modes of Criticism." *Commonweal*, 6 February 1959, 502–3.

Waterhouse, E. K. "A Master of Method." *The Listener*, 24 December 1959, 1120–21.

Werner, Alfred. "Bernard Berenson, 1865–1959." *Arts* 34 (November 1959): 13.

1960

Alexander, Sidney. "A Complete Life." *Reporter,* 1 September 1960, 39–44.

Clark, Kenneth. "Bernard Berenson." *Burlington Magazine* 102 (September 1960): 381–86.

Garlick, Kenneth. "The Life-Enhancing Gift of 'B.B.' " Rev. of *The Passionate Sightseer;* and *Berenson: A Biography,* by Sylvia Sprigge. *Manchester Guardian Weekly,* 9 April 1960.

Gilbert, Creighton. "The Classics: Berenson . . . How Can We Use Him?" *Arts* 34 (June 1960): 15.

Hardwick, Elizabeth. "Living in Italy: Reflections on Bernard Berenson." *Partisan Review* 27 (Winter 1960): 73–82.

"The 'Institootion.' " Rev. of *Berenson: A Biography,* by Sylvia Sprigge. *Newsweek,* 15 August 1960, 81–82.

Jacobsen, Herbert. "Being with Berenson." *Columbia University Forum* 3 (Fall 1960): 32–36.

"Landscape of the Mind." Rev. of *One Year's Reading for Fun: 1942. Time,* 15 February 1960, 112.

Origo, Iris. "The Insatiable Traveler." *Atlantic Monthly* 205 (April 1960): 56–62.

Petrie, Sir Charles. "A Citizen of the World." Rev. of *The Passionate Sightseer;* and *Berenson: A Biography,* by Sylvia Sprigge. *London Illustrated News,* 2 April 1960, 547.

Pope-Hennessey, John. "Portrait of an Art Historian." Rev. of *Berenson: A Biography,* by Sylvia Sprigge; *The Passionate Sightseer;* and *One Years Reading for Fun: 1942. Times Literary Supplement,* 25 March 1960, 185–87.

Prichard, Theodore J. Rev. of *Berenson: A Biography,* by Sylvia Sprigge. *AIA Journal* 34 (November 1960): 52–54.

Temko, Allan. "Life Was a Gallery to Explore." Rev. of *The Passionate Sightseer. New York Times Book Review,* 15 May 1960, 1.

Werner, Alfred. "Berenson's Achievement." *Chicago Review* 14 (Summer 1960): 95–102.

———. "The Constant Esthete." Rev. of *The Passionate Sightseer;* and *Berenson: A Biography,* by Sylvia Sprigge. *Saturday Review,* 13 August 1960, 30–31.

Wollheim, Richard. "Berenson." Rev. of *Berenson: A Biography,* by Sylvia Sprigge. *Spectator,* 25 March 1960, 435–36,

1961

Frankfurter, Alfred. "I Tatti Emerges as an International Center." *Art News* 60 (Summer 1961): 25.

Hartt, Frederick. "Bernard Berenson, 1865–1959." *Art Quarterly* 24 (Spring 1961): 89–91.

Nicolson, Benedict. "Schapiro on Berenson." *Encounter* 16 (April 1961): 60–63.

Schapiro, Meyer. "Mr. Berenson's Values." *Encounter* 16 (January 1961): 57–65.

Trevor-Roper, Hugh. "Schapiro on Berenson." *Encounter* 16 (April 1961): 63–64.

1962

Hill, Derek. "Berenson and I Tatti." *Apollo* 76 (October 1962): 594–600.

1963

Alexander, Sidney. "The Last Aesthete?" Rev. of *The Bernard Berenson Treasury*, ed. Hanna Kiel. *Reporter*, 18 July 1963, 55–56.

Fixler, Michael. "Bernard Berenson of Butremanz." *Commentary* 36 (August 1963): 135–43.

Origo, Iris. "82 to 93: A Picture of Old Age." *Cornhill Magazine* 173 (Autumn 1963): 341–59.

1964

Clark, Eleanor. "Berenson's Last Years." Rev. of *Sunset and Twilight* and *The Selected Letters of Bernard Berenson*, ed. A. K. McComb. *New York Review*, 5 March 1964, 3–4.

Edwards, Ralph. "The Value of Bernard Berenson's Life." Rev. of *Sunset and Twilight*; and *The Bernard Berenson Treasury*, ed. A. K. McComb. *Connoisseur* 157 (September 1964): 52–53.

"Half of B.B." Rev. of *The Selected Letters of Bernard Berenson*, ed. A. K. McComb. *Newsweek*, 24 February 1964, 92–93.

Lange, Victor. "Monologue of an Old Man." Rev. of *Sunset and Twilight*. *New Republic*, 1 February 1964, 17–19.

Rev. of *The Bernard Berenson Treasury*, ed. Hanna Kiel. *Studio* 167 (May 1964): 222.

Rev. of *The Selected Letters of Bernard Berenson*, ed. A. K. McComb. *AIA Journal* 41 (June 1964): 72–73.

Rich, Daniel Cotton. "Reflections of a Self-Curious Savant." Rev. *Sunset and Twilight*; and *The Selected Letters of Bernard Berenson*, ed. A. K. McComb. *Saturday Review*, 29 February 1964, 30–31.

Sutton, Denys. "The House of Life." *Apollo* n.s. 79 (March 1964): 176–82.

1965

Darack, Arthur. "In Love with the Renaissance." Rev. of *Conversations with Berenson. Saturday Review,* 9 October 1965, 53.

De Gennaro, Angelo. "Berenson's Aesthetics." *Journal of Aesthetics and Art Criticism* 24 (Winter 1965): 256–62.

Frankfurter, Alfred. "Two Centenarians." *Art News* 63 (February 1965): 23.

"The Game of the Spirit." Rev. of *Conversations with Berenson. Time,* 22 October 1965, 122.

Herney, Donald. Rev. of *Conversations with Berenson. Christian Science Monitor,* 17 October 1965, 14.

Mostyn-Owen, William. Rev. of *The Bernard Berenson Treasury,* ed. Hanna Kiel; *Conversations with Berenson* It. ed. and *Sunset and Twilight. Burlington Magazine* 107 (June 1965): 328–29.

Saisselin, Remy. Rev. of *Berenson et André Malraux,* by Bernard Halda. *Journal of Aesthetics and Art Criticism* 23 (Summer 1965): 514–15.

Steinberg, Leo. " 'BB' as Collector." Rev. of *The Berenson Collection. Harper's* 230 (March 1965): 154–56.

Werner, Alfred. "The Goddess and the Prophet." Rev. of *Conversations with Berenson;* and *Mrs. Jack,* by Louise Hall Tharp. *Reporter,* 4 November 1965, 50–52.

1966

Biddle, Francis. "A Life with the Berensons." Rev. of *Forty Years with Berenson,* by Nicki Mariano. *New Republic,* 24 December 1966, 29–32.

Diamonstein, Barbaralee. "Life True to Art." Rev. of *Forty Years with Berenson,* by Nicki Mariano. *Saturday Review,* 29 October 1966, 30.

Fasanelli, James. "A Letter from Berenson's Early Years." *Burlington Magazine* 108 (February 1966): 85.

1967

Brower, Reuben A. "Parallel Lives." Rev. of *Forty Years with Berenson,* by Nicki Mariano; and *Robert Frost: The Early Years,* by Lawrence Thompson. *Partisan Review* 34 (Winter 1967): 116–24.

1968

Laws, Frederick. "Eyes and No Eyes." Rev. of *Seeing and Knowing. New Statesman,* 2 August 1968, 148.

"Unwelcome Reprise." Rev. of *Seeing and Knowing. Art in America* 56 (November–December 1968): 118.

1969

Alexander, Sidney. "Is 'I Tatti' the Keeper of the Flame?" *Holiday* 46 (September 1969): 36.

Masciotta, Michelangelo. "Incontro con Berenson." *Antichita Viva* 8 (1969): 45–47.

1971

Clark, Kenneth. "Bernard Berenson." *The Listener*, 18 February 1971, 193–96.

Neumeyer, Alfred. "Four Art Historians Remembered: Woelfflin, Goldschmidt, Warburg, Berenson." *Art Journal* 31 (Fall 1971): 33–36.

1975

Delamar, Alice. "Some Little Known Facts About Bernard Berenson and the Art World." *Forum* 12 (1975): 23.

1976

Gilmore, Myron. "The Berenson's and Villa I Tatti." *Proceedings of the American Philosophical Society* 120 (January 1976): 7–12.

Nicolson, Benedict. "The Burlington Magazine." *Connoisseur* 191 (March 1976): 177–83.

1979

Beck, James. "Berenson, 20 Years Later." *Art Forum* 17 (April 1979): 46–48.

Bradbury, Ray. "The Renaissance Prince and the Baptist Martian." *Horizon* 22 (July 1979): 56–66.

Brink, Andrew. "The Russell-Berenson Connection." Rev. of *Bernard Berenson: The Making of a Connoisseur*, by Ernest Samuels. *Russell* 35–36 (Autumn–Winter 1979–80): 43–49.

Eliot, Alexander. "Berenson's Life as a Connoisseur Was a Fine Art." *Smithsonian* 9 (January 1979): 46–55.

Friedlaender, Marc. Rev. of *Bernard Berenson: The Making of a Connoisseur*, by Ernest Samuels. *New England Quarterly* 52 (December 1979): 560–64.

Hughes, Robert. "Only in America." Rev. of *Bernard Berenson: The Making of a Connoisseur*, by Ernest Samuels, and *Being Bernard Berenson*, by Meryle Secrest. *New York Review*, 20 December 1979, 19.

Knapp, B. Rev. of *Bernard Berenson: The Making of a Connoisseur*, by Ernest Samuels. *Modernist Studies–Literature and Culture, 1920–1940* 3 (1979): 159–61.

Kramer, Hilton. "Grappling with the Mysteries of Taste." *New York Times*, 11 February 1979, sec. D, p. 29.

Russell, John. "Devotee of Beauty." Rev. of *Being Bernard Berenson*, by Meryle Secrest. *New York Times Book Review*, 4 November 1979, 7.

Sutton, Denys. "Revaluations." *Apollo* 110 (August 1979): 88–93.

Tighe, Mary Ann. "The Art Lover." Rev. of *Bernard Berenson: The Making of a Connoisseur,* by Ernest Samuels. *New York Times Book Review,* 1 April 1979, 1.

1980

Berman, Avis. Rev. of *Bernard Berenson: The Making of a Connoisseur,* by Ernest Samuels; and *Being Bernard Berenson,* by Meryle Secrest. *Art News* 79 (April 1980): 37.

Brookner, Anita. "The Master of Attributions." Rev. of *Being Bernard Berenson,* by Meryle Secrest; and *Bernard Berenson: The Making of a Connoisseur,* by Ernest Samuels. *Times Literary Supplement,* 18 January 1980, 51–52.

Campbell, Malcolm. Rev. of *Bernard Berenson: The Making of a Connoisseur,* by Ernest Samuels. *Wintertur Portfolio* 15 (Summer 1980): 169–71.

Evans, Bruce H. Rev. of *Being Bernard Berenson,* by Meryle Secrest. *Museum News* 58 (1980): 90.

Mauries, P. Rev. of *Being Bernard Berenson,* by Meryle Secrest; and *Bernard Berenson: The Making of a Connoisseur,* by Ernest Samuels. *Critique* 36 (1980): 580–94.

Plagens, Peter. Rev. of *Being Bernard Berenson,* by Meryle Secrest; and *Bernard Berenson: The Making of a Connoisseur,* by Ernest Samuels. *Art in America* 68 (October 1980): 13–14.

Sutton, Denys. "Passionate Vision: Bernard Berenson and Roger Fry." Rev. of *Being Bernard Berenson,* by Meryle Secrest; and *Roger Fry: Art and Life,* by Francis Spalding. *Apollo* 112 (December 1980): 368–71.

1981

Bryson, Norman. Rev. of *Being Bernard Berenson,* by Meryle Secrest; and *Bernard Berenson: The Making of a Connoisseur,* by Ernest Samuels. *Journal of American Studies* 15 (April 1981): 139–40.

Mostyn-Owen, William. Rev. of *Bernard Berenson: The Making of a Connoisseur,* by Ernest Samuels. *Burlington Magazine* 123 (May 1981): 317–18.

Rump, Gerhard C. Rev. of *Bernard Berenson: The Making of a Connoisseur,* by Ernest Samuels. *Leonardo* 14 (Winter 1981): 77.

1982

Elevitch, Bernard. "A Pilgrim of Culture." Rev. of *Bernard Berenson: The Making of a Connoisseur,* by Ernest Samuels, and *Being Bernard Berenson,* by Meryle Secrest. *Massachusetts Review* 23 (Summer 1982): 245–52.

Price, A. Rev. of *Lo Specchio Doppio: Carteggio 1927–1955 di Bernard Berenson, Clotilde Marghieri. Times Literary Supplement,* 1982, 1109.

1983

Court, Franklin E. "The Matter of Pater's 'Influence' on Bernard Berenson: Setting the Record Straight." *English Literature in Transition* 26 (1983): 16–22.

Samuels, Ernest. "Henry Adams and Bernard Berenson: Two Boston Exiles." *Proceedings of the Massachusetts Historical Society* 95 (1983): 100–113.

1984

Barolsky, Paul. "Walter Pater and Bernard Berenson." *New Criterion* 2 (April 1984): 47–57.

Emanuel, Angela. "Julia Cartwright and Bernard Berenson." *Apollo* n.s. 120 (October 1984): 273–77.

Pizzorusso, Claudio. "Un Affresco per Villa 'I Tatti'; Rene Piot da Gide a Berenson." *Paragone Arte* 35 (May 1984): 41–73.

1986

Hoving, Thomas. "The Berenson Scandals: An interview with Colin Simpson." *Connoisseur* 216 (October 1986): 132–37.

1987

Berman, Avis. "Artful Schemers." Rev. of *Artful Partners: Bernard Berenson and Joseph Duveen,* by Colin Simpson. *Art News* 86 (November 1987): 74.

Dinnage, Rosemary. "Fanning the Gemlike Flame." Rev. of *Bernard Berenson: The Making of a Legend,* by Ernest Samuels. *New York Review,* 8 October 1987, 3.

Garstang, Donald Rev. of *The Partnership: The Secret Association of Bernard Berenson and Joseph Duveen,* by Colin Simpson. *Apollo* n.s. 126 (October 1987): 299.

Haskell, Francis. "Compromises of a Connoisseur." Rev. of *Bernard Berenson: The Making of a Legend,* by Ernest Samuels, and *The Partnership: The Secret Association of Bernard Berenson and Joseph Duveen,* by Colin Simpson. *Times Literary Supplement,* 5 June 1987, 595–96.

McGill, D. C. Rev. of *The Letters of Bernard Berenson and Isabella Stewart Gardner 1887–1924,* ed. Rollin Hadley. *New York Times Book Review,* 00 November 1987, 33.

Pope-Hennessy, John. "Berenson's Certificate." Rev. of *Artful Partners,* by Colin Simpson. *New York Review of Books,* 12 March 1987, 19–20.

Sutton, Denys. Rev. of *Bernard Berenson: The Making of a Legend,* by Ernest Samuels; and *The Partnership: The Secret Association of Bernard Berenson and Joseph Duveen,* by Colin Simpson. *Burlington Magazine* 129 (December 1987): 815–16.

Updike, John. "How to Milk a Millionaire." Rev. of *Artful Partners*, by Colin Simpson. *New York Times Book Review*, 29 March 1987, 1.

1988

Vance, William. "Berenson and Mrs. Gardner: 'A Rivalry of Aspirations.'" *New England Quarterly* 61 (December 1988): 575–95.

1989

Freedberg, Sydney. "Berenson, Connoisseurship, and the History of Art." *New Criterion* 7 (February 1989): 7–16.

Garstang, Donald. Rev. of *The Letters of Bernard Berenson and Isabella Stuart Gardner, 1887–1924*, ed. Rollin Hadley. *Apollo* 129 (February 1989): 135–36.

1990

Lauritzen, Peter. "The Legacy of I Tatti: Bernard Berenson's Renaissance Villa near Florence." *Architectural Digest* 47 (January 1990): 112.

Maginnis, Hayden B. J. "The Role of Perceptual Learning in Connoisseurship: Morelli, Berenson, and Beyond." *Art History* 13 (March 1990): 104–17.

Rotily, Jocelyne. "Bernard Berenson et Marcel Proust." *Gazette des Beaux Arts* 115 (January 1990): 45–51.

Other Works Consulted

Alsberg, John. *Modern Art and Its Enigma: Art Theories from 1800–1950 Based on the Writings of This Period's Artist's and Philosophers*. London: Weidenfeld and Nicolson, 1983.

Barolsky, Paul. *Walter Pater's Renaissance*. University Park, Pa.: Pennsylvania State University Press, 1987.

Barr, Alfred. *Matisse: His Art and His Public*. New York: Museum of Modern Art, 1951.

Brantlinger, Patrick. *Bread and Circuses: Theories of Mass Culture and Social Decay*. Ithaca, N.Y.: Cornell University Press, 1983.

Brooks, Van Wyck. *The Confident Years, 1885–1915*. New York: E. P. Dutton, 1952.

———. *The Dream of Arcadia*. New York: E. P. Dutton, 1958.

Clark, Kenneth. *Another Part of the Wood*. New York: Harper and Row, 1974.

———. Introduction to *Last Lectures of Roger Fry*. New York: Macmillan, 1939.

———. *Moments of Vision*. New York: Harper and Row, 1981.

———. *The Other Half: A Self Portrait*. London: John Murray, 1977.

Cortissoz, Royal. *Art and Common Sense*. New York: Charles Scribner's Sons, 1913.

Cox, Kenyon. *Artist and Public and Other Essays*. New York: Charles Scribner's Sons, 1914.

——. *The Classic Point of View*. 1911; reprint, New York: Books for Libraries Press, 1968.

Craven, Thomas. *Men of Art*. 1931; Garden City, N.Y.: Halcyon House, 1950.

Epstein, Helen. "Meyer Schapiro: A Passion to Know and Make Known.' *Art News* 82 (1983): 60–85.

Falkenheim, Jacqueline. *Roger Fry and the Beginnings of Formalist Criticism*. Ann Arbor: UMI Research Press, 1980.

Finch, Margaret. *Style in Art History*. Metuchen, N.J.: Scarecrow Press, 1974.

Fishman, Solomon R. *The Interpretation of Art: Essays on the Art Criticism of John Ruskin, Walter Pater, Clive Bell, Roger Fry, and Herbert Read*. Berkeley and Los Angeles: University of California Press, 1963.

The Forum Exhibition of American Painters. New York: Anderson Galleries, 1916.

Four Americans in Paris. New York: Museum of Modern Art, 1970.

Freud, Sigmund. *On Creativity and the Unconscious*. Selected with introduction and annotations by Benjamin Nelson. 1925; reprint, New York: Harper, 1958.

Fried, Michael. "Art and Objecthood." *Artforum* 5 (Summer 1967): 12–23.

Fry, Roger. *Vision and Design*. London: Chatto and Windus, 1920.

——. *Letters of Roger Fry*. 2 vols. Ed. Denys Sutton. London: Chatto and Windus, 1972.

Frye, Northrop. "*The Decline of the West* by Oswald Spengler." *Daedalus* 103 (Winter 1974): 1–13.

Gallup, Donald., ed. *The Flowers of Friendship: Letters Written to Gertrude Stein*. New York: Alfred A. Knopf, 1953.

Gaunt, William. *The Aesthetic Adventure*. New York: Harcourt, Brace, 1945.

Gibson-Wood, Carol. *Studies in the Theory of Connoisseurship from Vasari to Morelli*. New York: Garland, 1988.

Gombrich, E. H. *Art and Illusion*. Princeton: Princeton University Press, 1956.

Green, Christopher. *Cubism and Its Enemies* New Haven: Yale University Press, 1987.

Greenfeld, Howard. *The Devil and Dr. Barnes*. New York: Viking, 1987.

Guggenheim, Peggy. *Out of This Century: The Informal Memories of Peggy Guggenheim*. New York: Dial Press, 1949.

Gumm, Peter. *Vernon Lee: Violet Paget*. London: Oxford University Press, 1964.

Hamilton, George Heard. "Cézanne and His Critics." In *Cézanne: The Late Work*. New York: Museum of Modern Art, 1977.

Hapgood, Hutchins. *A Victorian in the Modern World*. New York: Harcourt, Brace, 1939.

Hauptman, William. "The Suppression of Art in the McCarthy Decade." *Art Forum* 12 (October 1973): 48–52.

Hobhouse, Janet. *Everybody Who Was Anybody: A Biography of Gertrude Stein*. New York: Putnam, 1975.

Hyland, Douglas. "Agnes Ernst Meyer, Patron of American Modernism." *American Art Journal* 12 (Winter 1980): 64–81.

Johnson, Martha. "Clive Bell's Formalism in Historical Perspective." Ph.D. diss., University of Georgia, 1985.

Kleinbauer, W. E. *Modern Perspectives in Western Art History*. New York: Holt, Rinehart and Winston, 1971.

Kramer, Hilton. *The Age of the Avant-Garde: An Art Chronicle of 1956–1972*. New York: Farrar, Straus, and Giroux, 1973.

―――. *The Revenge of the Philistines: Art and Culture, 1972–1984*. New York: Free Press, 1985.

Kuspit, Donald. *Clement Greenberg*. Madison: University of Wisconsin Press, 1979.

La Farge, Mabel. *Egisto Fabbri*. New Haven: privately printed, 1937.

Lang, Berel. "Roger Fry: Significance or Form." *Journal of Aesthetics and Art Criticism* 21 (Winter 1962): 167–76.

Lewis, R.W.B. *Edith Wharton*. New York: Harper and Row, 1975.

Luhan, Mabel Dodge. *European Experiences*. New York: Harcourt, Brace, 1935.

McCormick, John. *George Santayana*. New York: Alfred A. Knopf, 1987.

MacDonald, Dwight. "A Theory of Popular Culture." *Politics* 1 (February 1944): 20–23.

McGrath, F. C. *The Sensible Spirit: Walter Pater and the Modernist Paradigm*. Tampa: University of South Florida Press, 1986.

McLaughlin, Thomas. "Clive Bell's Aesthetic: Tradition and Significant Form." *Journal of Aesthetics and Art Criticism* 35 (Summer 1977): 433–43.

Martin, Marianne. "Some American Contributions to Early 20th Century Abstraction." *Arts* 54 (June 1980): 158–65.

Mathews, Jane De Hart. "Art and Politics in Cold War America." *American Historical Review* 81 (October 1976): 762–87.

Mecklenburg, Virginia. "American Aesthetic Theory, 1908–1917: Issues in Conservative and Avant-Garde Thought." Ph.D. diss., University of Maryland, 1983.

Mellow, James. *Charmed Circle: Gertrude Stein and Company.* New York: Praeger, 1974.

Meyerson, Charlotte, ed. *Shadow and Light: The Life and Opinions of Maurice Sterne.* New York: Harcourt, Brace and World, 1965.

Morelli, Giovanni. *Italian Painters: Borghese and Dorai Pamfili Galleries in Rome.* London, 1910.

Nicolson, Benedict. "Post-Impressionism and Roger Fry." *Burlington Magazine* 93 (January 1951): 11–15.

Nochlin, Linda. "The Realist Criminal and the Abstract Law." *Art in America* 61 (September–October 1973): 54–61.

Pach, Walter. *Queer Thing, Painting.* New York: Harper and Brothers, 1938.

Pavolini, Corrado. *Cubismo, Futurismo, Espressionismo.* Bologna: Nicola Zanichelli, 1926.

Phillips, Duncan. "Fallacies of the New Dogmatism in Art." *American Magazine of Art* 9 (December 1917 and January 1918): pt. 1, 43–106; pt. 2, 101–6.

Phillips, Sandra S. "The Art Criticism of Walter Pach." *Art Bulletin* 65 (March 1983): 106–22.

Platt, Susan Noyes. *Modernism in the 1920's: Interpretations of Modern Art in New York from Expressionism to Constructivism.* Ann Arbor: UMI Research Press, 1985.

———. "Modernism, Formalism, and Politics: The Cubism and Abstract Art Exhibition of 1936." *Art Journal* 47 (Winter 1988): 284–95.

Podro, Michael. *The Critical Historians of Art.* New Haven: Yale University Press, 1982.

Porter, Fairfield. *Art in its Own Terms: Selected Criticism, 1935–1975.* New York: Taplinger, 1979.

Reise, Barbara. "Greenberg and the Group: A Retrospective View." *Studio International* 175 (May–June 1968), pt. 1, 254–57; pt. 2, 314–16.

Rewald, John. *Cézanne and America: Dealers, Collectors, Artists and Critics.* Princeton: Princeton University Press, 1989.

———. *The Steins and Their Circle.* New York: Thames and Hudson, 1986.

Robinson, Alan. *Symbol to Vortex: Painting, Poetry and Ideas, 1885–1914.* New York: St. Martin's Press, 1985.

Roskill, Mark. *What Is Art History?* Amherst: University of Massachusetts Press, 1989.

Ross, Denman. *A Theory of Pure Design: Harmony, Balance, Rhythm.* 1907; reprint, New York: Peter Smith, 1933.

Rothenstein, John. *Brave Day, Hideous Night: Autobiography, 1939–1965*. New York: Holt, Rinehart and Winston, 1967.

———. *Summer's Lease: Autobiography, 1901–1938*. London: Hamish Hamilton, 1965.

Rothenstein, William. *Men and Memories*. 3 vols. New York: Coward-McCann, 1931–1940.

Rubin, William, ed. *Picasso*. New York: Museum of Modern Art, 1980.

Saarinen, Aline. *The Proud Possessors*. New York: Random House, 1958.

Saisselin, Remy. *The Bourgeois and the Bibelot*. New Brunswick, N.J.: Rutgers University Press, 1984.

Santayana, George. *The Letters of George Santayana*. Ed. Daniel Cory. New York: Charles Scribner's Sons, 1955.

Schapiro, Meyer. "On the Humanity of Abstract Painting." In *Modern Art: 19th and 20th Centuries*. New York: George Braziller, 1978.

Shiff, Richard. *Cézanne and the End of Impressionism*. Chicago: University of Chicago Press, 1984.

Shone, Richard. *Bloomsbury Portraits*. New York: E. P. Dutton, 1976.

Spadoni, Carl. "Bertrand Russell on Aesthetics." *Russell* n.s. 4 (Summer 1984): 49–82.

Spalding, Francis. *Roger Fry: Art and Life*. Berkeley and Los Angeles: University of California Press, 1980.

Stein, Gertrude. *The Autobiography of Alice B. Toklas*. New York: Harcourt, Brace and Co., 1933.

Stein, Leo. *The ABC of Aesthetics*. New York: Boni and Liveright, 1927.

———. *Appreciation: Painting, Poetry and Prose*. New York: Crown Publishers, 1947.

———. *Journey into the Self: Being the Letters, Papers and Journals of Leo Stein*. Ed. Edmund Fuller. New York: Crown Publishers, 1950.

———. "Pablo Picasso." *New Republic*, 23 April 1924, 229–30.

Stein, Richard. *The Ritual of Interpretation: Fine Arts as Literature*. Cambridge: Harvard University Press, 1975.

Swan, Michael. *A Small Part of Time*. London: J. Cape, 1957.

Taylor, Henry Fitch. *Babel's Tower: The Dilemma of the Modern Museum*. New York: Columbia University Press, 1945.

Twitchell, Beverly. *Cézanne and Formalism in Bloomsbury*. Ann Arbor: UMI Research Press, 1987.

Venturi, Lionello. *History of Art Criticism*. Trans. Charles Marriott. New York: E. P. Dutton, 1936.

Walker, John. *Self-Portrait with Donors*. Boston: Little, Brown, 1974.

Wayward Muse. Buffalo: Albright-Knox Art Gallery, 1987.

Weiss, Peg. *Kandinsky in Munich: The Formative Jugenstil Years*. Princeton: Princeton University Press, 1979.

Wellek, René. "Vernon Lee, Bernard Berenson and Aesthetics." In *Friendship's Garland: Essays in Honor of Mario Praz on His Seventieth Birthday,* ed. Vittorio Gabrieli. Rome: Edizioni di storia e letteratura, 1966.

Wharton, Edith. *The Letters of Edith Wharton.* Ed. R.W.B. Lewis and Nancy Lewis. New York: Scribner's, 1988.

Wickes, George. *The Amazon of Letters: The Life and Loves of Natalie Barney.* New York: G. P. Putnam's Sons, 1976.

Wind, Edgar. *Art and Anarchy.* New York: Alfred A. Knopf, 1964.

Worringer, Wilhelm. *Abstraction and Empathy.* Trans. Michael Bullock. New York: International Universities Press, 1953.

Wright, Willard Huntington. "The Aesthetic Struggle in America." *Forum* 55 (February 1916): 201–20.

Index